YEADON'S REGISTER

of

L N E R

LOCOMOTIVES

Volume Twenty-Three

**Class Q5, Q6, Q7 and Q10
The North Eastern 0-8-0's**

Copyright Booklaw/Railbus 2002
ISBN 1 899624 55 4

YEADON'S REGISTER OF L.N.E.R. LOCOMOTIVES - VOLUME 23

EDITOR'S NOTE & ACKNOWLEDGEMENTS

In this, the twenty-third volume of *Yeadon's Register of LNER Locomotives* we review the heavy goods engines of the former North Eastern Railway, the 0-8-0 tender engines of classes Q5, Q6, Q7 and Q10. Of course the latter class only just qualified as NER locomotives on account of the Hull & Barnsley Railway being taken over by the NER on the eve of Grouping. Situated as it was atop the then vast and productive coalfield of Durham and Northumberland, the North Eastern had reason to require some of the most powerful large goods engines of the pre-Group period. Besides the coal hauling business, the NER also had a vast through traffic not to mention the large iron and steel concerns along with a growing chemical industry within its boundaries. Although well-off for powerful 0-6-0's, the goods traffic required in many cases reliable and more powerful 0-8-0's. The first NER 0-8-0 appeared in 1901, these engines became LNER Class Q5 and were followed in 1913 by the Q6 class. Over a hundred of these versatile and popular locomotives were produced and were followed up in 1919 with yet another 0-8-0 design, the Q7, which continued to be built after the formation of the LNER though not in the large numbers of the Q6 class. All of these engines served the LNER faithfully and the Q6 and Q7's went on to serve British Railways equally well. The same cannot be said for the Q10 class. This small class of fifteen engines was delivered to the Hull & Barnsley Railway in 1907 to help that railway cope with its growing mineral traffic. When the class became NER property in 1922 they were already requiring new boilers which although built and fitted, did not prolong the life of the ex-H&BR engines. By the end of 1931 all of the Q10's had been withdrawn subject no doubt to a recession in trade and their non-standardisation within the LNER.

Eric Fry continues to prop up the editorial department with his wisdom and knowledge of LNER locomotive matters. His contribution to each volume is now a requirement without which much of this work would seem to be incomplete.

The Archive staff at the University of Hull seem to come and go more often these days. Are we wearing them out or are they going on to better things in the outside world. Good luck to them anyway and thanks to all of you. Meanwhile we shall continue to try and wear down the present friendly and patient staff members of the department.

Amadeus have been associated with this series from the earliest days and they have virtually as much enthusiasm for the *Register* as we have. May we all live to see the last volume published. Annie, Jean and Simon are once again thanked for their continued support - the last sentiment applies to them also.

And not forgetting you the reader for your loyalty too.

The next Register, Volume 24A, will feature the first five Parts of the Class O4 2-8-0's - the second and final installment of this two-part work, Volume 24B, will contain the continuing story of the O4 development, Parts 6 to 8, the Class O5 and the Thompson development of the O4, the erstwhile O1.

The Yeadon Collection is available for inspection and anyone who wishes to inspect it should contact:-
The Archivist
Brynmor Jones Library
University of Hull
Hull
HU6 7RX
Tel: 01482-465265
A catalogue of the Yeadon collection is available.

First published in the United Kingdom by
BOOKLAW/RAILBUS 2002 in association with CHALLENGER
382 Carlton Hill, Nottingham, NG4 1JA.
Printed and bound by The Amadeus Press, Cleckheaton, West Yorkshire.

INTRODUCTION

Q5

In 1901 the North Eastern Railway introduced the first batch of Wilson Wordsell's successful outside cylinder 0-8-0 goods engines to handle the growing mineral traffic of the period. The first ten (NER Class T) emerged from Gateshead works during that year and all had piston valves. Between March and June 1902 ten more engines, to the same design but this time with slide valves, were constructed by Gateshead and given the classification T1.

Gateshead continued construction of Class T engines and from December 1902 to May 1904 turned out another thirty of the type. Darlington added another twenty slide valve Class T1's during 1907 and 1908, and a final batch of twenty in 1911. All these engines became Class Q5 under the LNER whether fitted with piston or slide valves.

None of the ninety engines were ever superheated but two different parts of the class emerged from 1932 onwards when fourteen engines received larger diameter boilers. Those which got the 5ft 6in. boilers became Part 2 of the class whilst those retaining the original 4ft 9in. boilers were designated Part 1 engines. The larger boilers were surplus from withdrawn Class Q10 engines (*see* Class Q10). Three Part 2 engines reverted to 4ft 9in. boilers during 1943/5 and so became Part 1 again; the other eleven kept the Q10 boilers until withdrawal.

Three different boilers were used by this class: Diagram 56, Diagram 56A (from the withdrawn Q10 engines) and Diagram 56B. *Diagram 56*: This was the original boiler type which had a 15ft long, 4ft 9in. diameter barrel with a 7ft 6in. firebox. No less than 187 examples were built by Darlington and Gateshead works. These included the initial ninety plus six spares all built between 1901 and 1911. From 1916 to 1929 another 91 replacements were built, all at Darlington. Fourteen engines kept the Diagram 56 boiler throughout whilst ten more engines were withdrawn with one after previously carrying either a 56A or 56B type. *Diagram 56A*: These were second-hand boilers from the Class Q10 engines which were withdrawn en masse in 1931. They had been built at Darlington as replacements for the H&B boilers originally carried by the Q10's. Five had been built in 1924, five in 1925 and a

further five in 1927. When used by the Q10 they were designated Diagram 51 and had 5ft 6in. diameter barrels which were 14ft long and with a 7ft 6in. firebox. Fourteen of these boilers were used on the Q5's (reclassified Q5/2) with one kept as spare. The spare was first used on No.658, which thus carried two consecutively ex Q10. Three of the Q5/2's (644, 658, 939) reverted back to Diagram 56 boilers in 1943 and 1945; No.658 finished its life as it began with a Diagram 56 boiler, new in 1922. *Diagram 56B:* This was a 1935 redesign of the Diagram 56 and had the same dimensions but had a single plate barrel. The dome was also in the same place but there were detail differences such as blower control and, in the last thirty, handholes. Twenty were made during 1936 and 1937, numbered 2794 upwards. Between 1940 and 1945 another thirty were built. All except fourteen Q5's carried a 56B boiler at some time.

Of the three reversions from Q5/2, two got 56B boilers which they carried to withdrawal whilst No.658 got a 56B before receiving a 56 as its final boiler.

Two different tenders were used with this class. The first five had the shorter wheelbase 3701 gallon tender which was initially built for the S class 4-6-0's (LNER B13) whilst the other eighty-five had the standard 3940 gallon tender with an eight inch longer wheelbase. Water scoops were fitted until the early 1930's but these were removed then onwards.

The fifty slide valve engines served with the ROD in France during WWI and all of them returned to the North Eastern ready to become LNER property at Grouping. Those fifty were accorded recognition of their three years of war service when each engine had a cast brass flaming grenade fixed to the cab sides. Each of the symbols was placed above three chevrons. All fifty kept these momentos to withdrawal.

Forty piston valve engines, Nos.2116 to 2125, 1682, 1684, 1685, 1694, 1696, 83, 410, 474, 1186, 1757, 162, 650, 651, 1009, 1731, 715, 785, 792, 1128, 1218, 1110, 1669, 411, 430, 443, 444, 1111, 1149, 1150, and 1173 were built at Gateshead between August 1901 and May 1904. Note that at Grouping only No.2118 was fitted with a Westinghouse brake.

The Q5's could be found working in virtually every part of what became the NE Area during LNER days and none of the class strayed far from the former NER territory except for a handful which found employment in the Southern Area during the early years of the 1930's when the Depression had set in. However, the majority were stationed in County Durham, the area which required their pulling power for the coal hauls from the mines to the ports and was the reason for their existence. Hull had some twenty of the class by Grouping, again employed by Dairycoates and Springhead on coal hauls from the Barnsley coalfield to Hull for export though post war tonnage's of this traffic had declined somewhat from the pre-1914 levels. Eventually the Q5's gave way to Q6's on this work and by 1935 the Q5's were all gone from the Hull area. The five which went to the Southern Area in October 1931 went to March shed from Dairycoates but had all returned to the NE Area within five months. Mexborough and Doncaster were two other sheds which found employment for a three Q5's in the 30's but again these engines returned to the North East once traffic levels had risen. On the eve of WW2 most of the class could be found at sheds on Teesside, still hauling coal from the pits but also now helping with the growing chemical traffic in that area. Other than these allocations, there were a couple at Kirkby Stephen shed, two each at Tyne Dock and Gateshead, three at Heaton, and one each at Malton and York. Towards the end of the LNER period the greater proportion of the class had moved to sheds in the Tyne/Tees area but Cudworth had a couple and Selby eight, all working mineral traffic. Right to the end of their working lives the Q5's were associated with working coal trains from the collieries to yards and ports. It was a job that they were built to perform and one that they carried out superbly.

All except one, No.769 a Q5/2 withdrawn in December 1946, took up their new LNER numbers in the 1946 scheme. Of the ninety original engines some seventy-seven entered the BR period though only nine of these received the 60000 addition to their numbers.

Withdrawals started in the last month of 1946; at first it was gradual but when the WD 2-8-0's became available the withdrawals started in earnest and on 6th October 1951 Class Q5 became extinct with the condemnation of Q5/1 No.3326. The last Q5/2, No.3305, had been withdrawn in May 1949.

Q6

The NER Class T2 0-8-0 mineral engine (LNER Class Q6) was an enlarged version of the Wordsell Class T (LNER Class Q5), at least as far as the boiler was concerned. Raven basically retained the frames, wheels and piston valves of the earlier design but put on a larger 5ft 6in. superheated boiler with a saddle for the smokebox. The result was an engine more than capable of performing the work it was designed for - heavy mineral haulage. That it was a complete success can be borne out by the fact that these engines were still doing the same arduous work some fifty-odd years after their introduction.

Between February 1913 and March 1921, one hundred and twenty T2's were produced, the first seventy at Darlington up to 1919, and the final fifty by Armstrong Whitworth from 1919 to 1921. Wartime had delayed the production process of the class and none were built during the year 1914 to 1916.

The boiler used at first on the class was designated Diagram 50 and one-hundred and forty-three examples were constructed up to Grouping. This same boiler, with three butt-jointed rings forming the barrel, was also used on the twenty B15 class 4-6-0's (see also Volume 17) and included in the total number of boilers used by the two classes were three spares. In 1923 two more spares were made followed by twenty replacement boilers during the period from 1927 to 1929. These twenty were equipped with Schmidt superheaters whilst a further seventy-three replacement boilers built between 1930 and 1937 had Robinson superheaters. Altogether two hundred and thirty-eight Diagram 50 boilers were produced.

In October 1938 the Diagram 50A boiler first appeared. This boiler consisted of two telescopic rings to form the barrel and the dome was somewhat flatter than the Diagram 50 dome and, was

Thirty engines which were the first of the North Eastern Class T2, were built at Darlington from February to September 1913 comprising Nos.1247 to 1254, 1257, 1261, 1262, 1264, 1271, 1276, 1278, 1279, 1280, 1283, 1284, 1285, 1288, 1291 to 1294, 1311, 1335, 1361, 1362 and 1363. These had the large brass numberplate until shopped from 1917, and their tender was the 3940 gallons type. Note that Ross 'pop' safety valves were used from the start of this class.

set further back. One hundred and thirty-four Diagram 50A boilers were produced up to November 1960 but they were never used on the B15's. All the Q6's except one ended their days with Diagram 50A boilers; the odd man out was 63360 (withdrawn in June 1966) which, although fitted with a 50A boiler from January 1953 to April 1955, reverted to the Diagram 50 type.

The fifty boilers built by Armstrong Whitworth for engines 2253 to 2302 were numbered E4/1 to E4/50 but from June 1934 the LNER decided to renumber these contractor built boilers in line with the Darlington Boiler Register series. Because so many of the earlier Darlington boilers had long been scrapped, the Armstrong Whitworth boilers simply had the prefix E4 erased and took up the numbers 1 to 50 which were mostly vacant. However, only forty numbers were eventually required because ten of the E4 series boilers had already been scrapped. Hawthorn Leslie & Co. had made ten of the replacement Diagram 50 boilers in 1929/30 and these then carried the numbers 982 to 991 but in the 1934 renumbering they were allocated 103 to 112. Perusal of the tables will show the progress of these boiler renumberings and there origins are prefixed AW or HL even after 1934 for clarity.

Before and immediately after Grouping both Darlington and Gateshead works maintained the Q6's whilst the B15's were mainly Darlington's responsibility, so spare boilers were allocated three to Darlington and two to Gateshead.

Neither intended for nor pressed into passenger service, the Q6's were supplied with only a steam brake for the engine and tender.

Five different tenders were used on the Q6 class, three different types were provided when new and the other two resulted from interchanging with Class C7 from 1932. All five types could still be seen on the Q6's up to withdrawal of the class. Further details of these tenders used by the Q6 engines can be found in the captions.

Prior to Grouping these 0-8-0's were painted black with single red lining and, up to 1928, the LNER carried on this livery. Because of the painting economies the lining disappeared after 1928 and none were ever lined again throughout their long lives.

Because the NER numbering was adopted by the LNER at Grouping the engines kept their original numbers up to the 1946 general renumbering when the Q6's took up the numbers 3340 to 3459. When BR came into being these numbers were increased by 60000.

Like the Q5's, the Q6's were engaged for all of their working lives hauling coal trains and heavy freight. By 1923 the class could be found on this work throughout the former NER area and eleven sheds shared the class with over fifty stationed on Tyneside whilst the two Humberside sheds at Dairycoates and Springhead had twenty-five between them. During 1923 two Q6's ventured into Scotland for some months work from Thornton shed hauling coal from the Fife coalfield up to Aberdeen; first No.2263 went in March until May then No.2253 took its place until October. An O4 was tried out on this work at the same time but that story will be subject to scrutiny in Volume 24.

The Q6's saw regular work on the Newcastle to Carlisle line and six were stationed at Carlisle London Road shed by Grouping. They could also be seen working into Manchester, via Woodhead, right into BR days on trains from Hull but none were ever stationed in Lancashire. In the late LNER period they ventured further west to Liverpool and Northwich over the Cheshire Lines routes but again they were not stationed at either place. During the 1930's Doncaster shed used visiting Q6's on trains to New England and also to Immingham. Mexborough shed had two on the allocation from 1933 to 1937 and these took on

the normal work of that sheds eight coupled engines. In March 1943 the class was concentrated at only seven sheds with no fewer than fifty at Newport and thirty at Neville Hill. Lesser numbers could be found at Dairycoates (15), Stockton (10), Borough Gardens (5), Consett (5), and Selby (5).

The demands of wartime took the class to places to where they did not normally work and Edinburgh was one such venue where a Q6 would work via the ECML to Tweedmouth where a crew change would take place for the final stretch to Edinburgh. Colwick, Lincoln, March and Peterborough saw regular Q6 visits whilst there were two sighting, in 1942 and 1945, at Woodford.

In early BR days the engines had mainly migrated to Tees-side and County Durham and that remained the case up to withdrawal except for small numbers being allocated for short periods to places such as Neville Hill, Normanton and York; even Scarborough and Whitby had their services during this period. Hull had lost its Q6's in 1947 but half a dozen returned to Dairycoates in late 1949 for a matter of weeks. After that they became only visitors. Two went to Kirkby Stephen in April 1955 to take over the Q5 workings but in May of the same year the two engines, when coupled together, derailed whilst working a Tebay to Kirkby Stephen mineral train at Smardale. Both were badly damaged (see later illustrations) and neither returned to the line, being sent instead to Middlesbrough after repair.

The first withdrawal was 63372 in May 1960. This condemnation was due to an accident and it was December the following year before another Q6 was withdrawn, this time 63457. However, the class stayed pretty much intact until April 1963 when inroads started. September 1967 brought the demise of Class Q6 when the last three, 63344, 63387 and 63395 were condemned. Happily the latter engine was purchased for preservation and, in NER livery carrying its old number 2238, it is now working on the North Yorkshire Moors Railway fitted with a vacuum brake for passenger working.

Q7

The NER built only five of the Raven designed Class T3 0-8-0's, all in 1919 at Darlington. They were numbered 901 to 905. This three cylinder design culminated from the use of other three cylinder designs on the large goods tank engines of classes X and Y and on the Atlantic express passenger engines of Class Z.

The boiler used for the T3 engines was a modified version of that used on the Z class engines which was particularly free steaming. Virtually at the same time as the order for the five T3's was sanctioned, an order for ten express goods 4-6-0's (Class S3, LNER B16), using the same boiler type and having three cylinders also, was given (see also Volume 17).

Why the NER should want a more powerful 0-8-0 mineral engine seems strange especially when the T2's were still being delivered and those already working were doing a superb job. However, what is even stranger is the fact that a further ten T3's, by now LNER Class Q7, were ordered in 1924 when the LNER had more heavy goods engines than it actually required and when numerous ex R.O.D. 2-8-0s were becoming available at virtually a third of the price of the new Q7's.

The ten new Q7's were built at Darlington between March and May 1924 and numbered 624, 625, 626, and 628 to 634.

As mentioned earlier, the original Diagram 49 boilers were the same as fitted to Class B16 and interchange between the two classes began in November 1927. The Q7's had Schmidt superheaters when new and these were also fitted to the replacement boilers built in 1929. The next replacement boilers built in 1933/34 had Robinson superheaters.

A new boiler, Diagram 49A, was introduced in 1939 and was first used on the Q7 class from March 1941 (No.902). The firebox had a sloping throat plate and the barrel was 6 inches shorter, constructed from two plates in place of the previous three. The dome was set 2ft 8in. further back. All the Q7's finished with 49A boilers, although No.63470 carried a Diagram 49 boiler until February 1962, only ten months before the demise of the class.

On the first five engines, 901 to 905, the chimney was set just to the rear of the centre line of the smokebox but on the ten engines built in 1924 the chimney was set just forward of the centre line. This latter position was found necessary to fit the Gresley snifting valve on the smokebox behind the chimney. The problem did not arise with the B16's as they had a longer smokebox than the Q7's. Nos.901, 902, 904 and 905 changed from steam circulating to snifting valves, for element protection, in 1927/28 and their former boilers, D962, D976, D980 and D983 respectively, went to B16 class never to be used again on Q7's. Meanwhile No.903 kept its first boiler, D977, until October 1935 when it was condemned but it is not known if it received a Gresley anti-vacuum valve at that shopping or earlier.

Red lining complimented the black livery until 1928 and after that they remained simply plain black. All got the BR emblem before withdrawal.

In the 1946 renumbering they became 3460 to 3474 whilst BR added 60000 to these numbers.

The first three engines were sent to Blaydon when new and the other two to Gateshead shed. All worked main line goods trains south to York or across to Carlisle in the case of the Blaydon engines. By Grouping four of them had moved to Dairycoates for work on the coal trains from the South Yorkshire mines to Hull Alexandra Docks whilst No.903 remained on Tyneside but now at Tyne Dock shed. The ten 1924 engines were initially sent to

Five engines Nos.901 to 905 were built at Darlington during October and November 1919. The prototype No.901 shown here on 10th November 1919 is being tested on the Newcastle to Carlisle line at Prudhoe.

York (624 and 625), Hull (626, 628, 629, 630) and Tyne Dock (6311 to 634). By 1st August of that year the pair at York had joined the Hull engines at Dairycoates, giving that shed a total of ten Q7's, whilst Nos.631 and 634 were at Borough Gardens and No.632 was being used at Annfield Plain. Between April 1926 and July 1928 the Dairycoates Q7's were dispersed to other sheds as the Hull depot found that their Q6 power was adequate. The recipients were Haverton Hill and Stockton sheds which got them to work the steel traffic in the area. Throughout the 1930's these engines were forever moving from shed to shed and Darlington, Selby and West Hartlepool all used them. Unlike the Q6's which could trip work to collieries, the Q7's were restricted by their route availability so that work was mainly closed off to them.

During the war they ventured south with trains to Grantham and Colwick even the Woodhead route was used by most of the class with westbound trains to Manchester and on occasion Liverpool. In March 1943 the whole class congregated at Tyne Dock shed from where, over the next nineteen years, they were to do most of their work. During the late 1950's they did some work from other sheds such as Blaydon and Sunderland but they returned to Tyne Dock. It was from the latter shed where perhaps their immense power was best tested on the heavy iron ore trains from Tyne Dock to Consett steelworks.

Before the advent of the 56-ton bogie hopper wagons used from 1951, the Q7's were familiar with the stiff grades on the route to Consett whilst hauling iron ore trains and, with banking assistance they could lift trains of up to 700 tons on the climb to Consett. The introduction of the bogie hopper wagons meant that five of the Q7's had to be equipped with two second-hand Westinghouse air pumps each operating an independent system, one to keep the wagon doors closed and one for generating air to open them whilst over the unloading hoppers at the steelworks. The pumps were positioned on each side of the firebox with an associated air tank between each pump and the cab. The first engine equipped had the pumps mounted either side of the smokebox but that was later altered so that it too had them mounted at the firebox end of the running plate. Vacuum ejector equipment was also fitted to these engines for working the wagon

brakes and screw couplings were provided. From 1957 BR Standard 9F 2-10-0's began to take over the iron ore train workings and the Westinghouse pumps were gradually removed from the Q7s and fitted to the 9F's. By 1959 this task was completed and the Q7's were relegated to banking duties on these trains.

Withdrawal started in November 1962 when two of the 1924 batch engines were condemned. In December the rest of the class joined them at Darlington as surplus and Class Q7 became extinct. However, the story did not quite end at North Road scrap yard as the first of the powerful 0-8-0's, No.63460, was preserved and can now be found on the NYMR.

Q10

All fifteen of LNER Class Q10 were built and delivered to the Hull & Barnsley Railway in 1907. Ordered in two batches from the Yorkshire Engine Co., Sheffield, these inside cylinder 0-8-0 mineral engines were the largest and only ones of their type on that railway.

Classified A by the H&B, they had been constructed to cope with the growing coal traffic along the company's main line from Cudworth to Hull where the South Yorkshire coal was shipped mainly to Continental Europe via the railway's own facility at Alexandra Dock. In 1922 the Hull & Barnsley Railway was taken over by the North Eastern Railway

These were the only engines on the H&B which had Belpaire fireboxes. The saturated boilers which at first had a working pressure of 200 lb per. sq. in., later reduced to 175 lb., were of 5ft 6in. diameter and were without domes. By the time that the NER took over the H&B in 1922, these boilers were becoming due for replacement. During their fifteen years of work on the H&B the Q10's had not had new boilers or even a boiler change for there was no spare boiler. A new design was prepared at Darlington, to the same basic dimensions but with a dome and a round-top firebox. Five were constructed in 1924, five in 1925 and five in 1927. Again no spare was provided (perhaps with foresight). These new boilers were given LNER Diagram No.51 and were fitted between October 1924 and March 1928 (the originals did not last long enough to be included in the LNER diagram numbering scheme). Following the mass withdrawal of the class in 1931, these boilers found further employment on Class Q5 (see above). When the Q10's were reboilered they were classified Q10 Part 2 whilst those with the original boilers were Part 1.

No numbers for the original boilers were shown on LNER record cards. On the H&BR some of their engines had the same number for the boiler as for the engine, whilst others used the maker's works number to identify the boiler (all H&B engines and boilers were built by contractors). What the position was with Class Q10 we do not know.

A final word on the Q10 boilers. In the tables (*see* page 119) engine number 3124/2505 has an entry date into Darlington as 11/5/23 and an ex works date of 27/10/24 - nearly eighteen months - which at first glance looks wrong, however, these dates are correct. The reason behind such a long stay in shops probably stems from the fact that this engine was the first to receive the new Diagram 51 boiler. No doubt it took Darlington some time to accept that they had to design a fresh boiler for the class having first tried to adapt the Q10 to carry a Q6 boiler.

Numbered 117 to 131 by the H&B, they were renumbered 3117 to 3131 by the NER but at Grouping these numbers conflicted with those allocated to former Great Northern engines and so they were renumbered yet again, this time becoming LNER 2498 to 2512.

The usual haunt of the Q10's was between Hull and Cudworth hauling full loads of coal to the docks and empties, sometimes with loads of pit props too, back to the coalfield. This went on through H&B, NER and early LNER days until 1928 when recently purchased O4 2-8-0's from the R.O.D. became the normal motive power on the Cudworth-Hull hauls ousting the Q10's from that work. Other similar work was sought for them but it seems that everything was against them - cheap alternative engines, world recession, extended miners strike - even footplatemen at Selby shed refused to man them. Their allocation was Springhead shed up to Grouping but then some went to Cudworth followed by Selby and Dairycoates shed. In January 1931 Mexborough shed received ten of them but they were under utilised there. In July six went to March but their stay there was measured in weeks and by September all the class were back at either Dairycoates or Selby where withdrawal of the survivors took place forthwith. No.2502 became the last Q10, being withdrawn in November 1931.

Ten engines No.117 to 126 were built for the Hull & Barnsley Railway from February to June 1907 by Yorkshire Engine Co., Sheffield. Note that from new these had no cab roof ventilator and, both of the sandbox fillers were outside of the running plate.

Ten slide valve engines, Nos.130, 527, 1002, 1320, 1700, 1704, 1708, 1709, 1717, and 1729 were built at Gateshead from March to June 1902. They were similar to the forty piston valve engines except for valves.

Forty more slide valve engines similar to the ten Gateshead built engines were built at Darlington between June 1907 and May 1908 and from June to November 1911: Nos.578, 660, 939, 1031, 1032, 1054, 1062, 1177, 1178, 1215, 644, 645, 646, 647, 648, 652, 653, 654, 655, 656, 642, 643, 657, 658, 659, 661, 669, 764, 767, 769, 770, 771, 772, 773, 774, 781, 783, 789, 793, and 794.

During the 1914-18 war all fifty of the slide valve engines served in France, the ROD simply adding 5000 to their running number. All survived and, in due course, all worked through the 1939-45 war, but on the Home Front.

CLASS Q5

2116

Gateshead 10.01.

To traffic 8/1901.

REPAIRS:
???. ?/?—?/6/15.**G.**
Ghd. 13/5—25/8/25.**G.**
Ghd. 24/8—19/9/28.**L.**
Ghd. 26/2—16/4/30.**G.**
Dar. 28/5—11/7/35.**G.**
Dar. 14/7—27/9/38.**G.**
Dar. 8/10—10/11/41.**G.**
Dar. 8—27/11/43.**G.**
Dar. 7—12/11/44.**L.**
Dar. 7—30/3/46.**G.**
Dar. 11/6/48. *Not repaired.*

BOILERS:
G72.
G77 ?/?/??.
D35 ?/6/15.
2270 (new) 16/4/30.
2167 (ex1178) 11/7/35.
D994 (ex1684) 27/9/38.
2800 (ex764) 10/11/41 (56B).
2811 (ex767) 27/11/43 (56B).
3375 (ex1149) 30/3/46 (56B).

SHEDS:
Annfield Plain.
Tyne Dock. 24/6/37.
York 23/6/39.
Malton. 20/5/40.
West Hartlepool. 28/3/43.

RENUMBERED:
3250 30/3/46.

CONDEMNED: 26/6/48.
Cut up at Darlington.

2117

Gateshead 11.01.

To traffic 9/1901.

REPAIRS:
???. ?/?—?/10/16.**G.**
Dar. 3/8—18/10/23.**G.**
Dar. 16/11—22/12/23.**L.**
Dar. 22/9/26—7/1/27.**G.**
Dar. 14/10—26/11/29.**G.**
Dar. 17/3—19/4/32.**G.**
Dar. 21/11/34—9/1/35.**G.**

Dar. 12/10—19/11/36.**H.**
Dar. 27/4—8/6/38.**G.**
Dar. 22/8—6/10/41.**G.**
Dar. 16/11—11/12/43.**G.**
Ghd. 17/3—5/4/45.**L.**
Dar. 25/1—22/3/47.**G.**

BOILERS:
G74.
G80 ?/?/??.
D602 (new) 10/16.
D1769 (ex162) 19/4/32.
2085 (ex789) 9/1/35.
3226 (new) 6/10/41 (56B).
3135 (ex1684) 11/12/43 (56B).
2279 (ex3255) 22/3/47.

SHEDS:
Newport.
Borough Gardens 28/3/43.

RENUMBERED:
3251 15/12/46.

CONDEMNED: 20/12/50.
Cut up at Darlington.

2118

Gateshead 12.01.

To traffic 10/1901.

REPAIRS:
???. ?/?—?/9/07.**G.**
???. ?/?—?/10/12.**G.**
???. ?/?—?/5/18.**G.**
Dar. 3/7—20/9/23.**G.**
Dar. 1/12/27—14/2/28.**G.**
Dar. 12/6—20/8/30.**G.**
Dar. 28/3—3/5/33.**G.**
Dar. 11/9—20/10/36.**G.**
Dar. 23/6/39—4/1/40.**H.**
Dar. 6/8—11/9/40.**G.**
Dar. 10/7—19/8/42.**G.**
Dar. 23/6—3/7/43.**L.**
Dar. 23/6—10/8/44.**G.**
Ghd. 20/3—4/4/46.**L.**
Dar. 21/12/46—9/1/47.**L.**
Dar. 12/1/48. *Not repaired.*

BOILERS:
G76.
G138 ?/?/??.
G615 9/07.
G159 10/12.
D726 (new) 5/18.

D1485 (ex774) 3/5/33.
D1757 (ex1685) 20/10/36.
2278 (ex1215) 19/8/42.
2797 (ex1685) 10/8/44 (56B).

SHEDS:
Shildon.
Kirkby Stephen 6/1/31.
Darlington 2/9/40.
Kirkby Stephen 14/11/40.
Darlington 30/3/42.
Blaydon 28/3/43.
Haverton Hill 27/7/47.

RENUMBERED:
3252 4/4/46.

CONDEMNED: 7/2/48.
Cut up at Darlington.

2119

Gateshead 13.01.

To traffic 10/1901.

REPAIRS:
???. ?/?—?/11/13.**G.**
???. ?/?—?/3/19.**G.**
???. ?/?—?/7/22.**G.**
Dar. 4/12/25—27/2/26.**G.**
Dar. 3/3—22/4/30.**G.**
Dar. 27/9—27/10/32.**G.**
Rebuilt to Part 2.
Dar. 21/2—1/4/36.**G.**
Dar. 22/12/38—17/3/39.**G.**
Dar. 26/9—7/11/39.**H.**
Dar. 13/11—2/12/40.**L.**
Dar. 13/8—16/9/41.**G.**
Dar. 28/9—30/10/43.**G.**
Dar. 11/1—9/2/46.**G.**
Dar. 8—18/11/47.**L.**
Dar. 11/11/48. *Not repaired.*

BOILERS:
G98.
G291 11/13.
D722 (new) 3/19.
D1670 (exQ10 2507) 27/10/32 (56A).
D1997 (ex661) 1/4/36 (56A).
D1988 (ex769) 16/9/41 (56A).
D1670 (ex644) 9/2/46 (56A).

SHEDS:
Shildon.
Newport 7/1/35.
Middlesbrough 6/2/37.

West Hartlepool 28/3/43.

RENUMBERED:
3253 8/9/46.

CONDEMNED: 22/11/48.
Cut up at Darlington.

2120

Gateshead 14.01.

To traffic 10/1901.

REPAIRS:
???. ?/?—?/4/19.**G.**
Dar. 1/3—25/5/23.**G.**
Dar. 17/9—30/11/25.**G.**
Dar. 2/11—18/12/28.**G.**
Dar. 13/6—5/8/32.**G.**
Dar. 6/2—8/3/35.**G.**
Dar. 23/5—2/7/38.**G.**
Dar. 11/9—11/10/40.**G.**
Dar. 17—18/9/42.
Tender only.
Dar. 26/11—31/12/42.**G.**
Dar. 17/4—11/6/45.**G.**
Ghd. 6—19/8/46.**L.**
Ghd. 26/6—23/8/47.**L.**
Dar. 25/5/48. *Not repaired.*

BOILERS:
G100.
D714 (new) 4/19.
D737 (ex646) 30/11/25.
2227 (ex658) 5/8/32.
D1769 (ex2117) 8/3/35.
D1004 (ex1110) 2/7/38.
2159 (ex1178) 11/10/40.
2271 (ex1178) 31/12/42.
2904 (ex1729) 11/6/45 (56B).

SHEDS:
Newport.
Middlesbrough 6/2/37.
Newport 7/11/38.
Borough Gardens 28/3/43.

RENUMBERED:
3254 22/8/46.

CONDEMNED: 11/6/48.
Cut up at Darlington.

WORKS CODES:- Cw - Cowlairs. Dar- Darlington. Don - Doncaster. Ghd - Gateshead. Gor - Gorton. Hsi - Hull Springhead. Inv - Inverurie. Str - Stratford.
REPAIR CODES:- **C/H** - Casual Heavy. **C/L** - Casual Light. **G** - General. **H**- Heavy. **H/I** - Heavy Intermediate. **L** - Light. **L/I** - Light Intermediate. **N/C** - Non-Classified.

(*above*) Until 1929 all the boilers built were to Diagram 56, which *was* not suitable for interchanging with any other class. It had two handholes for washout purposes on the left hand side, and three (*see* page 6, bottom) on the right hand side.

(*left*) After the 1935 re-design of the boiler from three butt-jointed to two telescopic rings, only small external differences were apparent, the dome remaining in the same position. When building of replacement boilers resumed, they were to Diagram 56B, and twenty built from July 1936 to December 1937 had the same handhole arrangement as on Diagram 56. A final batch of thirty built February 1940 to December 1945 had only two handholes on both sides, and those on the left hand side were more widely spaced than hitherto. Note the lamp bracket duplication.

2121

Gateshead 15.01.

To traffic 10/1901.

REPAIRS:
???. ?/?—?/1/17.**G.**
Dar. 18/3—27/5/24.**G.**
Ghd. 9/7—19/9/27.**G.**
Ghd. 15/10—19/11/30.**G.**
Dar. 27/9—25/10/34.**G.**
Dar. 13/10—17/11/37.**G.**
Dar. 17/2—20/3/41.**G.**
Dar. 26/5—13/6/42.**N/C.**
Dar. 12/8—3/9/42.**L.**
Dar. 20/11—21/12/42.**L.**
Dar. 17/9—16/10/43.**G.**
Ghd. 29/1—10/2/45.**L.**
Dar. 28/12/46—15/2/47.**G.**
Dar. 4—14/3/47.**N/C.**

BOILERS:
G104.
D593 *(new)* ?/1/17.
2150 *(ex648)* 25/10/34.
D1457 *(ex1173)* 17/11/37.
2270 *(ex1150)* 20/3/41.
2279 *(ex1215)* 16/10/43.
2889 *(ex3291)* 15/2/47 (56B).

SHEDS:
Newport.
Shildon 9/1/26.
North Blyth 27/1/27.
Blaydon 28/3/43.
Darlington 5/10/47.
Neville Hill 29/8/48.
Selby 6/2/49.

RENUMBERED:
3255 25/8/46.

CONDEMNED: 3/11/49.
Cut up at Darlington.

2122

Gateshead 16.01.

To traffic 11/1901.

REPAIRS:
???. ?/?—?/12/12.**G.**
Dar. 28/5—31/7/23.**G.**
Dar. 21/10/25—30/1/26.**G.**
Dar. 2/4—17/5/29.**G.**
Dar. 28/9—31/10/32.**G.**
Dar. 31/10—13/12/33.
In store at Paint Shop.
Dar. 25/6—6/8/36.**G.**
Dar. 29/6—15/7/37.**N/C.**
Dar. 16/12/38—28/1/39.**G.**
Dar. 6/10—5/11/41.**G.**
Dar. 21/2—13/3/44.**G.**

Dar. 5—25/4/45.**L.**
After collision.
Ghd. 24/12/45—12/1/46.**L.**
Dar. 22/3—7/6/47.**G.**
Dar. 27/6—4/7/47.**N/C.**

BOILERS:
G110.
D2100 12/12.
2225 *(new)* 17/5/29.
2798 *(new)* 6/8/36 (56B).
3228 *(new)* 5/11/41 (56B).
2798 *(ex1696)* 13/3/44 (56B).

SHEDS:
Newport.
Mexborough 15/12/33.
Doncaster 19/2/34.
Mexborough 5/12/36.
Newport 8/5/37.
Middlesbrough 7/11/38.
West Hartlepool 28/3/43.
Borough Gardens 27/6/48.
Newport 6/2/49.
Middlesbrough 22/1/50.

RENUMBERED:
3256 8/9/46.

CONDEMNED: 12/6/50.
Cut up at Darlington.

2123

Gateshead 17.01.

To traffic 12/1901.

REPAIRS:
???. ?/?—?/5/14.**G.**
???. ?/?—?/8/16.**G.**
Dar. 18/7—29/9/23.**G.**
Dar. 10/8—23/11/26.**G.**
Dar. 8/7—27/8/29.**G.**
Dar. 25/11—22/12/32.**G.**
Dar. 7/6—30/7/35.**G.**
Dar. 31/8—20/10/38.**G.**
Dar. 31/3—3/5/41.**G.**
Dar. 25/10—17/11/43.**G.**
Dar. 3/4—19/5/44.**L.**
Ghd. 20/4—11/5/45.**L.**
Dar. 9/3—1/4/46.**L.**
Dar. 26/10—21/12/46.**G.**

BOILERS:
G116.
G98 5/14.
D579 *(new)* 8/16.
D1006 *(ex1032)* 23/11/26.
D1046 *(ex1110)* 27/8/29.
D1014 *(ex474)* 22/12/32.
D2270 *(ex2116)* 30/7/35.
D1074 *(ex792)* 20/10/38.
2167 *(ex772)* 3/5/41.
2168 *(ex162)* 17/11/43.

2227 *(ex3308)* 21/12/46.

SHEDS:
Newport.
Borough Gardens 28/3/43.

RENUMBERED:
3257 1/4/46.

CONDEMNED: 27/11/50.
Cut up at Darlington.

2124

Gateshead 18.01.

To traffic 12/1901.

REPAIRS:
???. ?/?—?/5/18.**G.**
Ghd. 12/9—19/11/23.**G.**
Ghd. 15/6—7/9/26.**G.**
Ghd. 24/11—31/12/30.**G.**
Dar. 11/3—6/8/36.**G.**
Dar. 10—24/5/37.**N/C.**
Dar. 19/10—2/11/38.**N/C.**
Dar. 18/10—23/11/39.**G.**
Dar. 12/12/41—7/1/42.**G.**
Dar. 3—25/3/44.**G.**
Ghd. 15/9—3/10/45.**L.**
Dar. 3/4/47. *Not repaired.*

BOILERS:
G139.
D727 *(new)* 5/18.
D35 *(ex2116)* 31/12/30.
2797 *(new)* 6/8/36 (56B).
2902 *(ex2125)* 7/1/42 (56B).
2906 *(ex781)* 25/3/44 (56B).

SHEDS:
Annfield Plain.
Tyne Dock 24/6/37.
Middlesbrough 29/3/38.
West Hartlepool 28/3/43.

RENUMBERED:
3258 8/9/46.

CONDEMNED: 26/4/47.
Cut up at Darlington.

2125

Gateshead 19.01.

To traffic 12/1901.

REPAIRS:
???. ?/?—?/2/11.**G.**
Dar. 13/6—30/8/23.**G.**
Dar. 7/12/23—12/1/24.**L.**
Dar. 23/4—29/5/25.**G.**
Dar. 4/1—21/2/27.**G.**

Dar. 8/8—26/9/28.**G.**
Dar. 30/10—30/11/31.**G.**
Dar. 13/4—22/5/35.**G.**
Dar. 8/8—7/9/38.**G.**
Dar. 28/12/38—21/1/39.**N/C.**
Dar. 7/11—8/12/41.**G.**
Dar. 8/5—3/6/44.**G.**
Dar. 26/7—21/8/44.**L.**
Dar. 19/9—29/10/47.**G.**

BOILERS:
G142.
D2098 ?/2/11.
D1919 30/8/23.
D1758 *(new)* 21/2/27.
2902 *(new)* 7/9/38 (56B).
2911 *(ex643)* 8/12/41 (56B).
D1768 *(ex474)* 3/6/44.
2800 *(ex3276)* 29/10/47 (56B).

SHEDS:
Shildon.
Darlington 7/1/35.
Blaydon 28/3/43.
Borough Gardens 20/7/47.

RENUMBERED:
3259 12/5/46.

CONDEMNED: 9/5/51.
Cut up at Darlington.

130

Gateshead 20.01.

To traffic 3/1902.

REPAIRS:
???. ?/?—?/4/17.**G.**
???. ?/?—?/11/19.**G.**
???. ?/?—?/11/22.**G.**
Dar. 13/12/24—30/4/25.**G.**
Dar. 19/3—23/5/28.**G.**
Dar. 15/5—16/6/31.**G.**
Dar. 13/12/34—22/1/35.**G.**
Dar. 8/6—27/8/37.**L.**
Dar. 2/2—6/3/39.**G.**
Dar. 31/3—28/4/42.**G.**
Dar. 17/11—13/12/44.**G.**
Ghd. 10—23/5/46.**L.**
Dar. 6—31/12/46.**L.**
Dar. 8/12/47—6/2/48.**G.**
Ghd. 4—20/5/49.**C/L.**

BOILERS:
G149.
G252 ?/4/17.
D1006 *(new)* 11/19.
D1037 *(ex1700)* 30/4/25.
D854 *(ex654)* 16/6/31.
D1454 *(ex1696)* 22/1/35.
2080 *(ex770)* 6/3/39.
2225 *(ex1685)* 28/4/42.
2073 *(ex1178)* 13/12/44.

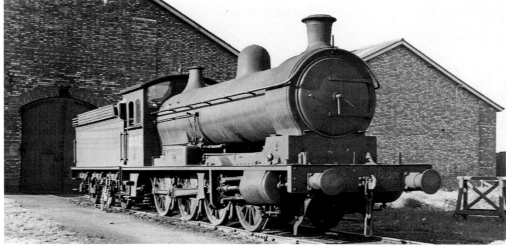

The first twenty built at Gateshead had a polished brass cap on the chimney. By Grouping, most had been removed, but No.1002 still had one when it went for repair on 4th June 1940.

Replacement chimneys were 3/16in. taller but less tapered than the original Worsdell design and no separate cap was fitted. This is a July 1936 built Diagram 56B boiler with its left hand washout plugs on the original close spacing. Only two were noted as fitted with windjabber, No.645 from August 1931 and No.3251 from March 1947, both shedded at Borough Gardens (*see* top two illustrations page 22).

Some replacement chimneys fitted in the 1930's were almost parallel sided.

The ninety original boilers and replacements built to December 1918 had Ramsbottom safety valves enclosed in the customary polished brass trumpet shaped casing. The last one, built in June 1916 and on No.1002 (*see* top illustration) from May 1938 worked until May 1941.

130 cont/.
2806 (*ex3280*) 6/2/48 (56B).

SHEDS:
Dairycoates.
Haverton Hill 18/6/31.
Blaydon 23/7/45.
Middlesbrough 20/7/47.

RENUMBERED:
3260 1/5/46.
E3260 6/2/48.

CONDEMNED: 21/6/50.
Cut up at Darlington.

527

Gateshead 1.02.

To traffic 3/1902.

REPAIRS:
???. ?/?—?/2/09.**G.**
???. ?/?—?/11/11.**G.**
???. ?/?—?/12/19.**G.**
Dar. 16/5—30/7/23.**G.**
Dar. 13/1—4/26.**G.**
Dar. 19/8—8/10/29.**G.**
Dar. 15/8—25/9/33.**G.**
Dar. 15/4—10/6/36.**G.**
Dar. 2/12/38—17/1/39.**G.**
Dar. 26/5—30/6/41.**G.**
Dar. 21/2—14/3/44.**G.**
Ghd. 10/8—22/8/45.**L.**
Dar. 26/11—28/12/46.**G.**
Ghd. 15/1—24/2/48.**L.**

BOILERS:
G72.
G255 2/09.
G331 11/11.
D1013 (*new*) 12/19.
2269 (*ex1149*) 25/9/33.
2068 (*ex767*) 17/1/39.
2232 (*ex1731*) 14/3/44.
2281 (*ex3309*) 28/12/46.

SHEDS:
Newport.
Tyne Dock 28/3/43.
Borough Gardens 13/4/47.

RENUMBERED:
3261 19/5/46.
E3261 24/2/48.

CONDEMNED: 31/10/50.
Cut up at Darlington.

1002

Gateshead 2.02.

To traffic 3/1902.

REPAIRS:
???. ?/?—?/2/10.**G.**
???. ?/?—?/5/10.**G.**
???. ?/?—?/12/19.**G.**
Dar. 22/4—31/7/24.**G.**
Dar. 30/3—25/5/26.**L.**
Ghd. 19/10/27—14/1/28.**G.**
Ghd. 14/1—6/2/30.**L.**
Ghd. 10/3—26/4/32.**G.**
Dar. 30/7—23/9/35.**G.**
Dar. 30/3—9/5/38.**G.**
Dar. 9—17/5/38.**N/C.**
Dar. 4/6—6/8/40.**L.**
Dar. 20/5—22/7/41.**G.**
Dar. 12/8—2/9/42.**N/C.**
Dar. 16/11—11/12/43.**G.**
Dar. 4—14/12/45.**L.**
Dar. 28/1—28/2/46.**L.**
Dar. 13/11—19/12/47.**G.**

BOILERS:
G74.
G72 ?/2/10.
G74 ?/5/10.
D1010 (*new*) 12/19.
D2159 (*ex474*) 23/9/35.
D572 (*ex656*) 9/5/38.
D1955 (*ex793*) 22/7/41.
D1441 (*ex770*) 11/12/43.
2804 (*ex3266*) 19/12/47 (56B).

SHEDS:
Dairycoates.
Springhead 26/8/24.
Blaydon 26/5/27.
North Blyth 9/10/34.
Blaydon 28/3/43.
Selby 20/7/47

RENUMBERED:
3262 20/1/46.

CONDEMNED: 22/8/50.
Cut up at Darlington.

1320

Gateshead 3.02.

To traffic 3/1902.

REPAIRS:
???. ?/?—?/4/12.**G.**
???. ?/?—?/7/19.**G.**
Dar. 1/4—31/5/24.**G.**
Dar. 1/7—11/10/27.**G.**
Dar. 11/9—24/10/30.**G.**
Dar. 10—23/1/33.**L.**
Dar. 19/4—15/5/34.**G.**
Rebuilt to Part 2.
Dar. 27/2—5/6/36.**G.**
Dar. 2/2—22/3/39.**G.**
Dar. 9—19/12/40.**N/C.**
Dar. 6/10—8/11/41.**G.**
Dar. 17/1—3/3/44.**G.**

Ghd. 27/6—21/7/45.**L.**
Dar. 13/7—14/9/46.**G.**
Dar. 21—24/9/46.**N/C.**
Dar. 5/10/48. *Not repaired.*

BOILERS:
G159.
G182 ?/4/12.
D882 (*new*) 7/19.
D1815 (*exQ10 2508*) 15/5/34 (56A).
D1670 (*ex2119*) 5/6/36 (56A).
D1997 (*ex2119*) 8/11/41 (56A).
D1674 (*ex653*) 14/9/46 (56A).

SHEDS:
Newport.
Middlesbrough 7/11/38.

RENUMBERED:
3263 14/4/46.

CONDEMNED: 1/11/48.
Cut up at Darlington.

1700

Gateshead 4.02.

To traffic 4/1902.

REPAIRS:
???. ?/?—?/2/20.**G.**
Dar. 29/10/24—21/1/25.**G.**
Dar. 11/6—13/8/28.**G.**
Dar. 10/2—18/3/31.**G.**
Dar. 13/3—9/4/34.**G.**
Dar. 24/11/37—20/1/38.**G.**
Dar. 24/9—24/10/40.**G.**
Dar. 17/12/42—21/1/43.**G.**
Ghd. 8—23/10/44.**L.**
Dar. 18/10—14/11/45.**G.**
Ghd. 10—25/10/46.**L.**
Dar. 11/6/48. *Not repaired.*

BOILERS:
G76.
D1037 (*new*) 2/20.
D11 (*ex661*) 21/1/25.
D587 (*ex653*) 13/8/28.
D1046 (*ex2123*) 9/4/34.
2150 (*ex2121*) 20/1/38.
D1004 (*ex2120*) 24/10/40.
2794 (*ex443*) 21/1/43 (56B).
3372 (*ex1708*) 14/11/45 (56B).

SHEDS:
Newport.
Haverton Hill 5/5/31.
Tyne Dock 28/3/43.
Borough Gardens 13/4/47.

RENUMBERED:
3264 1/9/46.

CONDEMNED: 26/6/48.
Cut up at Darlington.

1704

Gateshead 5.02.

To traffic 4/1902.

REPAIRS:
???. ?/?—?/11/19.**G.**
Dar. 23/1—14/4/23.**G.**
Dar. 7/9—11/12/25.**G.**
Dar. 3/11/27—6/1/28.**L.**
Dar. 3/7—29/8/29.**G.**
Dar. 1/8—4/9/33.**G.**
Dar. 4/4—26/6/34.**H.**
Dar. 1/10—18/11/36.**G.**
Dar. 12/12/39—29/1/40.**G.**
Dar. 12/12/41—9/1/42.**G.**
Dar. 7/10—1/12/43.**G.**
Dar. 5—6/1/44.**N/C.**
Ghd. 14—29/3/46.**L.**
Dar. 25/3/47. *Not repaired.*

BOILERS:
G176.
D1004 (*new*) ?/11/19.
D1364 (*ex1186*) 4/9/33.
D1768 (*ex1177*) 26/6/34.
2153 (*ex1032*) 9/1/42.
D1955 (*ex1002*) 1/12/43.

SHEDS:
Newport.
Middlesbrough 6/2/37.
Newport 22/9/44.

RENUMBERED:
3265 29/3/46.

CONDEMNED: 26/4/47.
Cut up at Darlington.

1708

Gateshead 6.02.

To traffic 5/1902.

REPAIRS:
???. ?/?—?/4/11.**G.**
???. ?/?—?/12/19.**G.**
Dar. 12/8—20/10/24.**G.**
Dar. 3/6—9/9/27.**G.**
Dar. 4/11—23/12/29.**G.**
Dar. 17/11—23/12/31.**G.**
Dar. 23/8—2/10/35.**G.**
Dar. 1/11—13/12/37.**G.**
Dar. 8—30/11/38.**N/C.**
Dar. 8/7—5/8/40.**G.**
Dar. 29/4—27/5/43.**G.**
Dar. 17/8—7/9/44.**L.**
Dar. 2—27/10/45.**G.**
Ghd. 16—24/12/46.**L.**

1708 cont/.
Dar. 13/10/47. *Not repaired.*

BOILERS:
 G179.
 G328 ?/4/11.
 D1007 *(new)* 12/19.
 D988 *(ex1731)* 23/12/29.
 2904 *(new)* 13/12/37 (56B).
 3126 *(new)* 5/8/40 (56B).
 3372 *(new)* 27/5/43 (56B).
 2804 *(ex1009)* 27/10/45 (56B).

SHEDS:
Starbeck.
Newport 9/4/31.
Middlesbrough 5/5/31.
Newport 7/11/38.
Middlesbrough 5/6/39.

RENUMBERED:
3266 30/6/46.

CONDEMNED: 22/11/47.
Cut up at Darlington.

1709

Gateshead 7.02.

To traffic 5/1902.

REPAIRS:
???. ?/?—?/11/11.G.
???. ?/?—?/7/14.G.
Ghd. 9/2—23/4/23.G.
Dar. 1/4—29/7/26.G.
Dar. 29/5—17/7/29.G.
Ghd. 7/7—15/8/32.G.
Dar. 8/6—12/7/33.H.
Dar. 27/8—17/10/35.G.
Dar. 9/11—22/12/39.G.
Dar. 13/2—14/3/42.G.
Dar. 12/1—3/2/43.
Tender only.
Dar. 28/9—16/10/43.L.
Dar. 2—24/6/44.G.
Dar. 26/9—12/10/44.N/C.
Ghd. 4—16/4/46.L.
Dar. 19/9—23/10/47.G.

BOILERS:
 G182.
 G329 ?/11/11.
 D1914 ?/7/14.
 D1745 *(new)* 29/7/26.
 D1453 *(ex578)* 17/7/29.
 D1010 *(ex1002)* 17/10/35.
 D1454 *(ex474)* 14/3/42.
 D1961 *(ex1757)* 24/6/44.
 D1427 *(ex3337)* 23/10/47.

SHEDS:
Borough Gardens.
Doncaster 13/1/26.

Borough Gardens 27/5/29.
Heaton 14/11/30.
North Blyth 12/7/34.
Heaton 28/3/43.
Darlington 4/11/44.
Tyne Dock 12/5/46.
Borough Gardens 13/4/47.

RENUMBERED:
3267 16/4/46.

CONDEMNED: 6/6/51.
Cut up at Darlington.

1717

Gateshead 8.02.

To traffic 6/1902.

REPAIRS:
???. ?/?—?/9/10.G.
???. ?/?—?/1/14.G.
???. ?/?—?/10/19.G.
???. ?/?—?/9/22.G.
Dar. 24/10—23/11/23.G.
Dar. 4/2—17/4/25.G.
Dar. 22/9—30/11/27.G.
Dar. 24/2—15/4/30.G.
Dar. 27/10—28/11/32.G.
Dar. 1/4—11/6/36.G.
Dar. 24/10—30/12/39.G.
Dar. 17/1—9/2/42.G.
Dar. 21/4—11/5/44.G.
Ghd. 22/3—9/4/45.L.
Dar. 5—30/3/46.G.
Ghd. 26/3—11/4/47.L.
Dar. 23/1/48. *Not repaired.*

BOILERS:
 G185.
 G72 ?/9/10.
 G258 ?/1/14.
 D1921 ?/10/19.
 D1427 *(new)* ?/9/22.
 D1432 *(ex430)* 9/2/42.
 2080 *(ex647)* 11/5/44.
 3132 *(ex794)* 30/3/46 (56B).

SHEDS:
Starbeck.
Newport 9/4/31.
Middlesbrough 5/5/31.

RENUMBERED:
3268 30/3/46.

CONDEMNED: 7/2/48.
Cut up at Darlington.

1729

Gateshead 9.02.

To traffic 6/1902.

REPAIRS:
???. ?/?—?/10/19.G.
Dar. 15/9—22/11/24.G.
Dar. 25/7—19/10/27.G.
Dar. 14/4—18/6/30.G.
Dar. 13/6—9/7/34.G.
Dar. 11/12/37—4/2/38.G.
Dar. 13—20/3/39.N/C.
Dar. 12/8—14/9/40.G.
Dar. 24/12/42—25/2/43.G.
Dar. 7/3—7/4/45.G.
Ghd. 4—18/7/46.L.
Dar. 6/6/47. *Not repaired.*

BOILERS:
 G188.
 D994 *(new)* ?/10/19.
 D1365 *(ex656)* 18/6/30.
 D859 *(ex654)* 9/7/34.
 2929 *(new)* 4/2/38 (56B).
 2904 *(ex1708)* 14/9/40 (56B).
 3128 *(ex645)* 7/4/45 (56B).

SHEDS:
Stockton.
Haverton Hill 15/12/30.
Middlesbrough 27/5/37.

RENUMBERED:
3269 14/4/46.

CONDEMNED: 19/7/47.
Cut up at Darlington.

1682

Gateshead 30.02.

To traffic 12/1902.

REPAIRS:
???. ?/?—?/3/20.G.
Dar. 28/3—12/6/23.G.
Dar. 12/3—28/7/26.G.
Dar. 17/9—5/10/26.L.
Dar. 8/10—28/11/28.G.
Dar. 26/1—24/2/32.G.
Dar. 3/9—16/10/36.G.
Dar. 4—29/3/40.G.
Dar. 28/10—25/11/42.G.
Dar. 6/3—6/4/45.G.
Ghd. 30/9—15/10/46.L.
Dar. 22/10—21/11/47.G.
Dar. 10/8/51. *Not repaired.*

BOILERS:
 G249.
 D1043 *(new)* ?/3/20.
 D1403 *(ex1669)* 16/10/36.

D1470 *(ex655)* 29/3/40.
 2233 *(ex774)* 25/11/42.
 2886 *(ex3284)* 21/11/47 (56B).

SHEDS:
Dairycoates.
Haverton Hill 19/3/28.
Normanton 14/11/48.
Malton 14/1/51.
York 11/3/51.

RENUMBERED:
3270 18/8/46

CONDEMNED: 10/8/51.
Cut up at Darlington.

1684

Gateshead 31.02.

To traffic 12/1902.

REPAIRS:
???. ?/?—?/5/14.G.
???. ?/?—?/10/16.G.
Dar. 18/7—28/9/23.G.
Dar. 22/12/24—17/3/25.G.
Dar. 11/4—11/6/28.G.
Dar. 14/10—20/11/30.G.
Dar. 17/8—1/10/34.H.
Dar. 30/7—3/9/35.G.
Dar. 5/8—13/9/38.G.
Dar. 10/3—5/5/41.G.
Dar. 2—25/11/43.G.
Ghd. 28/3—17/4/45.L.
Dar. 9/6—19/7/47.G.

BOILERS:
 G250.
 G72 ?/5/14.
 D601 *(new)* ?/10/16.
 D994 *(ex1729)* 20/11/30.
 2811 *(new)* 13/9/38 (56B).
 3135 *(new)* 5/5/41 (56B).
 3127 *(ex650)* 25/11/43 (56B).
 3249 *(ex3303)* 19/7/47 (56B).

SHEDS:
Newport.
Borough Gardens 28/3/43.

RENUMBERED:
3271 1/9/46.

CONDEMNED: 22/11/50.
Cut up at Darlington.

There were variations on the Ramsbottom mounting. From December 1930 to March 1936, No.2124 had a September 1911 built boiler with Ramsbottom valves and a truncated trumpet only about one-third of the usual height.

No.769, from May 1930 to March 1934, had a boiler built in February 1923 with a similar cover and 'pop' safety valves on what was ostensibly a Ramsbottom base.

Beginning with replacement boilers, built September 1919 onwards, two 2½in. Ross 'pop' valves were the standard fitting with a shallow cover around the base mounting stool.

The last twenty-three Diagram 56 boilers, built in 1928/29, omitted the mounting but retained the casing, which gave the impression that shorter valves had been used.

Until April 1934 normal whistle fitting was one large, and one smaller bell-shape on pipes which protruded through the cab roof. No.651 was the only one seen in LNER days, still with original circular front windows. It had them when it went to works 30th April 1936 but by August 1947 had been duly changed to the shaped pattern like all the others most of which had been fitted by the NER.

There were three noted, Nos.653, 1717 and 2117 (two at Newport and one at Middlesbrough sheds) which had the larger bell-shape replaced by an organ pipe.

(below) Starting with No.410, ex works 9th April 1934, the whistle position was changed to the front plate of the cab and all then seem to have had organ pipe on the right hand side flanked by small bell shape.

1685

Gateshead 32.02.

To traffic 12/1902.

REPAIRS:
???. ?/?—?/9/14.**G.**
???. ?/?—?/11/18.**G.**
Dar. 30/4—30/6/24.**G.**
Dar. 24/10—31/12/27.**G.**
Dar. 25/9—31/10/30.**G.**
Dar. 25/4—24/5/34.**G.**
Dar. 28/8—3/10/36.**G.**
Dar. 23/8—22/9/39.**G.**
Dar. 22/12/41—23/1/42.**G.**
Dar. 1—24/6/44.**G.**
Dar. 10/8—2/9/46.**L.**
Dar. 2/9—2/10/47.**G.**

BOILERS:
G251.
G250 ?/9/14.
D721 *(new)* ?/11/18.
D1757 *(ex644)* 24/5/34.
  2225 *(ex2122)* 3/10/36.
  2797 *(ex2124)* 23/1/42 (56B).
  2802 *(ex1031)* 24/6/44 (56B).
  2809 *(ex3201)* 2/10/47 (56B).

SHEDS:
Newport.
Darlington 21/7/32.
Ferryhill 18/1/36.
Darlington 7/11/38.
Blaydon 28/3/43.
Cudworth 20/7/47.
Middlesbrough 13/2/49.

RENUMBERED:
3272 20/10/46.

CONDEMNED: 3/7/50.
Cut up at Darlington.

1694

Gateshead 1.03.

To traffic 2/1903.

REPAIRS:
???. ?/?—?/8/14.**G.**
???. ?/?—?/9/20.**G.**
Dar. 6/11/22—31/1/23.**G.**
Dar. 13/11/25—4/2/26.**G.**
Dar. 24/5—30/7/28.**G.**
Dar. 16/1—2/3/31.**G.**
Dar. 11/6—7/8/35.**G.**
Dar. 2/8—1/9/38.**G.**
Dar. 20/5—21/6/41.**G.**

Dar. 5/11—4/12/43.**G.**
Ghd. 10—25/1/46.**L.**
Dar. 19/2—29/3/47.**G.**

BOILERS:
G252.
G615 ?/8/14.
D1061 *(new)* ?/9/20.
D714 *(ex2120)* 4/2/26.
D1014 *(ex2123)* 7/8/35.
  2916 *(new)* 1/9/38 (56B).
  3224 *(ex792)* 4/12/43 (56B).

SHEDS:
Dairycoates.
Haverton Hill 19/3/28.
Newport 25/1/35.
Middlesbrough 6/2/37.
Newport 22/9/44.
Middlesbrough 2/11/47.

RENUMBERED:
3273 15/12/46.

CONDEMNED: 28/3/49.
Cut up at Darlington.

83

Gateshead 3.03.

To traffic 3/1903.

REPAIRS:
???. ?/?—?/7/20.**G.**
Dar. 29/10/23—4/1/24.**G.**
Dar. 6/9—26/11/27.**G.**
Dar. 3/2—12/3/31.**G.**
Dar. 22/5—16/6/34.**G.**
Dar. 18/2—18/3/37.**G.**
Dar. 11—25/5/37.**N/C.**
Dar. 9—27/4/40.**G.**
Dar. 31/7—4/9/42.**G.**
Dar. 13/7—13/8/43.**G.**
Dar. 5—26/4/45.**L.**
Ghd. 18/12/45—5/1/46.**L.**
Dar. 3/4—7/6/47.**G.**
Dar. 18/9/50. *Not repaired.*

BOILERS:
G254.
D1066 *(new)* ?/7/20.
D1392 *(ex660)* 16/6/34.
  2809 *(new)* 18/3/37 (56B).
  2804 *(ex410)* 27/4/40 (56B).
  3117 *(ex1031)* 4/9/42 (56B).
  2807 *(ex1149)* 13/8/43 (56B).

SHEDS:
Shildon.
Ferryhill 15/8/32.

Darlington 7/11/38.
Newport 15/4/39.
Tyne Dock 28/3/43.
Newport 6/2/49.

RENUMBERED:
3274 1/9/46.

CONDEMNED: 18/9/50.
Cut up at Darlington.

162

Gateshead 11.03.

To traffic 6/1903.

REPAIRS:
???. ?/?—?/2/11.**G.**
Dar. 21/8—29/10/23.**G.**
Dar. 16/5—10/6/24.**L.**
Dar. 14/1—30/3/27.**G.**
Dar. 14/10—29/11/29.**G.**
Dar. 11—26/2/32.**H.**
Dar. 5/10—2/11/34.**G.**
Dar. 25/10—24/11/38.**G.**
Dar. 10/3—5/5/41.**G.**
Dar. 16/6—15/7/43.**G.**
Ghd. 27/6—5/7/45.**L.**
Dar. 31/10—30/11/46.**G.**

BOILERS:
G287.
D2097 ?/2/11.
D1769 *(new)* 30/3/27.
D1380 *(ex652)* 26/2/32.
D1441 *(ex793)* 2/11/34.
  2168 *(ex785)* 24/11/38.
  3126 *(ex1708)* 15/7/43 (56B).
  2929 *(ex578)* 30/11/46 (56B).

SHEDS:
Haverton Hill.
Tyne Dock 28/3/43.
Borough Gardens 13/4/47.
Haverton Hill 15/2/48.

RENUMBERED:
3275 27/10/46.

CONDEMNED: 18/4/49.
Cut up at Darlington.

1696

Gateshead 2.03.

To traffic 3/1903.

REPAIRS:
???. ?/?—?/2/13.**G.**

Dar. 19/2—26/5/25.**G.**
Dar. 7/8—7/9/25.**L.**
Dar. 7/1—19/2/29.**G.**
Dar. 30/11/31—11/1/32.**G.**
Dar. 14/11—7/12/34.**G.**
Dar. 25/5—9/7/38.**G.**
Dar. 25/10—28/12/39.**H.**
Dar. 21/10—22/11/41.**G.**
Dar. 26/11—23/12/43.**G.**
Dar. 22/5—7/6/45.**L.**
Ghd. 3—17/12/45.**L.**
Dar. 23/2—27/3/46.**L.**
Dar. 6/8—12/9/47.**G.**

BOILERS:
G253.
D1918 ?/2/13.
D1454 *(new)* 26/5/25.
D1380 *(ex162)* 7/12/34.
  2798 *(ex2122)* 22/11/41 (56B).
  2800 *(ex2116)* 23/12/43 (56B).
  2153 *(ex3285)* 12/9/47.

SHEDS:
Shildon.
Ferryhill 15/8/32.
Darlington 7/11/38.
Selby 29/6/39.
Neville Hill 28/3/43.
Selby 23/7/45.

RENUMBERED:
3276 26/3/46.

CONDEMNED: 20/2/50.
Cut up at Darlington.

410

Gateshead 4/03.

To traffic 4/1903.

REPAIRS:
???. ?/?—?/2/08.**G.**
???. ?/?—?/10/18.**G.**
Dar. 9/1—19/3/24.**G.**
Dar. 28/2—30/5/27.**G.**
Dar. 28/10—27/11/30.**G.**
Dar. 12/3—9/4/34.**G.**
Dar. 8/12/36—22/1/37.**G.**
Dar. 7—16/7/37.**N/C.**
Dar. 20/1—2/2/39.**N/C.**
Dar. 21/2—13/3/40.**G.**
Dar. 3/11—2/12/42.**G.**
Ghd. 28/8—15/9/44.**L.**
Dar. 17/4—17/5/46.**G.**
Dar. 30/5—3/6/46.**N/C.**
Ghd. 1—13/5/47.**N/C.**

WORKS CODES:- Cw - Cowlairs. Dar- Darlington. Don - Doncaster. Ghd - Gateshead. Gor - Gorton. Hsi - Hull Springhead. Inv - Inverurie. Str - Stratford.
REPAIR CODES:- **C/H** - Casual Heavy. **C/L** - Casual Light. **G** - General. **H** - Heavy. **H/I** - Heavy Intermediate. **L** - Light. **L/I** - Light Intermediate. **N/C** - Non-Classified.

410 cont/.

BOILERS:
G255.
G138 ?/2/08.
D731 (new) ?/10/18.
 2272 (ex653) 9/4/34.
 2804 (new) 22/1/37 (56B).
 3123 (new) 13/3/40 (56B).
 3120 (ex655) 2/12/42 (56B).
 3117 (ex650) 17/5/46 (56B).

SHEDS:
Newport.
Shildon 9/1/26.
Darlington 7/1/35.
Heaton 28/12/35.
Blaydon 27/5/40.
Darlington 20/7/47.

RENUMBERED:
3277 17/5/46.

CONDEMNED: 2/5/49.
Cut up at Darlington.

474

Gateshead 5.03.

To traffic 4/1903.

REPAIRS:
???. ?/?—?/12/19.G.
Dar. 3/8—6/11/23.G.
Dar. 15/3—15/7/26.G.
Dar. 25/3—9/5/29.G.
Dar. 15/11—16/12/32.G.
Dar. 31/7—30/8/35.G.
Dar. 23/2—30/3/39.G.
Dar. 24/12/41—24/1/42.G.
Dar. 17—24/11/42.N/C.
Dar. 22/4—13/5/44.G.
Ghd. 7—22/3/46.L.
Dar. 13/8—19/9/47.G.

BOILERS:
 G256.
D1014 (new) ?/12/19.
D2159 (ex659) 16/12/32.
D2153 (ex794) 30/8/35.
D1454 (ex130) 30/3/39.
D1768 (ex1704) 24/1/42.
 2085 (ex764) 13/5/44.

SHEDS:
Newport.
Darlington 14/3/33.
Ferryhill 7/1/35.
Darlington 7/11/38.
Blaydon 28/3/43.
Darlington 27/7/47.
Neville Hill 11/7/48.
Selby 10/7/49.

RENUMBERED:
3278 19/3/46.

CONDEMNED: 30/8/50.
Cut up at Darlington.

1186

Gateshead 6.03.

To traffic 5/1903.

REPAIRS:
???. ?/?—?/4/19.G.
Ghd. 19/6—27/8/23.G.
Dar. 9/11—30/4/27.G.
Dar. 20/1—10/3/30.G.
Dar. 15/5—23/6/33.G.
Dar. 4/12/35—17/1/36.G.
Dar. 20/7—22/8/38.G.
Dar. 7/4—13/5/41.G.
Dar. 16/2—17/3/43.G.
Dar. 24/7—6/8/43.L.
Dar. 8/10/43—10/2/44.
Tender only.
Ghd. 31/7—21/8/44.L.
Dar. 27/3—13/4/45.L.
Dar. 10/10—3/11/45.G.
Ghd. 28/12/46—9/1/47.L.
Dar. 4/2/48. Not repaired.

BOILERS:
 G257.
D862 (new) ?/4/19.
D1364 (ex1215) 10/3/30.
 2232 (ex642) 23/6/33.
D716 (ex1731) 17/1/36.
D1769 (ex2120) 22/8/38.
 2806 (ex767) 13/5/41 (56B).
 3121 (ex654) 17/3/43 (56B).
 2930 (ex648) 13/4/45 (56B).
 2159 (ex656) 3/11/45.

SHEDS:
Newport.
Shildon 18/11/31.
Ferryhill 15/8/32.
Darlington 7/11/38.
Selby 26/6/39.

RENUMBERED:
3279 24/2/46.

CONDEMNED: 14/2/48.
Cut up at Darlington.

650

Gateshead 12.03.

To traffic 6/1903.

REPAIRS:
???. ?/?—?/4/13.G.
???. ?/?—?/12/17.G.

Dar. 1/11/23—11/1/24.G.
Dar. 25/7—13/10/27.G.
Dar. 24/9—6/11/29.G.
Dar. 3/5—3/6/32.G.
Dar. 26/2—29/3/35.G.
Dar. 2/2—4/3/38.G.
Dar. 11/1—17/2/39.L.
Dar. 19/12/40—18/1/41.G.
Dar. 23/11—12/12/42.N/C.
Dar. 8/9—2/10/43.G.
Ghd. 25/11—9/12/44.L.
Dar. 30/1—23/2/46.G.
Dar. 2/12/47—2/1/48.G.

BOILERS:
G288.
G253 ?/4/13.
D716 (new) ?/12/17.
D562 (ex715) 6/11/29.
D602 (ex2117) 3/6/32.
 2227 (ex2120) 29/3/35.
 2906 (new) 4/3/38 (56B).
 3127 (new) 18/1/41 (56B).
 3117 (ex83) 2/10/43 (56B).
 2806 (ex772) 23/2/46 (56B).
 2225 (ex3289) 2/1/48.

SHEDS:
Newport.
Selby 12/6/39.
Neville Hill 6/2/49.
Selby 10/7/49.

RENUMBERED:
3280 17/11/46.

CONDEMNED: 25/10/50.
Cut up at Darlington.

651

Gateshead 10.03.

To traffic 6/1903.

REPAIRS:
???. ?/?—?/4/19.G.
???. ?/?—?/1/22.G.
Ghd. 3—30/1/24.L.
Ghd. 19/11/25—16/2/26.G.
Ghd. 2/5—6/7/28.G.
Ghd. 22/5—14/7/31.G.
Dar. 30/4—11/7/36.G.
Dar. 7/7—16/7/37.N/C.
Dar. 2—28/12/38.N/C.
Dar. 19/8—21/9/40.G.
Dar. 30/9—24/10/41.L.
Dar. 24/3—5/5/43.G.
Dar. 1/7—16/8/44.G.
Ghd. 28/2—15/3/46.L.
Dar. 24/6—15/8/47.G.
Dar.27/1—20/2/48.L.

BOILERS:
G286.
D856 (new) ?/4/19.
D727 (ex2124) 14/7/31.
 2794 (new) 11/7/36 (56B).
 2929 (ex1729) 21/9/40 (56B).
 2914 (ex772) 5/5/43 (56B).
 2809 (ex783) 16/8/44 (56B).
 3241 (ex1002) 15/8/47 (56B).

SHEDS:
East Hartlepool.
Haverton Hill 10/12/38.
West Hartlepool 28/3/43.
Newport 6/2/49.
Middlesbrough 1/5/49.

RENUMBERED:
 3281 22/12/46.
E3281 20/2/48.

CONDEMNED: 12/6/50.
Cut up at Darlington.

1009

Gateshead 9.03.

To traffic 6/1903.

REPAIRS:
???. ?/?—?/12/17.G.
Dar. 5/1—20/3/24.G.
Dar. 7/3—15/6/27.G.
Dar. 25/7—19/9/30.G.
Dar. 4/4—3/5/34.G.
Dar. 27/4—2/6/37.G.
Dar. 1—25/5/40.G.
Dar. 9/9—9/10/42.G.
Dar. 8/9—6/10/45.G.
Ghd. 3—23/9/46.L.
Dar. 29/4—21/5/48.G.

BOILERS:
G285.
D698 (new) ?/12/17.
D1745 (ex1110) 3/5/34.
D1392 (ex83) 2/6/37.
 2804 (ex83) 9/10/42 (56B).
 3238 (ex669) 6/10/45 (56B).
 3235 (ex3311) 21/5/48 (56B).

SHEDS:
Newport.
Borough Gardens 28/3/43.
Tyne Dock 19/10/44.
Borough Gardens 13/4/47.
Middlesbrough 15/2/48.

RENUMBERED:
3282 24/2/46.
63282 21/5/48

CONDEMNED: 11/12/50.
Cut up at Darlington.

On the Diagram 56B boiler built from July 1936, there was only one whistle, a bell-shape above an isolating valve and mounted on the firebox between the safety valves and cab front plate. This was the clearest indication of a 56B boiler especially the first batch which had similar handholes to Diagram 56.

Replacement of the wheel by a second handle had clearly begun by 23rd January 1933 when No.1320 was last ex-works prior to rebuilding with larger boiler. The wheel had certainly gone by 1938.

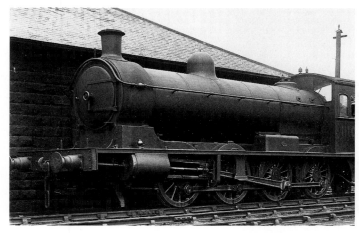

Until the mid-1930's the smokebox door had a wheel and handle for fastening. This photograph is after November 1933 as it shows No.1110 fitted at that repair with Group Standard buffers. It next went for repair on 5th May 1938.

All the original smokebox doors had a flat flange, which fitted flush against a sealing ring in the front plate.

Beginning with No.644, ex works 11th December 1945, at least twelve more acquired a larger diameter and more dished door, which did not have the wide flat flange. The pressed joint ring fitted into a recess in the front plate of the smokebox and which had asbestos packing in it.

Until about 1930 all kept the original taper-shank buffers, which had an end collar, and the drawhook was the NER design. Some of the last withdrawals were still so fitted.

From 1930, increasing use was made of Group Standard type buffers and drawhook.

Prior to the LNER taking over the standard front butter beam was the wood sandwich type, the insert being tapered at the ends to give greater flexibility.

After Grouping a few were changed to single steel plate, Nos.656, 764 and 774 being noted, and still with taper shank buffers.

1731

Gateshead 8.03.

To traffic 6/1903.

REPAIRS:
???. ?/?—?/10/19.**G.**
Ghd. 13/6—25/8/23.**G.**
Dar. 5/10/26—20/1/27.**G.**
Dar. 9/2—4/3/27.**L.**
Dar. 14/10—3/12/29.**G.**
Dar. 12/5—27/6/33.**G.**
Dar. 28/11/35—30/1/36.**G.**
Dar. 9/8—15/9/38.**G.**
Dar. 2/6—14/7/41.**G.**
Dar. 9/12/43—6/1/44.**G.**
Ghd. 3—19/4/45.**L.**
Dar. 9/8—19/9/47.**G.**

BOILERS:
G284.
D988 (new) ?/10/19.
D716 (ex650) 3/12/29.
 2232 (ex1186) 30/1/36.
 2270 (ex2121) 6/1/44.

SHEDS:
Newport.
Stockton 16/10/39.
Newport 1/2/43.
Borough Gardens 28/3/43.

RENUMBERED:
3283 8/12/46.

CONDEMNED: 19/12/50.
Cut up at Darlington.

1757

Gateshead 7.03.

To traffic 6/1903.

REPAIRS:
???. ?/?—?/10/13.**G.**
???. ?/?—?/8/17.**G.**
???. ?/?—?/6/20.**G.**
Dar. 10/7—15/10/23.**G.**
Dar. 17/8—29/9/25.**L.**
Dar. 25/11/26—23/2/27.**G.**
Dar. 18/7—16/8/28.**L.**
Dar. 10/2—29/3/30.**G.**
Dar. 8/8—7/9/33.**G.**
Dar. 23/4—23/6/36.**G.**
Dar. 10/1—3/2/39.**G.**
Dar. 28/7—6/9/41.**G.**
Dar. 26/4—20/5/44.**G.**
Ghd. 9—26/10/45.**L.**
Dar. 1/2—7/3/46.**L.**
Dar. 10/9—10/10/47.**G.**
Dar. 13/6/51. Not repaired.

BOILERS:
G258.
D1929 ?/10/13.
 G295 ?/8/17.
D1053 (new) ?/6/20.
D1961 (ex661) 7/9/33.
 2886 (ex411) 20/5/44 (56B).
 3371 (ex3302) 10/10/47 (56B).

SHEDS:
Newport.
Borough Gardens 28/3/43.

RENUMBERED:
3284 1/9/46.

CONDEMNED: 13/6/51.
Cut up at Darlington.

715

Gateshead 15.03.

To traffic 9/1903.

REPAIRS:
???. ?/?—?/6/16.**G.**
Dar. 9/2—28/4/23.**G.**
Dar. 21/9/26—9/4/27.**G.**
Dar. 2—20/9/29.**G.**
Dar. 11/2—20/3/31.**G.**
Dar. 5/10—4/11/33.**G.**
Dar. 12/12/35—22/2/36.**G.**
Dar. 24—26/2/36.**N/C.**
Dar. 8/8—9/9/38.**G.**
Dar. 9—12/9/38.**N/C.**
Dar. 26/5—11/7/41.**G.**
Dar. 17—28/5/43.**L.**
Dar. 19/6—2/7/43.**L.**
Dar. 1/2—2/3/44.**G.**
Ghd. 22—31/1/46.**L.**
Dar. 26/6—30/8/47.**G.**

BOILERS:
G289.
 D562 (new) ?/6/16.
D1080 (ex430) 20/9/29.
D1013 (ex527) 4/11/33.
D1758 (ex2125) 9/9/38.
 2153 (ex1704) 2/3/44.
 3128 (ex3269) 30/8/47 (56B).

SHEDS:
Dairycoates.
Springhead 30/1/25.
Thirsk 24/11/27.
Starbeck 9/8/29.
Neville Hill 27/7/37.
Darlington 14/12/37.
Kirkby Stephen 2/9/40.
Darlington 21/5/41.
Blaydon 28/3/43.
Middlesbrough 5/10/47.
Neville Hill 13/6/48.
Selby 10/7/49.

RENUMBERED:
3285 5/6/46.

CONDEMNED: 27/9/50.
Cut up at Darlington.

785

Gateshead 16.03.

To traffic 9/1903.

REPAIRS:
???. ?/?—?/2/20.**G.**
Dar. 19/6—30/8/23.**G.**
Dar. 28/5—29/9/26.**G.**
Dar. 3/12/28—18/1/29.**G.**
Ghd. 22/1—6/2/30.**L.**
Dar. 22/6—2/8/33.**G.**
Dar. 5/10—14/11/38.**G.**
Dar. 31/10—28/11/40.**G.**
Dar. 23/6—16/7/42.**L.**
Dar. 26/11/42—1/1/43.**G.**
Ghd. 30/8—21/9/44.**L.**
Dar. 10/7—24/8/46.**G.**
Dar. 3—6/4/48.Not repaired.
Ghd. 8/4—10/5/48.**L.**

BOILERS:
G290.
D1023 (new) ?/2/20.
 2168 (new) 18/1/29.
 2281 (ex772) 14/11/38.
 2150 (ex1700) 28/11/40.
D1392 (ex1009) 1/1/43.
 2080 (ex1717) 24/8/46.

SHEDS:
Dairycoates.
Springhead 10/10/24.
Dairycoates 30/1/25.
York 21/2/27.
Tyne Dock 13/5/29.
Annfield Plain 14/10/29.
Tyne Dock 24/6/37.
Newport 29/3/38.
Borough Gardens 28/3/43.
Selby 15/2/48.

RENUMBERED:
3286 5/1/47.
63286 10/5/48.

CONDEMNED: 11/4/49.
Cut up at Darlington.

792

Gateshead 17/03.

To traffic 10/1903.

REPAIRS:
???. ?/?—?/10/13.**G.**
???. ?/?—?/2/21.**G.**

Dar. 5/4—17/6/24.**G.**
Dar. 20/1—27/3/28.**G.**
Dar. 13/1—20/2/31.**G.**
Dar. 22/3—8/5/35.**G.**
Dar. 23/8—23/9/38.**G.**
Dar. 12/5—26/9/41.**G.**
Dar. 30/9—23/10/43.**G.**
Ghd. 18/8—7/9/44.**L.**
Dar. 25/6—20/8/47.**G.**

BOILERS:
G291.
 G185 ?/10/13.
D1074 (new) ?/2/21.
D1013 (ex715) 23/9/38.
 3224 (new) 26/9/41 (56B).
 2276 (ex652) 23/10/43.
 3127 (ex3271) 20/8/47 (56B).

SHEDS:
Newport.
Borough Gardens 28/3/43.

RENUMBERED:
3287 25/8/46.

CONDEMNED: 29/11/50.
Cut up at Darlington.

1128

Gateshead 18.03.

To traffic 10/1903.

REPAIRS:
???. ?/?—?/2/15.**G.**
???. ?/?—?/8/16.**G.**
???. ?/?—?/2/22.**G.**
Dar. 21/3—11/4/24.**N/C.**
Dar. 29/9—28/11/24.**G.**
Dar. 16/1—22/3/28.**G.**
Dar. 14—16/1/29.**N/C.**
Dar. 2/9—16/10/30.**G.**
Dar. 26/9—30/10/33.**G.**
Dar. 26/4—8/6/37.**G.**
Dar. 1—25/4/40.**G.**
Dar. 15—22/12/41.**L.**
Dar. 1/8—5/9/42.**G.**
Dar. 3/2—3/3/45.**G.**
Dar. 2/7/47. Not repaired.

BOILERS:
G294.
 G251 ?/2/15.
D589 (new) ?/8/16.
 2073 (new) 22/3/28.
D1053 (ex1757) 30/10/33.
D1365 (ex789) 8/6/37.
D1400 (ex444) 5/9/42.
D1757 (ex1218) 3/3/45.

SHEDS:
Stockton.
Dairycoates 7/2/25.

1128 cont/.
Haverton Hill 19/3/28.

RENUMBERED:
3288 24/2/46.

CONDEMNED: 2/8/47.
Cut up at Darlington.

1218

Gateshead 19.03.

To traffic 11/1903.

REPAIRS:
???. ?/?—?/10/14.**G.**
???. ?/?—?/10/19.**G.**
Dar. 26/6—20/9/22.**G.**
Dar. 21/9—9/12/25.**G.**
Dar. 19/12/28—7/2/29.**G.**
Dar. 29/6—5/8/32.**G.**
Dar. 10/2—23/3/36.**L.**
Dar. 11/3—17/4/37.**G.**
Dar. 27/4—14/5/37.**N/C.**
Dar. 5/12/39—31/1/40.**G.**
Dar. 24/7—1/9/42.**G.**
Dar. 20/12/44—26/1/45.**G.**
Ghd. 5—17/5/46.**L.**
Dar. 25/10—12/12/47.**G.**

BOILERS:
G295.
G329 ?/10/14.
D989 *(new)* ?/10/19.
D737 *(ex2120)* 5/8/32.
2073 *(ex444)* 17/4/37.
D1757 *(ex2118)* 1/9/42.
2225 *(ex130)* 26/1/45.
2911 *(ex3336)* 12/12/47 (56B).

SHEDS:
Newport.
Borough Gardens 28/3/43.
Middlesbrough 15/2/48.

RENUMBERED:
3289 7/4/46.

CONDEMNED: 21/8/50.
Cut up at Darlington.

1110

Gateshead 6.

To traffic 12/1903.

REPAIRS:
???. ?/?—?/4/20.**G.**
Dar. 12/4—29/6/23.**G.**
Dar. 28/1—18/6/26.**G.**
Dar. 22/5—2/8/29.**G.**
Dar. 27/10—28/11/33.**G.**
Dar. 5/5—17/6/38.**G.**

Dar. 20—27/6/38.**N/C.**
Dar. 11/6—2/7/40.**N/C.**
Dar. 1—27/1/41.**G.**
Dar. 24/2—26/3/43.**G.**
Ghd. 19/9—7/10/44.**L.**
Dar. 13/6—7/7/45.**L.**
Dar. 14/11—14/12/45.**G.**
Ghd. 30/1—8/2/47.**L.**
Dar. 18/5—11/6/48.**G.**
Dar. 15—24/6/48.**N/C.**

BOILERS:
G324.
D1046 *(new)* ?/4/20.
D1745 *(ex1709)* 2/8/29.
D1004 *(ex1704)* 28/11/33.
2278 *(ex781)* 17/6/38.
3132 *(new)* 27/1/41 (56B).
2086 *(ex771)* 26/3/43 (56).
2930 *(ex1186)* 14/12/45 (56B).
2794 *(ex3339)* 11/6/48 (56B).

SHEDS:
Newport.
Springhead 10/10/24.
Dairycoates 3/26.
York 21/2/27.
Tyne Dock 13/5/29.
Annfield Plain 14/10/29.
Tyne Dock 24/6/37.
Middlesbrough 29/3/38.
Newport 7/11/38.
Selby 16/6/39.
West Hartlepool 14/11/48.
Newport 6/2/49.
Middlesbrough 24/4/49.
Selby 15/1/50.

RENUMBERED:
3290 20/1/46.
63290 11/6/48.

CONDEMNED: 25/7/50.
Cut up at Darlington.

1669

Gateshead 1.

To traffic 12/1903.

REPAIRS:
???. ?/?—?/4/16.**G.**
???. ?/?—?/9/21.**G.**
Dar. 30/8—11/11/24.**G.**
Dar. 25/6—24/8/28.**G.**
Dar. 4/6—12/9/31.**G.**
Dar. 13/8—18/9/36.**G.**
Dar. 15/3—4/5/39.**G.**
Dar. 28/4—19/6/41.**G.**
Dar. 9—19/7/41.**N/C.**
Dar. 12/6—16/8/43.**G.**
Ghd. 19/11—1/12/45.**L.**
Dar. 30/1—1/3/46.**L.**
Dar. 11/12/46—1/2/47.**G.**

Dar. 5—10/2/47.**N/C.**
Dar. 3/1/49. *Not repaired.*

BOILERS:
G325.
D538 *(new)* ?/4/16.
D1403 *(ex1177)* 12/9/31.
D1382 *(ex645)* 18/9/36.
2229 *(ex1032)* 4/5/39.
2889 *(ex578)* 16/8/43 (56B).
3126 *(ex3275)* 1/2/47 (56B).

SHEDS:
Newport.
Middlesbrough 6/2/37.
Newport 20/9/44.
Middlesbrough 2/11/47.

RENUMBERED:
3291 20/1/46.

CONDEMNED: 12/2/49.
Cut up at Darlington.

411

Gateshead 2.

To traffic 3/1904.

REPAIRS:
???. ?/?—?/4/11.**G.**
???. ?/?—?/5/15.**G.**
???. ?/?—?/2/21.**G.**
Dar. 12/11/24—31/1/25.**G.**
Dar. 21/2—31/5/27.**G.**
Dar. 7—10/1/29.**N/C.**
Dar. 15/3—2/5/30.**G.**
Dar. 2—16/8/32.**N/C.**
Dar. 14/5—13/6/34.**G.**
Dar. 1/7—13/8/37.**G.**
Dar. 11/3—5/4/40.**G.**
Dar. 20/4—13/5/42.**G.**
Dar. 25/3—21/4/44.**G.**
Ghd. 27/5—9/6/45.**L.**
Dar. 10/7—23/8/46.**G.**
Ghd. 12—30/8/47.**L.**
Dar. 20/10/48. *Not repaired.*

BOILERS:
G327.
G142 ?/4/11.
G327 ?/5/15.
D1934 ?/2/21.
D27 *(ex783)* 31/5/27.
2271 *(new)* 2/5/30.
2233 *(ex939)* 13/6/34.
D1364 *(ex1177)* 13/8/37.
3128 *(new)* 5/4/40 (56B).
2886 *(ex789)* 13/5/42 (56B).
3228 *(ex2122)* 21/4/44 (56B).
3120 *(ex410)* 23/8/46 (56B).

SHEDS:
Haverton Hill.

Middlesbrough 27/5/37.

RENUMBERED:
3292 30/6/46.

CONDEMNED: 8/11/48.
Cut up at Darlington.

430

Gateshead 3.

To traffic 2/1904.

REPAIRS:
???. ?/?—?/7/11.**G.**
???. ?/?—?/11/15.**G.**
???. ?/?—?/4/19.**G.**
???. ?/?—?/11/20.**G.**
Dar. 13/10—18/12/23.**G.**
Dar. 25/11/26—30/4/27.**G.**
Dar. 7/8—18/9/29.**G.**
Dar. 3/11—5/12/32.**G.**
Dar. 6/9—22/11/35.**G.**
Dar. 18/9—21/10/39.**G.**
Dar. 13/12/41—13/1/42.**G.**
Dar. 30/3—26/4/44.**G.**
Dar. 4/9—5/10/45.**L.**
After collision.
Dar. 31/1—2/3/46.**L.**
Dar. 27/5—20/7/46.**L.**
Ghd. 10—23/1/47.**L.**
Dar. 13/8—14/10/47.**G.**

BOILERS:
G326.
G330 ?/7/11.
D1925 ?/11/15.
D1923 ?/4/19.
D1080 *(new)* ?/11/20.
D1006 *(ex2123)* 18/9/29.
D1432 *(ex1031)* 5/12/32.
3241 *(new)* 13/1/42 (56B).
2068 *(ex527)* 26/4/44.

SHEDS:
Newport.
Starbeck 21/1/31.
Neville Hill 6/5/31.
Mexborough 12/12/33.
Doncaster 20/2/34.
Mexborough 23/11/36.
Ferryhill 13/3/37.
Darlington 7/11/38.
Blaydon 28/3/43.
West Hartlepool 20/7/47.
Newport 5/12/48.
Middlesbrough 24/4/49.

RENUMBERED:
3293 1/12/46.

CONDEMNED: 9/1/50.
Cut up at Darlington.

Some others changed to single plate had the GS buffers. These included Nos.1215, 3335, 63282 and 63319 (ex656). Note No.1215 still had Raven fog signal apparatus which began to be removed from November 1933.

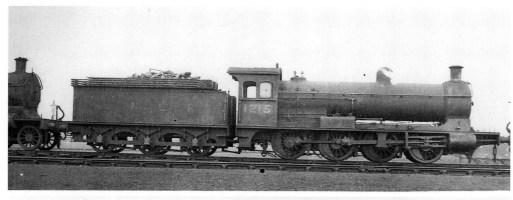

From new, the pistons were fitted with tail rods and almost all kept them to withdrawal.

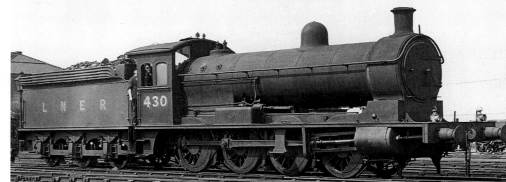

Just a few had the tail rods taken off but only from about 1945. No.3310 (*see* page 35, bottom) certainly lost them and No.3336 appears to have done so too.

The front buffer beam had holes in line with the tail rods which made it possible for the pistons to be drawn far enough forward for rings to be examined and/or replaced. The larger square flanges of GS buffers partially masked these holes.

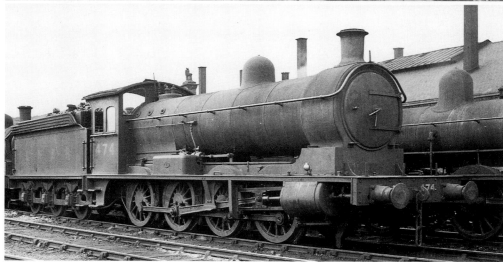

No.645, about 1934, had a chimney with windjabber of the type used by Q6 class but this had been taken off when it was ex-works 4th September 1936 (*see* page 10).

Only one other was noted with windjabber, No.3251 on 26th August 1950, again of Q6 type. This was probably fitted when ex-works 22nd March 1947 and kept to 20th December 1950 withdrawal. Note that the number is LNER but the tender carries BRITISH RAILWAYS. This tender had been put on at a Gateshead repair 26th February 1948, and the switch from 3296 to 3251 was on 20th August 1949.

No.3290 was an oddity. As No.1110 it was ex-works 14th December 1945 with a December 1937 built Diagram 56B boiler and on 20th January 1946 was re-numbered 3290 at Selby shed. It had a light repair at Gateshead works, out 8th February 1947, which is probably when a stool was put below its front 'pop' valve. Note Diagram 56B boilers had internal blower control instead of through the handrail as on the Diagram 56 boiler.

Ex works 24th August 1946, No.785 had a 1927 built Diagram 56 boiler which had twin whistle mounts on the cab front. The left hand outlet was blanked off, but the right hand had an extension pipe which put the single bell-shape above the cab roof. No.785 changed to 3286 on 5th January 1947.

443

Gateshead 4.

To traffic 3/1904.

REPAIRS:
???. ?/?—?/3/11.**G.**
???. ?/?—?/3/15.**G.**
???. ?/?—?/8/16.**G.**
???. ?/?—?/12/22.**G.**
Dar. 13/2—30/4/25.**G.**
Dar. 10/11/27—16/3/28.**G.**
Dar. 19—29/11/28.**N/C.**
Dar. 18/11—23/12/30.**G.**
Dar. 31/5—5/7/34.**G.**
Dar. 21/8—7/9/34.**N/C.**
Dar. 14/6—29/7/37.**G.**
Dar. 4/1—14/2/40.**N/C.**
Dar. 13/9—15/10/40.**G.**
Dar. 22/9—29/10/42.**G.**
Dar. 25/3—20/4/44.**G.**
Ghd. 21/12/45—10/1/46.**L.**
Dar. 22/3—7/6/47.**G.**
Dar. 10—21/6/47.**N/C.**
Dar. 31/10/49. *Not repaired.*

BOILERS:
G328.
G287 3/11.
D2101 3/15.
D1919 8/16.
D24 (*ex774*) 12/22.
D2068 (*new*) 16/3/28.
2271 (*ex411*) 5/7/34.
2086 (*ex783*) 29/7/37.
2794 (*ex651*) 15/10/40 (56B).
3249 (*new*) 29/10/42 (56B).
2909 (*ex2124*) 20/4/44 (56B).

SHEDS:
Dairycoates.
Springhead 10/10/24.
Dairycoates 7/2/25.
Thirsk 12/3/28.
Shildon 1/8/29.
Kirkby Stephen 4/11/29.
Shildon 6/1/31.
Ferryhill 5/10/33.
Darlington 7/11/38.
Selby 2/8/39.
West Hartlepool 28/3/43.
Selby 27/6/48.

RENUMBERED:
3294 1/12/46.

CONDEMNED: 3/11/49.
Cut up at Darlington.

444

Gateshead 5.

To traffic 3/1904.

REPAIRS:
???. ?/?—?/4/11.**G.**
???. ?/?—?/7/13.**G.**
???. ?/?—?/11/18.**G**
Dar. 1/5—7/8/24.**G.**
Dar. 6/9—24/11/27.**G.**
Dar. 3/2—6/3/31.**G.**
Dar. 17/10—10/11/33.**G.**
Dar. 29/1—24/2/37.**G.**
Dar. 30/8—7/9/37.**N/C.**
Dar. 27/11—23/12/39.**G.**
Dar. 8/5/41.*Weigh.*
Dar. 23/12/41.*Weigh.*
Dar. 17/7—27/8/42.**G.**
Ghd. 14/9—3/10/44.**L.**
Dar. 22/8—21/9/46.**G.**
Dar. 12/11/48. *Not repaired.*

BOILERS:
G329.
G185 ?/4/11.
G179 ?/7/13.
D707 (*new*) ?/11/18.
D2073 (*ex1128*) 10/11/33.
D1400 (*ex1215*) 24/2/37.
D1485 (*ex647*) 27/8/42.
3380 (*ex767*) 21/9/46 (56B).

SHEDS:
Shildon.
Kirkby Stephen 18/11/31.
Darlington 31/12/36.
Kirkby Stephen 21/5/41.
Darlington 17/11/41.
Blaydon 28/3/43.
Middlesbrough 5/10/47.

RENUMBERED:
3295 8/12/46.

CONDEMNED: 22/11/48.
Cut up at Darlington.

1111

Gateshead 7.

To traffic 3/1904.

REPAIRS:
???. ?/?—?/5/11.**G.**
???. ?/?—?/3/15.**G.**
Dar. 8/10—16/12/24.**G.**
Dar. 29/6—17/9/26.**G.**
Dar. 7—10/1/29.**N/C.**

Dar. 12/8—30/9/29.**G.**
Dar. 14/7—23/8/33.**G.**
Dar. 25/9—31/10/36.**G.**
Dar. 22/1—23/2/40.**G.**
Dar. 2/3—1/4/42.**G.**
Dar. 23/11—16/12/42.**N/C.**
Dar. 5/8—4/9/43.**L.**
Dar. 13/6—6/7/44.**G.**
Dar. 11/9—12/10/46.**G.**
Ghd. 13—26/2/48.**L.**

BOILERS:
G330.
G327 5/11.
D26 (*ex781*) 3/15.
2279 (*new*) 30/9/29.
D1427 (*ex1717*) 1/4/42.
D1453 (*ex646*) 6/7/44.
3123 (*ex3317*) 12/10/46 (56B).

SHEDS:
Haverton Hill.
Tyne Dock 28/3/43.
Borough Gardens 23/12/43.
Tyne Dock 22/9/44.
Borough Gardens 14/1/46.

RENUMBERED:
3296 20/1/46.
E3296 26/2/48.

CONDEMNED: 22/8/49.
Cut up at Darlington.

1149

Gateshead 8.

To traffic 4/1904.

REPAIRS:
???. ?/?—?/6/11.**G.**
???. ?/?—?/6/13.**G.**
???. ?/?—?/10/20.**G.**
???. ?/?—?/5/22.**G.**
Dar. 5/4—25/6/24.**G.**
Dar. 14/5—30/8/27.**G.**
Dar. 13/1—28/2/30.**G.**
Dar. 16/6—2/8/33.**G.**
Dar. 7/8—16/9/36.**G.**
Dar. 25/5—3/6/37.**N/C.**
Dar. 16/12/38—16/1/39.**N/C.**
Dar. 14/6—27/7/39.**G.**
Dar. 18/8—25/9/41.**G.**
Dar. 13/5—9/6/43.**G.**
Ghd. 14—31/8/44.**L.**
Dar. 21/11—29/12/45.**H.**
Ghd. 16—30/5/47.**L.**

BOILERS:
G331.

G179 ?/6/11.
D1934 ?/6/13.
D1928 ?/10/20.
D1392 (*new*) ?/5/22.
2269 (*new*) 28/2/30.
D726 (*ex2118*) 2/8/33.
2807 (*new*) 16/9/36 (56B).
3375 (*new*) 9/6/43 (56B).
3608 (*new*) 29/12/45 (56B).

SHEDS:
Scarborough.
York 15/7/24.
Scarborough 1/10/24.
Selby 17/2/25.
Newport 13/8/34.
Middlesbrough 7/11/38.
Northallerton 28/3/43.
West Hartlepool 19/2/44.

RENUMBERED:
3297 3/2/46.

CONDEMNED: 22/2/49.
Cut up at Darlington.

1150

Gateshead 9.

To traffic 4/1904.

REPAIRS:
???. ?/?—?/7/16.**G.**
Dar. 31/5—30/8/24.**G.**
Dar. 15/12/27—29/2/28.**G.**
Dar. 9/1—11/2/31.**G.**
Dar. 1/5—12/6/35.**G.**
Dar. 14/10—22/11/38.**G.**
Dar. 28/1—27/2/41.**G.**
Dar. 28/10—4/12/42.**G.**
Dar. 20/4—11/6/45.**G.**
Ghd. 2—7/11/46.**L.**
Dar. 6—9/5/47.**L.**
Dar. 29/1/48. *Not repaired.*

BOILERS:
G332.
D572 (*new*) ?/7/16.
D601 (*ex1684*) 11/2/31.
D615 (*ex669*) 12/6/35.
2270 (*ex2123*) 22/11/38.
2227 (*ex656*) 27/2/41.
D1470 (*ex1682*) 4/12/42.
D1400 (*ex1128*) 11/6/45.

SHEDS:
Newport.
Borough Gardens 28/3/43.

WORKS CODES:- Cw - Cowlairs. Dar- Darlington. Don - Doncaster. Ghd - Gateshead. Gor - Gorton. Hsi - Hull Springhead. Inv - Inverurie. Str - Stratford.
REPAIR CODES:- **C/H** - Casual Heavy. **C/L** - Casual Light. **G** - General. **H** - Heavy. **H/I** - Heavy Intermediate. **L** - Light. **L/I** - Light Intermediate. **N/C** - Non-Classified.

1150 cont/.

RENUMBERED:
3298 20/1/46.

CONDEMNED: 27/2/48.
Cut up at Darlington.

1173

Gateshead 10.

To traffic 5/1904.

REPAIRS:
???. ?/?—?/4/20.**G.**
Ghd. 6/6—17/8/23.**G.**
Dar. 20/6—12/10/27.**G.**
Dar. 24/3—6/5/30.**G.**
Dar. 6/12/32—5/1/33.**H.**
Dar. 12/4—10/5/34.**G.**
Dar. 2/9—7/10/37.**G.**
Dar. 2—26/7/40.**G.**
Dar. 2/2—4/3/43.**G.**

Ghd. 27/9—17/10/44.**L.**
Dar. 10/4—11/5/46.**G.**
Ghd. 16/8—5/9/47.**L.**
Dar. 4/1/49. *Not repaired.*

BOILERS:
G333.
D1052 *(new)* 4/20.
D1457 *(ex1054)* 10/5/34.
2271 *(ex443)* 7/10/37.
D1745 *(ex1177)* 26/7/40.
2150 *(ex785)* 4/3/43.
2272 *(ex652)* 11/5/46.

SHEDS:
Dairycoates.
Stockton 7/2/25.
Haverton Hill 25/6/30.

RENUMBERED:
3299 20/1/46.

CONDEMNED: 12/2/49.
Cut up at Darlington.

578

Darlington 516.

To traffic 6/1907.

REPAIRS:
???. ?/?—?/6/14.**G.**
???. ?/?—?/5/17.**G.**
Dar. 20/11/23—11/3/24.**G.**
Dar. 7/2—14/5/27.**G.**
Dar. 17/4—14/6/29.**G.**
Dar. 24/3—16/4/30.**N/C.**
Dar. 12/7—16/8/32.**G.**
Dar. 26/3—3/7/35.**G.**
Dar. 20/10—3/12/37.**G.**
Dar. 8/12/38—5/1/39.**N/C.**
Dar. 12/12/39—30/3/40.**H.**
Dar. 12/8—18/9/40.**G.**
Dar. 19/4—22/5/43.**G.**
Ghd. 10—24/8/44.**L.**
Dar. 25/9—2/11/46.**G.**

BOILERS:
D1914.
G116 ?/6/14.
D1927 ?/5/17.
D1453 *(new)* 11/3/24.
D1023 *(ex785)* 14/6/29.
D989 *(ex1218)*16/8/32.
2889 *(new)* 3/12/37 (56B).
2929 *(ex651)* 22/5/43 (56B).
3384 *(ex3323)* 2/11/46 (56B).

SHEDS:
Springhead.
Selby 22/3/24.
Gateshead 5/2/38.
Heaton 21/11/40.
Blaydon 22/10/44.
West Hartlepool 20/7/47.
Neville Hill 5/4/48.
Newport 30/5/48.

RENUMBERED:
3300 17/11/46.

CONDEMNED: 16/5/49.
Cut up at Darlington.

On the original smokeboxes the front plate and wrapper were joined by an internal angle iron, which produced a sharp right-angled corner externally.

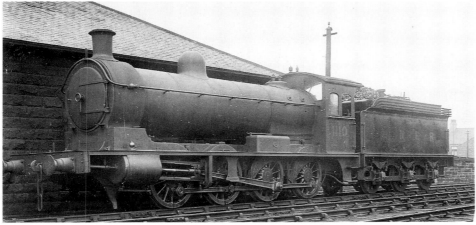

From about 1915 new front plates had a flanged edge to fit inside the wrapper which eliminated the sharp corner but this change was only completed during the 1939-45 war. When ex-works 6th March 1939, No.130 still had the original style of smokebox.

Lubrication for cylinders and valves was from globe holders on the running plate and from oilboxes to the axles. None had, or needed, mechanical lubrication.

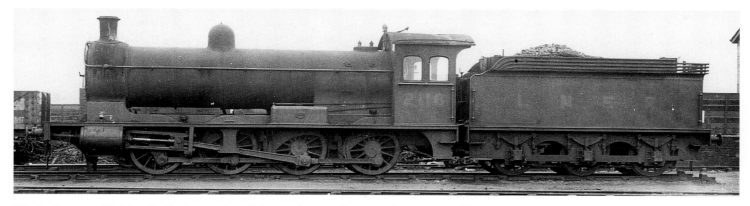

The tenders provided for the first five, Nos.2116 to 2120, were the same short type as built to keep Class B13 within the 50ft 0in. wheelbase. These had 8in. shorter frame and wheelbase than standard and the water capacity was cut from 3940 to 3701 gallons.

(right) The shorter main tank enabled the tender brake handle to be set back to suit, but its lower bracket then came where there was a small cut-out in the frame. Thus, on these five tenders the frames had to remain solid at their front end, giving a ready means to identify them. Three stayed with their original engines to withdrawal and the only significant change was 2120's tender to engine 1009 on the 9th October 1942 to 11th September 1947, and then to 63289 from 9th July 1949 to 21st August 1950.

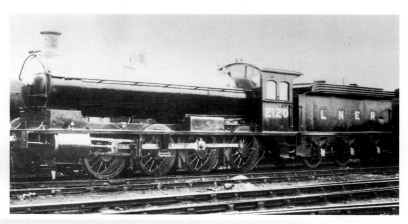

(below) Starting with No.2121, the other eight-five had the standard length 3940 gallons tender. This had the small cut-out in front of the leading axle, and the short vertical handrail matched that on the engine. Note the prominent air vents associated with the water pick-up apparatus.

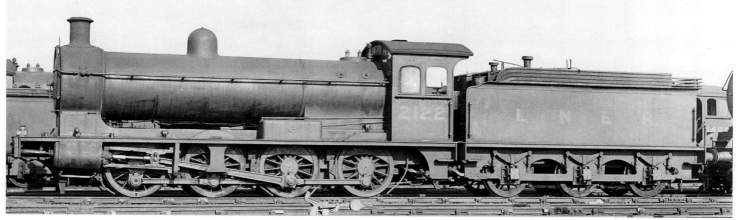

660

Darlington 517.

To traffic 6/1907.

REPAIRS:
???. ?/?—?/8/16.**G.**
???. ?/?—?/7/19.**G.**
???. ?/?—?/8/22.**G.**
Dar. 5/10/25—6/1/26.**G.**
Ghd. 21/6—27/8/28.**G.**
Dar. 17/6—29/7/29.**G.**
Dar. 26/3—30/5/30.**G.**
Dar. 9/5—5/6/34.**G.**
Rebuilt to Part 2.
Dar. 30/8—7/10/38.**G.**
Dar. 14/7—30/8/41.**G.**
Dar. 6—29/1/44.**G.**
Dar. 19/11—21/12/45.**L.**
After collision.
Dar. 10/12/46—1/2/47.**G.**
Ghd. 30/11/48. *Not repaired.*

BOILERS:
D1915.
  G288 8/16.
  D859 *(new)* 7/19.
D1392 *(ex1149)* 30/5/30.
D1991 *(exQ10 2510)* 5/6/34 (56A).
D1661 *(ex658)* 29/1/44 (56A).

SHEDS:
Stockton.
Haverton Hill 25/6/30.

RENUMBERED:
3301 12/1/47.

CONDEMNED: 31/12/48.
Cut up at Darlington.

939

Darlington 518.

To traffic 6/1907.

REPAIRS:
???. ?/?—?/12/15.**G.**
???. ?/?—?/11/22.**G.**
Dar. 13/1—20/4/27.**G.**
Dar. 4/11—12/12/30.**G.**
Dar. 2—28/5/34.**G.**
Rebuilt to Part 2.
Dar. 21/12/36—1/2/37.**G.**
Dar. 27/2—13/4/40.**G.**
Dar. 16—20/4/40.**N/C.**
Dar. 12/2—6/3/42.**G.**
Dar. 27/4—31/5/43.**G.**
Restored to Part 1.
Ghd. 24/6—9/7/45.**L.**
Dar. 20/8/47. *Not repaired.*

BOILERS:
D1916.
  D14 *(ex769)* ?/12/15.
  2233 *(new)* 12/12/30.
D1704 *(exQ10 2509)* 28/5/34 (56A).
D1994 *(ex653)* 1/2/37 (56A).
D1815 *(ex642)* 13/4/40 (56A).
D1670 *(ex1320)* 6/3/42 (56A).
  3371 *(new)* 31/5/43 (56B).

SHEDS:
Shildon.
Newport 7/1/35.
Blaydon 23/7/45.

RENUMBERED:
3302 17/11/46.

CONDEMNED: 18/9/47.
Cut up at Darlington.

1031

Darlington 519.

To traffic 8/1907.

REPAIRS:
???. ?/?—?/11/22.**G.**
Ghd. 23/8—28/10/27.**G.**
Dar. 12/7—25/8/32.**G.**
Dar. 25/10/35—10/1/36.**G.**
Dar. 19/7/39—19/2/40.**G.**
Dar. 1/7—11/8/42.**G.**
Dar. 10/8—29/9/43.**L.**
Dar. 3—25/5/44.**G.**
Dar. 9/5—21/6/47.**G.**

BOILERS:
D1917.
D1432 *(new)* ?/11/22.
D1023 *(ex578)* 25/8/32.
  3117 *(new)* 19/2/40 (56B).
  2802 *(ex645)* 11/8/42 (56B).
  3249 *(ex443)* 25/5/44 (56B).
D1955 *(ex3265)* 21/6/47.

SHEDS:
North Blyth.
Shildon 5/6/29.
Newport 7/1/35.
Selby 15/7/39.
West Hartlepool 28/3/43.
Borough Gardens 11/7/48.

RENUMBERED:
3303 20/1/46.

CONDEMNED: 23/4/51.
Cut up at Darlington.

1032

Darlington 520.

To traffic 9/1907.

REPAIRS:
???. ?/?—?/12/12.**G.**
???. ?/?—?/5/16.**G.**
???. ?/?—?/2/19.**G.**
???. ?/?—?/5/22.**G.**
Dar. 1/5—17/8/25.**G.**
Dar. 30/3—6/7/26.**G.**
Dar. 8/10—22/11/29.**G.**
Dar. 30/12/32—30/1/33.**G.**
Dar. 2/3—14/4/36.**G.**
Dar. 13/3—20/4/39.**G.**
Dar. 11/10—20/11/41.**G.**
Dar. 21/4—18/5/44.**G.**
Dar. 13/6/45.*Weigh.*
Dar. 3/6/47. *Not repaired.*

BOILERS:
D1918.
D1919 ?/12/12.
D1923 ?/5/16.
  D6 *(ex646)* ?/2/19.
D1006 *(ex130)* 17/8/25.
  G957 *(ex657)* 6/7/26.
  2229 *(new)* 22/11/29.
  2153 *(ex474)* 20/4/39.
  3232 *(new)* 20/11/41 (56B).
  3241 *(ex430)* 18/5/44 (56B).

SHEDS:
Springhead 6/9/22.
Selby 22/3/24.
Springhead 18/8/25.
Shildon 1/2/27.
Darlington 7/1/35.
Kirkby Stephen 31/12/36.
Darlington 14/11/40.

RENUMBERED:
3304 20/1/46.

CONDEMNED: 19/7/47.
Cut up at Darlington.

1054

Darlington 521.

To traffic 9/1907.

REPAIRS:
???. ?/?—?/10/12.**G.**
???. ?/?—?/5/17.**G.**
???. ?/?—22/12/22.**G.**
Ghd. 24/1—3/4/25.**G.**
Dar. 10/3—29/4/30.**G.**
Dar. 4—28/4/34.**G.**
Rebuilt to Part 2.
Dar. 1/6—15/7/37.**G.**
Dar. 26/7—23/8/38.**H.**
Dar. 23—31/12/38.**N/C.**
Dar. 17/6—13/7/40.**G.**
Dar. 23/11—29/12/42.**G.**
Dar. 3/1—14/2/45.**G.**
Ghd. 23/4—6/5/46.**L.**
Dar. 23/11—18/12/46.**L.**
Dar. 25/1—15/3/47.**G.**
Dar. 27/3—1/4/47.**N/C.**

BOILERS:
D1919.
D1927 ?/10/12.
D1915 ?/5/17.
D1457 *(new)* 3/4/25.
D1674 *(exQ10 2504)* 28/4/34 (56A).
D1805 *(ex1062)* 15/7/37 (56A).
D1994 *(ex939)* 13/7/40 (56A).

SHEDS:
North Blyth.
Shildon 5/6/29.
Newport 7/1/35.
Middlesbrough 8/1/44.

RENUMBERED:
3305 20/1/46.

CONDEMNED: 16/5/49.
Cut up at Darlington.

1062

Darlington 522.

To traffic 10/1907.

REPAIRS:
Dar. 15/8—7/11/23.
Dar. 28/2—9/6/27.**G.**
Dar. 24/3—13/5/30.**G.**
Dar. 18/1—16/2/34.**G.**
Rebuilt to Part 2.
Dar. 1/4—13/5/37.**G.**
Dar. 25/9—30/10/39.**G.**
Dar. 30/10—13/11/39.**N/C.**
Dar. 26/5—27/6/42.**G.**
Dar. 5/12/44—17/1/45.**G.**
Dar. 23—26/1/45.**N/C.**
Dar. 3—8/2/45.**N/C.**
Ghd. 5—15/11/46.**L.**
Dar. 19/11/48. *Not repaired.*

BOILERS:
D1920.
  D579 *(ex2123)* 9/6/27.
D1805 *(exQ10 2502)* 16/2/34 (56A).
D1809 *(ex657)* 13/5/37 (56A).
D1817 *(ex653)* 30/10/39 (56A).
D1815 *(ex939)* 27/6/42 (56A).

SHEDS:
Dairycoates.
Newport 19/6/24.
Blaydon 28/7/45.
Haverton Hill 5/10/47.

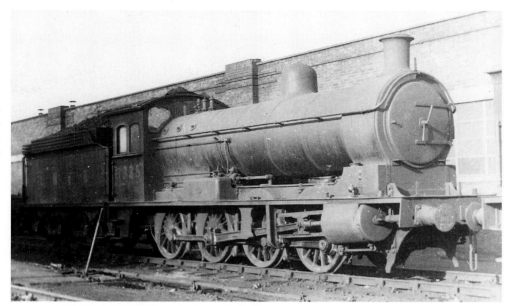

From 29th March 1947 to withdrawal, No.3335 had a longer vertical handrail as it acquired the tender which had been modified to run with Part 2 engine No.1054.

All were right hand drive and kept steam reversing gear to withdrawal. Apart from odd exceptions for trials they had only steam brake.

When the fifty slide valve engines returned from the ROD in 1919, their war service was recognised by the NER (*see* page 6, centre) fitting them with the badge of the Royal Engineers and three chevrons, one for each year of service. These were on the cabside until, from March 1929, that position was needed for the engine number.

The badge and chevrons were then fitted on the leading sandbox but were normally painted over. Photos on page 38 show they were carried to withdrawal.

For a brief period Nos.474 and 654 carried a small tender cab for crew protection when running in reverse. This was after 1909 because the tender has the extra coal rail and plating then introduced. The painting style shown was discarded in 1917.

The water pick-up apparatus was retained until well into the 1930's, although little used after most Q5 mainline duties were taken over by Q6 class.

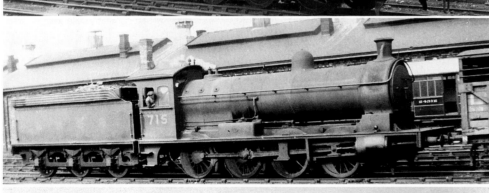

During the 1930's most Q5 tenders had their water pick-up apparatus removed as shown by absence of the mushroom type air vents.

From September 1902, No.2118 was changed to Westinghouse for engine and train brakes, for use with trains of high capacity wagons. In March 1904 new engines 411 and 443 were also Westinghouse fitted but they went to steam brake by June 1915. So at LNER take-over only No.2118 of Q5 class was Westinghouse braked.

1062 cont/.

RENUMBERED:
3306 27/1/46.

CONDEMNED: 20/12/48.
Cut up at Darlington.

1177

Darlington 523.

To traffic 10/1907.

REPAIRS:
Dar. ?/?—?/8/19.**G.**
Dar. ?/?—?/7/22.**G.**
Dar. 15/12/24—11/2/25.**G.**
Dar. 14/4—8/6/28.**G.**
Dar. 22/5—6/7/31.**G.**
Dar. 9/3—4/5/34.**H.**
Dar. 9/10—13/11/34.**L.**
Dar. 16/6—15/7/36.**L.**
Dar. 7/5—21/6/37.**G.**
Dar. 26/5—20/7/38.**L.**
Dar. 1/6—4/7/40.**G.**
Dar. 6/4—5/5/43.**G.**
Ghd. 7/3—7/4/45.**L.**
Dar. 4/9—28/9/46.**G.**
Ghd. 14/12/47—9/1/48.**L.**

BOILERS:
D1921.
D1929 ?/8/19.
D1403 *(new)* ?/7/22.
D1768 *(ex773)* 6/7/31.
D1364 *(ex1704)* 4/5/34.
D1745 *(ex1009)* 21/6/37.
  2809 *(ex83)* 4/7/40 (56B).
  2269 *(ex656)* 5/5/43.
  3226 *(ex3333)* 28/9/46 (56B).

SHEDS:
Dairycoates.
March 21/10/31.
Dairycoates 5/2/32.
Newport 20/9/34.
Stockton 16/10/39.
Newport 1/2/43.
Stockton 20/1/47.
Darlington 2/11/47.

RENUMBERED:
3307 20/1/46.

CONDEMNED: 16/5/49.
Cut up at Darlington.

1178

Darlington 524.

To traffic 10/1907.

REPAIRS:
???. ?/?—?/5/15.**G.**

Dar. 28/6—24/9/23.**G.**
Dar. 26/2—30/6/26.**G.**
Dar. 7/11—21/12/28.**G.**
Dar. 16/2—31/3/32.**G.**
Dar. 9/5—1/7/35.**G.**
Dar. 13/4—30/5/38.**G.**
Dar. 29/7—5/9/40.**G.**
Dar. 6/10—3/11/42.**G.**
Dar. 30/10—23/11/44.**G.**
Dar. 21/9—19/10/46.**G.**
Ghd. 8/8—11/9/47.**L.**
Dar. 13/1/49. *Not repaired.*

BOILERS:
D1922.
  D5 *(ex669)* ?/5/15.
  2167 *(new)* 21/12/28.
  D601 *(ex1150)* 1/7/35.
  2159 *(ex1002)* 30/5/38.
  2271 *(ex1173)* 5/9/40.
  2073 *(ex1218)* 3/11/42.
  2227 *(ex771)* 23/11/44.
  2269 *(ex3307)* 19/10/46.

SHEDS:
Newport.
Middlesbrough 6/2/37.
Newport 7/11/38.
Middlesbrough 3/1/44.

RENUMBERED:
3308 20/1/46.

CONDEMNED: 12/2/49.
Cut up at Darlington.

1215

Darlington 525.

To traffic 11/1907.

REPAIRS:
???. ?/?—?/12/15.**G.**
???. ?/?—?/2/22.**G.**
Dar. 10/4—24/6/24.**G.**
Dar. 2/3—30/5/27.**G.**
Dar. 15/1—28/2/30.**G.**
Dar. 8/10—24/11/36.**G.**
Dar. 9/2—22/3/39.**L.**
Dar. 29/5—22/6/40.**L.**
Dar. 14/1—26/2/41.**G.**
Dar. 23/4—11/5/42.**G.**
Dar. 30/6—7/8/43.**G.**
Ghd. 12/4—3/5/45.**L.**
Dar. 11/10/46. *Not repaired.*

BOILERS:
D1923.
D1932 ?/12/15.
D1364 *(new)* ?/2/22.
D1400 *(ex764)* 28/2/30.
D1043 *(ex1682)* 24/11/36.
  2278 *(ex1110)* 26/2/41.
  2279 *(ex1111)* 11/5/42.

2281 *(ex783)* 7/8/43.

SHEDS:
Dairycoates.
March 21/10/31.
Dairycoates 5/2/32.
West Hartlepool 13/6/35.
East Hartlepool 28/3/38.
West Hartlepool 17/4/39.
Darlington 13/5/39.
Selby 13/7/39.
West Hartlepool 28/3/43.

RENUMBERED:
3309 31/3/46.

CONDEMNED: 7/12/46.
Cut up at Darlington.

644

Darlington 526.

To traffic 12/1907.

REPAIRS:
???. ?/?—?/10/12.**G.**
Ghd. ?/?—14/9/22.**G.**
Ghd. 8/6—10/9/26.**G.**
Ghd. 14/3—29/4/30.**G.**
Ghd. 19/2—24/3/31.**L.**
After collision.
Dar. 11/4—8/5/34.**G.**
Rebuilt to Part 2.
Dar. 17/8—22/9/37.**G.**
Dar. 27/6—23/7/40.**G.**
Dar. 27/1—14/2/41.**L.**
Dar. 27/7—6/8/42.**L.**
Dar. 25/8—10/9/42.**L.**
Dar. 24/5—30/6/43.**G.**
Dar. 14/11—11/12/45.**G.**
Restored to Part 1.
Ghd. 19—28/2/47.**L.**
Dar. 21/5/48. *Not repaired.*

BOILERS:
D1925.
D1931 ?/10/12.
D1757 *(new)* 10/9/26.
D1988 *(exQ10 2506)* 8/5/34 (56A).
D1674 *(ex1054)* 22/9/37 (56A).
D1805 *(ex1054)* 23/7/40 (56A).
D1670 *(ex939)* 30/6/43 (56A).
  3602 *(new)* 11/12/45 (56B).

SHEDS:
North Blyth.
Heaton 28/3/43.
Selby 22/10/44.

RENUMBERED:
3310 14/7/46.

CONDEMNED: 11/6/48.
Cut up at Darlington.

645

Darlington 527.

To traffic 12/1907.

REPAIRS:
???. ?/?—?/4/22.**G.**
Dar. 15/5—18/7/24.**G.**
Dar. 18/2—26/5/27.**G.**
Ghd. 9/7—21/8/31.**G.**
Dar. 30/7—4/9/36.**G.**
Dar. 11—27/5/37.**N/C.**
Dar. 18/5—29/7/38.**L.**
After collision.
Dar. 19/12/38—11/1/39.**N/C.**
Dar. 12/3—8/4/40.**G.**
Dar. 12/5—6/6/42.**G.**
Dar. 9/8—9/9/44. *Tender.*
Dar. 14/2—9/3/45.**G.**
Dar. 15—22/3/45.**N/C.**
Ghd. 21/9—10/10/46.**L.**
Dar. 9/1—5/3/48.**G.**

BOILERS:
D1926.
D1382 *(new)* 4/22.
  2802 *(new)* 4/9/36 (56B).
  3128 *(ex411)* 6/6/42 (56B).
  3235 *(ex789)* 9/3/45 (56B).
  2914 *(ex3314)* 5/3/48 (56B).

SHEDS:
Dairycoates.
Springhead 26/8/24.
Borough Gardens 4/6/27.
Gateshead 5/10/36.
Heaton 21/11/40.
Darlington 4/11/44.
Middlesbrough 28/7/46.
Darlington 25/8/46.
Cudworth 29/9/46.
West Hartlepool 14/11/48.
Newport 6/2/49.
Haverton Hill 1/5/49.

RENUMBERED:
  3311 18/8/46.
ᴇ**3311** 5/3/48.

CONDEMNED: 29/9/51.
Cut up at Darlington.

646

Darlington 528.

To traffic 12/1907.

REPAIRS:
???. ?/?—9/12.**G.**
???. ?/?—4/16.**G.**
???. ?/?—9/18.**G.**
???. ?/?—11/22.**G.**
Dar. 29/7—14/10/25.**G.**

646 cont/.
Dar. 11/10—29/11/28.**G.**
Dar. 17/6—31/7/31.**G.**
Dar. 8/10—29/11/35.**G.**
Dar. 4/1—4/2/37.**L.**
Dar. 25/1—15/3/38.**L.**
Dar. 26/6—10/8/39.**G.**
Dar. 9/9—11/10/41.**G.**
Dar. 4—27/5/44.**G.**
Dar. 28/6—18/7/45.**L.**
Dar. 30/1—19/2/46.**L.**
Dar. 4/1—15/2/47.**G.**

BOILERS:
D1927.
 G326 9/12.
  D6 *(ex764)* 4/16.
 D737 *(new)* 9/18.
 G962 *(ex648)* 14/10/25.
 D589 *(ex647)* 31/7/31.
D1453 *(ex1709)* 29/11/35.
 3232 *(ex1632)* 27/5/44 (56B).
 2232 *(ex3261)* 15/2/47.

SHEDS:
Shildon.
Newport 30/1/24.
Middlesbrough 21/12/32.
Darlington 12/6/34.
Selby 24/6/39.

RENUMBERED:
3312 14/7/46.

CONDEMNED: 22/8/49.
Cut up at Darlington.

647

Darlington 529.

To traffic 12/1907.

REPAIRS:
???. ?/?—7/20.**G.**
Dar. 23/2—18/5/23.**G.**
Dar. 21/9—22/12/25.**G.**
Dar. 23/5—11/7/28.**G.**
Dar. 28/5—7/7/31.**G.**
Dar. 8/5—2/6/34.**G.**
Dar. 14/11—21/12/36.**G.**
Dar. 27/9—18/11/39.**G.**
Dar. 7/5—19/6/41.**N/C.**
Dar. 10/6—8/7/42.**G.**
Dar. 5—20/11/42.**N/C.**
Dar. 23/2—18/3/44.**G.**
Dar. 10—31/8/44.**L.**
Ghd. 16/10—2/11/45.**L.**
Dar. 12/2—29/3/47.**G.**
Ghd. 28/10—2/12/48.**L.**

BOILERS:
D1928.
D1060 *(new)* 7/20.
 D589 *(ex1128)* 11/7/28.

D1037 *(ex130)* 7/7/31.
D1052 *(ex1173)* 2/6/34.
D1485 *(ex2118)* 21/12/36.
 2080 *(ex130)* 8/7/42.
 3116 *(ex773)* 18/3/44 (56B).
 3135 *(ex3251)* 29/3/47 (56B).

SHEDS:
Selby.
Malton 28/3/38.
Selby 29/5/39.

RENUMBERED:
3313 24/11/46.
63313 2/12/48.

CONDEMNED: 21/11/49.
Cut up at Darlington.

648

Darlington 530.

To traffic 3/1908.

REPAIRS:
???. ?/?—10/13.**G.**
???. ?/?—11/15.**G.**
???. ?/?—10/22.**G.**
Dar. 1/5—17/9/25.**G.**
Dar. 25/1—14/3/29.**G.**
Dar. 1/12/31—15/1/32.**G.**
Dar. 29/9—17/10/32.**N/C.**
Dar. 6/7—18/8/34.**G.**
Dar. 18—28/2/35.**N/C.**
Dar. 1/4/36.*Weigh.*
Dar. 25/5—6/7/38.**G.**
Dar. 24/7—14/8/39.**N/C.**
Dar. 22/10—13/11/40.**N/C.**
Dar. 10—24/12/40.**N/C.**
Dar. 1/9—7/10/41.**G.**
Dar. 28/8—26/9/42.**N/C.**
Dar. 8—20/1/43.**L.**
Dar. 23/10—20/11/44.**G.**
Dar. 14/12/45—19/1/46.**L.**
Dar. 6/1—20/2/48.**G.**
Dar. 3/9/51. *Not repaired.*

BOILERS:
D1929.
D1932 10/13.
 G962 *(ex661)* 11/15.
  D6 *(ex1032)* 17/9/25.
 2150 *(new)* 14/3/29.
D1037 *(ex647)* 18/8/34.
 2930 *(new)* 6/7/38 (56B).
 2914 *(ex651)* 20/11/44 (56B).
 2073 *(ex3260)* 20/2/48.

SHEDS:
Newport.
Ferryhill 18/7/32.
Darlington 7/11/38.
West Auckland 17/8/46.
Neville Hill 4/1/48.

Normanton 30/5/48.
Haverton Hill 14/11/48.

RENUMBERED:
3314 11/8/46.
ᴇ**3314** 20/2/48.

CONDEMNED: 3/9/51.
Cut up at Darlington.

652

Darlington 531.

To traffic 3/1908.

REPAIRS:
???. ?/?—4/22.**G.**
Dar. 25/9—29/11/24.**G.**
Dar. 5/12/27—23/2/28.**G.**
Dar. 26/8—12/10/31.**G.**
Dar. 24/2—8/4/36.**G.**
Dar. 28/4—18/5/36.**L.**
Dar. 13/1—15/2/39.**G.**
Dar. 8/1—14/2/41.**G.**
Dar. 30/1—13/2/43.**L.**
Dar. 7/5—3/6/43.**G.**
Ghd. 7/9—26/9/44.**L.**
Dar. 22/2—23/3/46.**G.**
Ghd. 9/6—21/6/47.**L.**
Dar. 11/3/48 *Not repaired.*

BOILERS:
D1930.
D1380 *(new)* 4/22.
 D538 *(ex1669)* 12/10/31.
 2269 *(ex527)* 15/2/39.
 2276 *(ex771)* 14/2/41.
 2272 *(ex794)* 3/6/43.
 2086 *(ex1110)* 23/3/46.

SHEDS:
Dairycoates.
Springhead 30/1/25.
Dairycoates 14/12/25.
March 28/0/31.
Dairycoates 5/2/32.
Newport 20/9/34.
West Auckland 3/3/41.
Neville Hill 4/1/48.

RENUMBERED:
3315 23/3/46.

CONDEMNED: 25/3/48.
Cut up at Darlington.

653

Darlington 532.

To traffic 3/1908.

REPAIRS:
???. ?/?—8/12.**G.**

???. ?/?—8/16.**G.**
Dar. 15/11/22—20/2/23.**G.**
Dar. 12/5—19/8/25.**G.**
Dar. 26/3—30/5/28.**G.**
Dar. 6—19/6/29.**N/C.**
Dar. 10/4—24/6/30.**G.**
Dar. 14/11—23/12/33.**G.**
Rebuilt to Part 2.
Dar. 27/8—25/9/34.**L.**
Dar. 6/10—27/11/36.**G.**
Dar. 15/3—26/4/39.**G.**
Dar. 10/2—18/3/41.**G.**
Dar. 12/6—23/8/43.**G.**
Ghd. 24/9—11/10/45.**L.**
Dar. 13/7—21/8/46.**G.**
Dar. 28/9—1/10/46 **N/C.**
Dar. 19/11—23/12/46
Tender only.
Dar. 25/3/49. *Not repaired.*

BOILERS:
D1931.
 G255 8/12.
 D587 *(new)* 8/16.
  D30 *(ex789)* 30/5/28.
 2272 *(new)* 24/6/30.
D1994 *(exQ10 2499)* 23/12/33 (56A).
D1817 *(ex642)* 27/11/36 (56A).
 2003 *(ex659)* 26/4/39 (56A).
D1674 *(ex644)* 18/3/41 (56A).
D1997 *(ex3263)* 21/8/46 (56A).

SHEDS:
Shildon.
Newport 8/2/24.
Middlesbrough 7/11/38.
Newport 22/9/44.
Middlesbrough 2/11/47.

RENUMBERED:
3316 21/9/46.

CONDEMNED: 4/4/49.
Cut up at Darlington.

654

Darlington 533.

To traffic 4/1908.

REPAIRS:
???. ?/?—7/13.**G.**
???. ?/?—5/16.**G.**
???. ?/?—6/19.**G.**
Ghd. ?/?—8/12/22.**G.**
Dar. 19/8—10/9/25.**G.**
Ghd. 30/9—28/12/26.**G.**
Dar. 7—24/1/29.**L.**
Dar. 19/5—14/8/30.**G.**
Dar. 17/5—14/6/34.**G.**
Dar. 13/5—18/6/36.**G.**
Dar. 15/3—26/4/37.**L.**
Dar. 18/7—25/8/38.**H.**
Dar. 18/3—13/4/40.**G.**

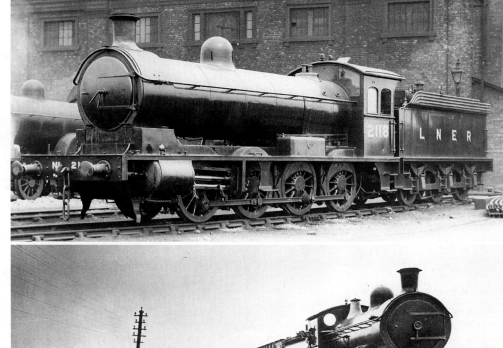

No.2118's odd brake seems to have been over-looked because it kept it until it went to works on 12th June 1930. Ex-works 20th August, it only had steam brake just like all the others.

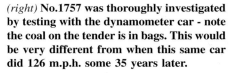

When new, Nos.162, 430, 651 and 1757 had steam brake on the engine but were also fitted with vacuum ejector for train brakes to work the 40 ton hopper mineral wagons. The vacuum brake was taken off Nos.162, 430 and 1757 in December 1913 and from No.651 by April 1919.

(right) No.1757 was thoroughly investigated by testing with the dynamometer car - note the coal on the tender is in bags. This would be very different from when this same car did 126 m.p.h. some 35 years later.

(below) From 1917 the 24in. wide brass number plates were taken off the cab sides and were replaced by 8⅝in. wide plates. So that the number could be identified, it was then put on the tender, in 12in. shaded transfers, between the N. and E. from the N.E.R. used previously. All were in this style when the LNER took them over.

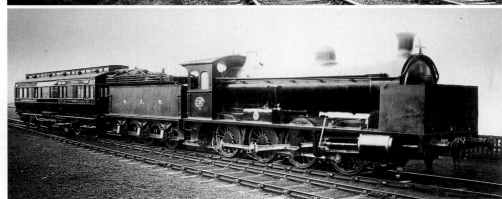

31

Indication of new owners took four forms before it achieved finality. Between 14th April and 12th June 1923 L.&N.E.R. was put on Nos. 1704, 793, 1709, 715, 647, 2120 and 1682, then 1110 and 1173 got L&NER without full points. From 23rd July to 30th August 1923 only LNER was used for Nos. 657, 527, 2122, 1186, 785 and 2125. From 13th September 1923 to 22nd January 1924 the suffix D was added, in the style shown, to Nos.658, 770, 2118, 1178, 1684, 2123, 794, 1757, 2117, 162, 474, 1062, 2124, 655, 1717, 430, 83, 650 and 1781. For some reason No.578 also got the suffix although it was not ex-works until 11th March 1924.

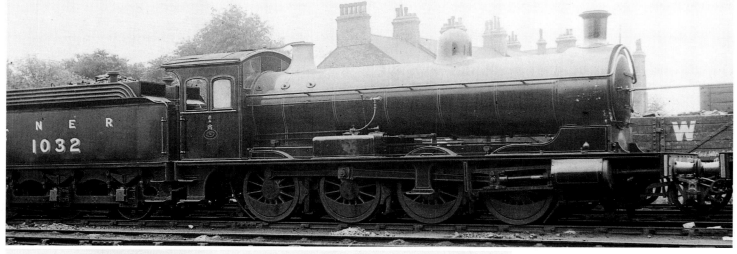

(above) **Until the June 1928 painting economies took effect, single lining in red was applied and Darlington put it on cylinder casings and boxes, splashers and even around the small number plate, in addition to where it would normally be expected. No reason has been found for No.1032 to be given special attention e.g. exhibition participation.**

(left) **No.1717 seems to be more representative of pre-1928 painting, shown as ex-works 30th November 1927. Normal photography at that time allowed almost no distinction between black and red.**

654 cont/.

Dar. 8/4—21/6/41.**G.**
Dar. 19—29/8/42.**N/C.**
Dar. 22/12/42—22/1/43.**G.**
Ghd. 10—28/9/44.**L.**
Dar. 2/8—6/9/46.**G.**
Dar. 10—12/9/46.**N/C.**
Dar. 7/1/49. *Not repaired.*

BOILERS:
D1932.
 G288 7/13.
 G330 5/16.
 D854 *(new)* 6/19.
 D859 *(ex660)* 14/8/30.
 D882 *(ex1320)* 14/6/34.
 3121 *(new)* 13/4/40 (56B).
 3123 *(ex410)* 22/1/43 (56B).
 3228 *(ex3292)* 6/9/46 (56B).

SHEDS:
Borough Gardens.
Shildon 27/1/27.
Darlington 7/1/35.
Blaydon 28/3/43.
Newport 20/7/47.
Middlesbrough 2/11/47.

RENUMBERED:
3317 24/4/46.

CONDEMNED: 12/2/49.
Cut up at Darlington.

655

Darlington 534.

To traffic 5/1908.

REPAIRS:
???. ?/?—1/13.**G.**
???. ?/?—10/15.**G.**
Ghd. 24/8—22/11/23.**G.**
Dar. 22/4—12/7/27.**G.**
Dar. 4/11—19/12/30.**G.**
Dar. 23/5—28/6/34.**G.**
Dar. 12—21/5/36.**N/C.**
Dar. 18/3—23/4/37.**G.**
Dar. 12/2—15/3/40.**G.**
Dar. 25/9—24/10/42.**G.**
Ghd. 19/9—7/10/44.**L.**
Dar. 20/7—31/8/46.**G.**
Ghd. 8—24/12/47.**L.**
Dar. 22/6/49. *Not repaired.*

BOILERS:
D1933.
D1925 1/13.
D1933 10/15.
D1955 *(new)* 12/7/27.

D1470 *(ex769)* 28/6/34.
 3120 *(new)* 15/3/40 (56B).
 3240 *(new)* 24/10/42 (56B).
 3615 *(new)* 31/8/46 (56B).

SHEDS:
Annfield Plain.
Borough Gardens 1/25.
Shildon 9/25.
Darlington 7/1/35.
Blaydon 28/3/43.
West Hartlepool 20/7/47.
Middlesbrough 5/12/48.

RENUMBERED:
3318 30/8/46.

CONDEMNED: 27/6/49.
Cut up at Darlington.

656

Darlington 535.

To traffic 5/1908.

REPAIRS:
???. ?/?—?/3/13.**G.**
???. ?/?—?/8/15.**G.**
???. ?/?—?/2/22.**G.**
Ghd. 27/8—23/10/24.**G.**
Dar. 4/8—26/10/27.**G.**
Dar. 8/3—29/4/30.**G.**
Dar. 26/2—30/3/35.**G.**
Dar. 22/2—30/3/38.**G.**
Dar. 31/3—5/4/38.**N/C.**
Dar. 22/1—22/2/41.**G.**
Dar. 23/1—26/2/43.**G.**
Ghd. 23/8—12/9/44.**L.**
Dar. 1—18/5/45.**L.**
Dar. 5/9—13/10/45.**G.**
Ghd. 19/12/46—11/1/47.**L.**
Ghd. 2—26/11/47.**L.**
Dar. 31/3—30/4/48.**G.**

BOILERS:
D1934.
D1933 3/13.
D1922 8/15.
D1365 *(new)* 2/22.
 D862 *(ex1186)* 29/4/30.
 D572 *(ex773)* 30/3/35.
 2227 *(ex650)* 30/3/38.
 2269 *(ex652)* 22/2/41.
 2159 *(ex2120)* 26/2/43.
 2271 *(ex2120)* 13/10/45.
 2797 *(ex3252)* 30/4/48 (56B).

SHEDS:
Springhead.
Dairycoates 24/12/25.

March 28/10/31.
Dairycoates 5/2/32.
Newport 20/9/34.
Middlesbrough 6/2/37.
Darlington 21/11/48.
Selby 20/11/49.

RENUMBERED:
 3319 18/8/46.
 63319 30/4/48.

CONDEMNED: 18/4/51.
Cut up at Darlington.

642

Darlington.

To traffic 6/1911.

REPAIRS:
???. ?/?—?/4/22.**G.**
Dar. 4/5—31/8/25.**G.**
Dar. 21/10—5/12/29.**G.**
Dar. 9/5—15/6/33.**G.**
Rebuilt to Part 2.
Dar. 9—16/8/34.**N/C.**
Dar. 2/6—4/7/36.**G.**
Dar. 9/2—14/3/40.**G.**
Dar. 13/6/40.**N/C.**
Dar. 28/6/40.**N/C.**
Dar. 12/8—26/9/40.**G.**
Dar. 10/11—18/12/42.**G.**
Ghd. 8—30/8/44.**L.**
Dar. 4/1/47. *Not repaired.*

BOILERS:
 G949.
 2232 *(new)* 5/12/29.
D1817 *(exQ10 2500)* 15/6/33 (56A).
D1815 *(ex1320)* 4/7/36 (56A).
D1809 *(ex1062)* 14/3/40 (56A).
D1704 *(ex657)* 18/12/42 (56A).

SHEDS:
Shildon.
Newport 7/1/35.
Stockton 16/10/39.
Newport 1/2/43.
Borough Gardens 28/3/43.

RENUMBERED:
3320 25/8/46.

CONDEMNED: 22/3/47.
Cut up at Darlington.

643

Darlington.

To traffic 6/1911.

REPAIRS:
???. ?/?—?/7/22.**G.**
Ghd. 16/9—11/12/25.**G.**
Ghd. 3/7—13/9/28.**G.**
Ghd. 11/8—4/10/32.**G.**
Dar. 28/9—29/10/37.**G.**
Dar. 19/7—2/8/39.**N/C.**
Dar. 18/9—23/10/40.**H.**
Dar. 20/10—21/11/41.**G.**
Dar. 16/11—18/12/43.**L.**
Dar. 18/12/44—20/1/45.**G.**
Ghd. 27/5—13/6/46.**L.**
Dar. 11/2/48. *Not repaired.*

BOILERS:
 G953.
D1060 *(ex647)* 13/9/28.
 2911 *(new)* 29/10/37 (56B).
 3233 *(new)* 21/11/41 (56B).

SHEDS:
Annfield Plain.
Tyne Dock 24/6/37.
Borough Gardens 1/3/40.

RENUMBERED:
3321 13/6/46.

CONDEMNED: 6/3/48.
Cut up at Darlington.

657

Darlington.

To traffic 6/1911.

REPAIRS:
Dar. 30/4—23/7/23.**G.**
Dar. 14/1—8/4/26.**G.**
Dar. 13/1—24/2/30.**G.**
Dar. 3—31/8/33.**G.**
Rebuilt to Part 2.
Dar. 14—20/9/33.**N/C.**
Dar. 12/3—27/4/37.**G.**
Dar. 19/3—19/4/40.**G.**
Dar. 23/4—14/5/40.**N/C.**
Dar. 3/3—21/4/42.**L.**
Dar. 28/10—23/11/42.**G.**
Dar. 6/12/44—19/1/45.**G.**
Dar. 28/12/46—8/3/47.**G.**
Dar. 11—22/3/47.**N/C.**
Ghd. 8/10—1/11/48.**L.**
Dar. 24/1/49. *Not repaired.*

WORKS CODES:- Cw - Cowlairs. Dar- Darlington. Don - Doncaster. Ghd - Gateshead. Gor - Gorton. Hsi - Hull Springhead. Inv - Inverurie. Str - Stratford.
REPAIR CODES:- **C/H** - Casual Heavy. **C/L** - Casual Light. **G** - General. **H**- Heavy. **H/I** - Heavy Intermediate. **L** - Light. **L/I** - Light Intermediate. **N/C** - Non-Classified.

657 cont/.

BOILERS:
 G957.
 D1061 *(ex1694)* 8/4/26.
 D1809 *(exQ10 2498)* 31/8/33 (56A).
 D1704 *(ex939)* 27/4/37 (56A).
 D1817 *(ex1062)* 23/11/42 (56A).

SHEDS:
 Shildon.
 Newport 7/1/35.
 Middlesbrough 8/1/44.

RENUMBERED:
 3322 18/8/46.
 63322 1/11/48.

CONDEMNED: 12/2/49.
Cut up at Darlington.

658

Darlington.

To Traffic 6/1911.

REPAIRS:
 Dar. 5/5—13/9/23.**G.**
 Dar. 29/6—27/10/26.**G.**
 Dar. 17/6—15/8/29.**G.**
 Dar. 31/5—11/7/32.**G.**
 Rebuilt to Part 2.
 Dar. 28/5—12/7/35.**G.**
 Dar. 17/8—20/9/38.**G.**
 Dar. 5/5—6/6/41.**G.**
 Dar. 31/3—10/4/42
 Tender only.
 Dar. 20/9—16/10/43.**G.**
 Restored to Part 1.
 Dar. 3—28/9/46.**G.**
 Dar. 13—24/12/47.**L.**
 Dar. 19/10/48. *Not repaired.*

BOILERS:
 G958.
 2227 *(new)* 15/8/29.
 D2003 *(exQ10 2512)* 11/7/32 (56A).
 D1685 *(exQ10 2511)* 12/7/35 (56A).
 D1808 *(ex769)* 20/9/38 (56A).
 D1661 *(ex661)* 6/6/41 (56A).
 3384 *(new)* 16/10/43 (56B).
 D1392 *(ex785)* 28/9/46.

SHEDS:
 Shildon.
 Newport 30/1/24.
 Middlesbrough 29/5/31.
 Newport 20/9/44.
 Middlesbrough 2/11/47.

RENUMBERED:
 3323 18/8/46.

CONDEMNED: 8/11/48.
Cut up at Darlington.

659

Darlington.

To traffic 6/1911.

REPAIRS:
 Dar. 27/9/22—27/1/23.**G.**
 Dar. 1/7—29/9/25.**G.**
 Dar. 27/9—22/11/28.**G.**
 Dar. 4/8—9/9/32.**G.**
 Rebuilt to Part 2.
 Dar. 26/9—28/10/35.**G.**
 Dar. 10/1—7/2/39.**G.**
 Dar. 1/9—9/10/41.**G.**
 Dar. 11—26/6/43.**L.**
 Dar. 15/4—6/5/44.**G.**
 Ghd. 31/10—17/11/45.**L.**
 Dar. 16/9/47. *Not repaired.*

BOILERS:
 D2099.
  2159 *(new)* 22/11/28.
 D1661 *(exQ10 2505)* 9/9/32
 (56A).
 D2003 *(ex658)* 28/10/35 (56A).
 D1685 *(ex658)* 7/2/39 (56A).
 D1991 *(ex660)* 6/5/44 (56A).

SHEDS:
 Newport.
 Tyne Dock 28/3/43.

RENUMBERED:
 3324 17/11/46.

CONDEMNED: 16/10/47.
Cut up at Darlington.

661

Darlington.

To traffic 7/1911.

REPAIRS:
 ???. ?/?—?/9/15.**G.**
 Dar. 5/2—22/4/24.**G.**
 Dar. 2/6—31/7/24.**H.**
 Dar. 4/8—21/10/27.**G.**
 Dar. 28/3—27/5/30.**G.**
 Dar. 2/6—13/7/33.**G.**
 Rebuilt to Part 2.
 Dar. 17/1—22/2/36.**G.**
 Dar. 30/3—14/5/38.**G.**
 Dar. 26/2—31/3/41.**G.**
 Dar. 7—23/4/42.**L.**
 Dar. 19/10—24/11/43.**G.**
 Dar. 12/2/47. *Not repaired.*

BOILERS:
 G962.
  D11 *(ex767)* 9/15.
  D22 *(ex773)* 31/7/24.
 D1961 *(new)* 21/10/27.

D1997 *(exQ10 2501)* 13/7/33 (56A).
D1661 *(ex659)* 22/2/36 (56A).
D2003 *(ex653)* 31/3/41 (56A).

SHEDS:
 Selby.
 Newport 25/4/38.
 Tyne Dock 28/3/43.

RENUMBERED:
 3325 1/9/46.

CONDEMNED: 22/3/47.
Cut up at Darlington.

669

Darlington.

To traffic 7/1911.

REPAIRS:
 ???. ?/?—?/8/15.**G.**
 ???. ?/?—?/12/16.**G.**
 Dar. 21/2—2/5/24.**G.**
 Ghd. 26/7—16/11/27.**G.**
 Ghd. 24/10—1/12/30.**G.**
 Ghd. 20—27/10/31.**N/C.**
 Dar. 4/3—8/4/35.**G.**
 Dar. 26/6—3/8/39.**G.**
 Dar. 23/4—16/5/42.**G.**
 Dar. 12/6—7/7/45.**G.**
 Ghd. 2—12/8/46.**L.**
 Dar. 11/2—19/3/48.**G.**

BOILERS:
 D5.
 G294 ?/8/15.
 D615 *(new)* ?/12/16.
 D854 *(ex130)* 8/4/35.
 D1382 *(ex1669)* 3/8/39.
  3228 *(new)* 16/5/42 (56B).
  3121 *(ex1186)* 7/7/45 (56B).
  3132 *(ex3268)* 19/3/48 (56B).

SHEDS:
 Dairycoates.
 Blaydon 24/5/27.
 Heaton 8/6/37.
 Tyne Dock 24/6/39.
 Borough Gardens 1/3/40.
 Tyne Dock 19/10/44.
 Borough Gardens 13/4/47.

RENUMBERED:
 3326 12/8/46.
 E3326 19/3/48.

CONDEMNED: 6/10/51.
Cut up at Darlington.

764

Darlington.

To traffic 8/1911.

REPAIRS:
 ???. ?/?—?/2/16.**G.**
 ???. ?/?—?/6/22.**G.**
 Dar. 21/3—30/5/24.**G.**
 Dar. 26/8—11/9/24.**L.**
 Dar. 16/2—3/6/27.**G.**
 Dar. 1/1—14/2/30.**G.**
 Dar. 18/6—21/8/34.**H.**
 Dar. 28/1—14/3/35.**G.**
 Dar. 6/10—7/11/38.**G.**
 Dar. 16—26/9/39.**N/C.**
 Dar. 8/9—21/10/41.**G.**
 Dar. 1—14/4/43.**L.**
 Dar. 13—25/9/43.**N/C.**
 Dar. 26/2—18/3/44.**G.**
 Ghd. 15—30/3/45.**L.**
 Dar. 6/9—4/10/46.**G.**
 Dar. 22/10—26/11/46.**N/C.**
 Dar. 12/11/48. *Not repaired.*

BOILERS:
 D6.
 D1916 ?/2/16.
 D1400 *(new)* ?/6/22.
 D1007 *(ex1708)* 14/2/30.
 D1066 *(ex83)* 21/8/34.
  2800 *(new)* 7/11/38 (56B).
  2085 *(ex2117)* 21/10/41.
 D1769 *(ex793)* 18/3/44.
  3240 *(ex653)* 4/10/46 (56B).

SHEDS:
 Springhead.
 Dairycoates 31/5/24.
 Tyne Dock 15/4/35.
 York 10/2/38.
 West Hartlepool 28/3/43.
 Newport 7/9/47.

RENUMBERED:
 3327 1/9/46.

CONDEMNED: 22/11/48.
Cut up at Darlington.

767

Darlington.

To traffic 8/1911.

REPAIRS:
 ???. ?/?—?/6/15.**G.**
 ???. ?/?—?/12/16.**G.**
 ???. ?/?—20/10/22.**G.**
 Ghd. 28/2—16/3/23.**L.**
 Ghd. 4/5—25/8/25.**G.**
 Ghd. 3/7—11/9/28.**G.**
 Ghd. 19/11—23/12/31.**G.**

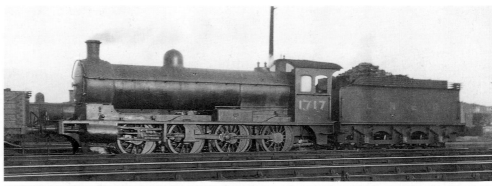

Beginning with No.648, ex Darlington 14th March 1929, the number was moved to the cab and 12in. LNER was used on the tender and by then only unlined black was being used.

When fresh from works, No.1218 was out 5th August 1932, at least the black paint had a glossy component to it, although it quickly disappeared from service and weather exposure.

From July 1942, only NE was put on the tender. No.2117 was so from 11th December 1943, and this 18th August 1946 photograph really illustrates how badly wartime had affected this class. Note that the inner rim of the chimney has gone completely.

In the 1946 re-numbering Q5 was allocated 3250 to 3339 and only No.769 (3329) failed to take up its new number. On Sunday 14th July 1946, No.644 was changed to 3310 at Selby shed in the style used by local painters doing this job.

LNER was applied to the tender again on engines ex works from January 1946 and, where the re-numbering was done by works, normal shaded transfers were used. No.774 was under repair at Darlington 9th July to 17th August 1946 and with effect from Sunday 14th July 1946 was changed to 3334.

The stock of transfers was exhausted during 1947 and they were regarded as too expensive to re-order. A change was made to yellow painted and unshaded letters and numbers in Gill sans style but with 6 and 9 modified as shown on Doncaster drawing No.16601 dated 21st February 1945. No.3256 was ex-works 7th June 1947 in that style.

No.3281 had been put into Gill sans style when ex-works 15th August 1947 from a general repair. It was in Darlington for a light repair 27th January to 20th February 1948 and came out with the BR 'E' prefix to its number but still with LNER on its tender.

In February and March 1948, Darlington turned out four Q5's with the prefix and BRITISH RAILWAYS on the tender: E3260 (6th February), E3311 (5th March), E3314 (20th February), and E3326 (19th March). It is probable that No.3296, ex-Gateshead 26th February, from a light repair also got the prefix. Its tender certainly carried BRITISH RAILWAYS. No.E3261, ex-Gateshead 24th February, also from light repair, was reported with the prefix.

767 cont/.

Dar. 12/11—6/12/34.**G**.
Dar. 27/9—29/10/38.**G**.
Dar. 24/3—22/4/41.**G**.
Dar. 8/9—9/10/43.**G**.
Ghd. 29/8—14/9/45.**L**.
Dar. 11/7—23/8/46.**G**.
Dar. 10—17/5/47.**L**.
Dar. 19/8/48. *Not repaired.*

BOILERS:
D11.
G142 6/15.
D607 *(new)* 12/16.
D856 *(ex651)* 23/12/31.
D2068 *(ex443)* 6/12/34.
2806 *(new)* 29/10/38 (56B).
2811 *(ex1684)* 22/4/41 (56B).
3380 *(new)* 9/10/43 (56B).
3609 *(new)* 23/8/46 (56B).
3121 *(ex3326)* 10/9/48 (56B).

SHEDS:
Tyne Dock.
Borough Gardens 12/1/23.
Heaton 14/11/30.
Darlington 4/11/44.
Middlesbrough 13/2/49.

RENUMBERED:
3328 23/8/46.
63328 10/9/48.

CONDEMNED: 13/1/51.
Cut up at Darlington.

769

Darlington.

To traffic 8/1911.

REPAIRS:
???. ?/?—?/11/15.**G**.
???. ?/?—?/7/19.**G**.
???. ?/?—4/5/22.**G**.
Ghd. 9/7—18/9/25.**G**.
Ghd. 14/3—1/5/30.**G**.
Dar. 12/3—11/4/34.**G**.
Rebuilt to Part 2.
Dar. 24/8—29/10/37.**G**.
Dar. 18/11/40—14/1/41.**H**.
Dar. 22/5—19/6/41.**G**.
Dar. 23/11—5/12/42.**N/C**.
Dar. 23/7—4/9/43.**G**.
Dar. 26/4—1/6/44.**G**.
Dar. 30/8—25/9/44.**L**.
Dar. 25/9/46. *Not repaired.*

BOILERS:
D14.
G287 11/15.
D1925 7/19.
D1470 *(new)* 18/9/25.
D1808 *(exQ10 2503)* 11/4/34 (56A).

D1988 *(ex644)* 29/10/37 (56A).
D1808 *(ex658)* 19/6/41 (56A).
D1685 *(ex659)* 1/6/44 (56A).

SHEDS:
East Hartlepool.
Darlington 22/4/39.
Selby 27/6/39.

RENUMBERED:
Allocated **3329**.

CONDEMNED: 21/12/46.
Cut up at Darlington.

770

Darlington.

To traffic 9/1911.

REPAIRS:
Ghd. 6/7—13/9/23.**G**.
Ghd. 12/5—2/6/25.**L**.
Ghd. 9/11—30/3/28.**G**.
Dar. 1—30/11/32.**G**.
Dar. 2/10—28/11/35.**G**.
Dar. 10/1—13/2/39.**G**.
Dar. 17/7—29/8/41.**G**.
Dar. 2—26/11/42.**N/C**.
Dar. 18/9—12/10/43.**G**.
Dar. 4—19/7/45.**L**.
Dar. 24/2—12/4/47.**G**.

BOILERS:
D15.
D2080 *(new)* 30/3/28.
D1441 *(ex162)* 13/2/39.
2229 *(ex1669)* 12/10/43.
3116 *(ex3313)* 12/4/47 (56B).

SHEDS:
North Blyth.
Haverton Hill 23/4/31.
Newport 25/1/35.
Stockton 20/1/47.
Darlington 2/11/47.

RENUMBERED:
3330 18/8/46.

CONDEMNED: 28/12/49.
Cut up at Darlington.

771

Darlington.

To traffic 9/1911.

REPAIRS:
???. ?/?—?/2/17.**G**.
Dar. 23/4—18/7/24.**G**.
Dar. 22/6—29/9/27.**G**.
Dar. 17/1—12/2/29.**N/C**.

Dar. 5/4—6/6/30.**G**.
Dar. 14/3—14/5/35.**G**.
Dar. 10/2—20/5/38.**G**.
Dar. 23/12/40—28/1/41.**G**.
Dar. 27/8—12/9/42.**N/C**.
Dar. 26/11/42—2/1/43.**G**.
Dar. 12/9—10/10/44.**G**.
Ghd. 17/2—1/3/46.**L**.
Dar. 12/6—9/8/47
Dar. 29/1/49. *Not repaired.*

BOILERS:
D17.
D19 *(ex772)* ?/2/17.
2276 *(new)* 6/6/30.
2086 *(ex443)* 28/1/41.
2227 *(ex1150)* 2/1/43.
2278 *(ex2118)* 10/10/44.
2906 *(ex3258)* 9/8/47 (56B).

SHEDS:
Dairycoates.
March 22/10/31.
Dairycoates 5/2/32.
Newport 20/9/34.
Middlesbrough 8/1/44.
Blaydon 23/7/45.
Haverton Hill 5/10/47.

RENUMBERED:
3331 27/1/46.

CONDEMNED: 12/2/49.
Cut up at Darlington.

772

Darlington.

To traffic 9/1911.

REPAIRS:
???. ?/?—?/1/17.**G**.
???. ?/?—?/9/22.**G**.
Dar. 27/7—30/9/25.**G**.
Dar. 29/8—28/9/27.**L**.
Dar. 20/8—18/10/28.**G**.
Dar. 7/4—20/5/31.**G**.
Dar. 30/10—29/11/34.**G**.
Dar. 9/9—21/10/38.**G**.
Dar. 6—29/3/41.**G**.
Dar. 10/3—5/4/43.**G**.
Ghd. 4—19/9/44.**L**.
Dar. 19/11—15/12/45.**G**.
Ghd. 24/6—15/7/47.**G**.
Dar. 28/2/49. *Not repaired.*

BOILERS:
D19.
D2101 ?/1/17.
2281 *(new)* 20/5/31.
2167 *(ex2116)* 21/10/38.
2914 *(ex781)* 29/3/41 (56B).
2806 *(ex1186)* 5/4/43 (56B).
3605 *(new)* 15/12/45 (56B).

SHEDS:
Shildon.
Newport 30/1/24.
Haverton Hill 5/5/31.
Tyne Dock 28/3/43.
Cudworth 29/9/46.
Middlesbrough 13/2/49.

RENUMBERED:
3332 15/12/46.

CONDEMNED: 22/3/49.
Cut up at Darlington.

773

Darlington.

To traffic 9/1911.

REPAIRS:
Dar. 21/4—28/6/24.**G**.
Dar. 11/11/26—11/2/27.**G**.
Dar. 2/9—22/10/29.**G**.
Dar. 21/4—5/5/31.**H**.
Dar. 31/1—27/2/35.**G**.
Dar. 1/8/39—14/2/40.**G**.
Dar. 11—25/4/40.**N/C**.
Dar. 7/3—9/4/42.**G**.
Dar. 18/12/43—19/1/44.**G**.
Dar. 21/12/44—2/2/45.**L**.
Dar. 10/7—24/8/46.**G**.
Ghd. 16/9—1/10/47.**L**.
Dar. 25/8—17/9/48.**G**.

BOILERS:
D22.
D2098 28/6/24.
D1768 *(new)* 11/2/27.
D572 *(ex1150)* 5/5/31.
D856 *(ex767)* 27/2/35.
3116 *(new)* 14/2/40 (56B).
3226 *(ex2117)* 19/1/44 (56B).
2811 *(ex2116)* 24/8/46 (56B).
3233 *(ex3321)* 17/9/48 (56B).

SHEDS:
Dairycoates.
Mexborough 15/12/33.
Doncaster 19/2/34.
Mexborough 22/11/36.
Ferryhill 1/4/37.
Darlington 7/11/38.
Middlesbrough 29/7/39.

RENUMBERED:
3333 30/6/46.
63333 17/9/48.

CONDEMNED: 21/12/50.
Cut up at Darlington.

(*above*) **Only eight Q5 got the full BR number and three of these were put on by Gateshead works at light repairs, Nos.63338 (13h April), 63286 (10th May), 63313 (2nd December), all 1948. None of these got a smokebox number plate. At Darlington 63319 (30th April 1948) and 63282 (21st May 1948) got a BR number but were too early for a smokebox plate.**

(*left*) **The last three to have general repair also had a smokebox plate fitted. Nos.63290 (11th June), 63328 (10th September), 63333 (17th September), all done at Darlington in 1948.**

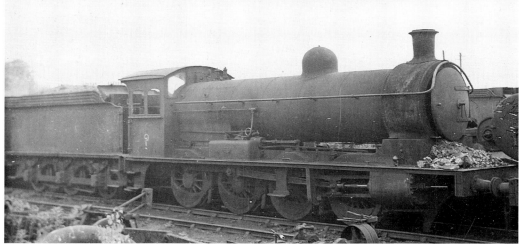

Withdrawal began with No.769 on 21st December 1946 and this was a Part 2 engine, although Part 1 No.3309 (ex1215) was actually the first to go - on 7th December 1946. When E3326 was taken out of stock on the 6th October 1951, Class Q5 was extinct. All were cut up at Darlington.

(above) The mass withdrawal of Q10 class late in 1931 provided fifteen Diagram 51 boilers only four to seven years of age and fourteen Q5 were modified to get further use from these boilers which then became Diagram 56A. No.658, ex-works 11th July 1932, was the first to be rebuilt, followed on 9th September 1932 by another slide valve engine No.659. The 9in. bigger boiler needed a new smokebox and a new cab to be put on and a shorter chimney.

(right) The other one rebuilt in 1932 was No.2119, the only piston valve engine to be converted. It was ex-works 27th October and also seems to have been the only one to keep the Raven fog signalling apparatus, although that system was still in use to October 1933 - the striker for it can be seen behind the cab step.

Four more were altered in 1933: 642 (15th June), 661 (13th July), 657 (31st August), 653 (23rd December). In 1934 seven more Q5's got the larger boiler: 1062 (16th February), 769 (11th April), 1054 (28th April), 644 (8th May), 1320 (15th May), 939 (28th May), and 660 (5th June). The fifteenth boiler was kept spare to permit interchange.

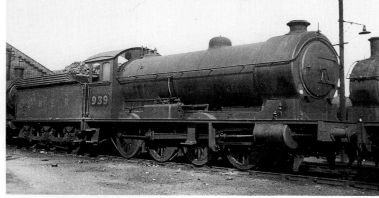

Withdrawal of the 5ft 6in. diameter boiler began in November 1942 and by May 1944 three had gone - all from the second batch of five built in October 1925. Three of the Part 2 engines then reverted to Part 1 as plenty of the 4ft 9in. boilers were available. These re-conversions were Nos.939 (31st May 1943), 658 (16th October 1943) and 644 (11th December 1945). Their only remnant from Part 2 was the longer vertical handrail on the tender. The other twelve Diagram 56A boilers were then used with the eleven Part 2 engines through to withdrawal.

774

Darlington.

To traffic 10/1911.

REPAIRS:
???. ?/?—?/10/22.**G.**
Dar. 8/7—30/9/25.**G.**
Dar. 1/7—16/8/29.**G.**
Dar. 31/8—28/9/31.**H.**
Dar. 9/2—23/3/33.**G.**
Dar. 22/5—1/7/36.**G.**
Dar. 6—27/7/36.**N/C.**
Dar. 11/10—10/11/37.**H.**
Dar. 6/11—18/12/39.**G.**
Dar. 6—13/9/40.**N/C.**
Dar. 19/9—10/11/42.**G.**
Dar. 29/8—18/9/44.**L.**
Ghd. 1—22/10/44.**L.**
Ghd. 13/1—5/2/48.**L.**

BOILERS:
D24.
D1921 10/22.
D1485 *(new)* 30/9/25.
D1006 *(ex430)* 23/3/33.
2233 *(ex411)* 10/11/37.
D1365 *(ex1128)* 10/11/42.
2150 *(ex3299)* 17/8/46.

SHEDS:
Shildon.
Darlington 7/1/35.

RENUMBERED:
3334 14/7/46.

CONDEMNED: 16/5/49.
Cut up at Darlington.

781

Darlington.

To traffic 10/1911.

REPAIRS:
???. ?/?—?/1/15.**G.**
???. ?/?—?/5/17.**G.**
Ghd. 8/12/24—19/2/25.**G.**
Ghd. 5/7—17/9/28.**G.**
Dar. 28/7—26/8/30.**G.**
Dar. 21/9—23/10/31.**G.**
Dar. 27/11/34—4/1/35.**G.**
Dar. 8/4—2/6/36.**H.**
Dar. 11/4—19/5/38.**G.**
Dar. 26/1—14/2/39.**N/C.**
Dar. 30/12/40—15/2/41.**G.**
Dar. 10/8—9/9/42.
Tender only.
Dar. 22/12/43—21/1/44.**G.**
Ghd. 11—30/10/45.**L.**
Dar. 31/1—29/3/47.**G.**

BOILERS:
D26.
G295 ?/1/15.
 D17 *(ex771)* 5/17.
2278 *(new)* 26/8/30.
2914 *(new)* 19/5/38 (56B).
2906 *(ex650)* 15/2/41 (56B).
2916 *(ex1694)* 21/1/44 (56B).

SHEDS:
Shildon.
Darlington 20/3/35.

RENUMBERED:
3335 8/9/46.

CONDEMNED: 29/8/49.
Cut up at Darlington.

783

Darlington.

To traffic 10/1911.

REPAIRS:
???. ?/?—?/2/22.**G.**
Ghd. 1/4—27/5/25.**G.**
Ghd. 26/5—2/8/28.**G.**
Ghd. 11/7—9/8/29.**L.**
Ghd. 12/1—15/2/32.**G.**
Dar. 24/2—8/4/37.**G.**
Dar. 5/11—2/12/40.**G.**
Dar. 11—22/8/41.**L.**
Dar. 14/5—8/6/43.**G.**
Dar. 15/6—3/8/44.**H.**
Ghd. 11—26/3/46.**L.**
Dar. 2/10—7/11/47.**G.**

BOILERS:
D27.
 D32 *(ex793)* 27/5/25.
D2086 *(new)* 2/8/28.
 2272 *(ex410)* 8/4/37.
 2281 *(ex785)* 2/12/40.
 2809 *(ex1177)* 8/6/43 (56B).
 2911 *(ex2125)* 3/8/44 (56B).
 2802 *(ex3272)* 7/11/47 (56B).

SHEDS:
East Hartlepool.
Haverton Hill 10/12/38.
West Hartlepool 28/3/43.
Selby 14/11/48.

RENUMBERED:
3336 8/12/46.

CONDEMNED: 16/10/50.
Cut up at Darlington.

789

Darlington.

To traffic 11/1911.

REPAIRS:
???. ?/?—?/9/22.**G.**
Dar. 22/12/24—28/2/25.**G.**
Dar. 24/6—29/7/25.**L.**
Dar. 12/3—19/5/28.**G.**
Dar. 23/12/30—16/2/31.**G.**
Dar. 28/9—22/10/34.**G.**
Dar. 3/3—10/5/37.**G.**
Dar. 11—19/5/37.**N/C.**
Dar. 8/12/38—5/1/39.**N/C.**
Dar. 10/8—14/9/39.**G.**
Dar. 14/6—8/7/40.**N/C.**
Dar. 25—28/8/40.**N/C.**
Dar. 6/3—7/4/42.**G.**
Dar. 22/6—2/7/43.**L.**
Dar. 14/9—7/10/44.**G.**
Dar. 12/2—9/3/46.**L.**
Ghd. 7—22/5/46.**L.**
Dar. 25/6/47. *Not repaired.*

BOILERS:
D30.
 2085 *(new)* 19/5/28.
D1365 *(ex1729)* 22/10/34.
 2886 *(new)* 10/5/37 (56B).
 3235 *(new)* 7/4/42 (56B).
D1427 *(ex1111)* 7/10/44.

SHEDS:
Newport.
Middlesbrough 7/11/38.
Darlington 19/8/39.

RENUMBERED:
3337 25/5/46.

CONDEMNED: 2/8/47.
Cut up at Darington.

793

Darlington.

To traffic 11/1911.

REPAIRS:
Ghd. 19/2—19/4/23.**G.**
Ghd. 22/3—7/4/24.**L.**
Ghd. 22/4—1/7/27.**G.**
Ghd. 28/8—10/10/30.**G.**
Dar. 16/8—15/9/34.**G.**
Dar. 21/10—23/12/38.**G.**
Dar. 21/4—29/5/41.**G.**
Dar. 15/12/43—8/1/44.**G.**
Dar. 8/1—8/3/47.**G.**
Dar. 11—22/3/47.**N/C.**
Ghd. 22/3—13/4/48.**L.**

BOILERS:
D32.
D1441 *(new)* 19/4/23.
D1955 *(ex655)* 15/9/34.
D1769 *(ex1186)* 29/5/41.
D2167 *(ex2123)* 8/1/44.
 3232 *(ex3312)* 8/3/47 (56B).

SHEDS:
North Blyth.
Newport 23/3/38.

RENUMBERED:
3338 18/8/46.
63338 13/4/48.

CONDEMNNED: 1/10/49.
Cut up at Darlington.

794

Darlington.

To traffic 11/1911.

REPAIRS:
Dar. 27/8—9/10/23.**G.**
Dar. 15/7—26/10/25.**G.**
Dar. 8/10—10/11/28.**G.**
Dar. 20/4—23/5/32.**G.**
Dar. 21/6—16/8/35.**G.**
Dar. 11/7—23/8/38.**G.**
Dar. 2—28/12/40.**G.**
Dar. 19/6—7/7/42.**L.**
Dar. 12/3—16/4/43.**G.**
Ghd. 19/8—4/9/44.**L.**
Dar. 19/3—14/4/45.**L.**
Dar. 21/11—21/12/45.**G.**
Ghd. 2—9/11/46.**L.**
Dar. 15/1/48. *Not repaired.*

BOILERS:
D34.
 2153 *(new)* 10/11/28.
D714 *(ex1694)* 16/8/35.
D1037 *(ex648)* 23/8/38.
 2272 *(ex783)* 28/12/40.
 3132 *(ex1110)* 16/4/43 (56B).
 2794 *(ex1700)* 21/12/45 (56B).

SHEDS:
Newport.
Middlesbrough 6/2/37.
Newport 7/11/38.
Middlesbrough 8/1/44.

RENUMBERED:
3339 18/8/46.

CONDEMNED: 7/2/48.
Cut up at Darlington.

Amongst only fourteen engines it was unusual to find three varieties of chimney. No.658 (*see* page 1) had one with a windjabber, almost certainly a B16 class pattern, and from November 1943 Nos.661, 3301 and 3324 had that style. Most had the style as carried by No.1054 which lacked windjabber and, late on, even this type could lose its inner rim as shown by the illustration of No.63322 (ex 657) on page 17.

No.657 started off with a taller chimney than seen on any of the others which it certainly had to March 1937 and may possibly have kept it to a March 1940 repair, when its more than 13ft 0in. height from rail would have more significance.

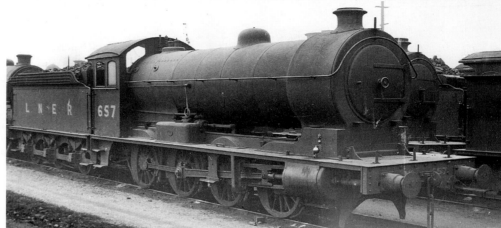

This 7th September 1942 photograph at Starbeck shows No.657 changed to a shorter chimney with inner rim which later wore away as shown by a photo when No.657 had become BR No.63322.

No.657 shared with No.658 the distinction of at first keeping wheel and handle fastening for the smokebox door. All others noted having changed to twin handles, as on No.1054. Although the smokebox diameter increased from 5ft 8⅛in. to 6ft 5⅛in., the door remained the same size as before, and not until December 1942 were any larger doors fitted.

During the war, three had new larger doors put on. Instead of the flat flange, they had pressed joint ring, and the straps were much closer to each other. Instead of the hinges being split, they were solid with an extension to service as a door stop. The three so altered were 1054 (29th December 1942), 661 (24th November 1943) and 660 (29th January 1944).

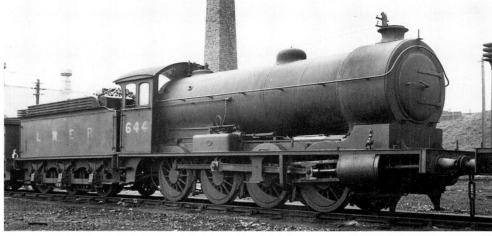

All retained steam reversing gear although, at re-boilering, this was altered to the single handle control type.

Most retained NER design draw gear and buffers which were taper shank and had a circular flange.

Nos.657, 659, 661 and 1320 are known to have changed to Group Standard hook and buffers. These had a square flange and stepped shank. All kept the wood sandwich type buffer beam.

(above) **Whilst the re-boilered engines were officially designated Part 2 from the December 1932 Diagram Book alterations, they remained simply 'Class Q5' on the front buffer beam.**

(right) **With the new cab and higher position of the side windows, longer vertical handrails were put on. New rails of matching length were also put on the tender.**

By 20th October 1945, No.661 had exchanged tenders with No.651 of Part 1 which still had short vertical handrails.

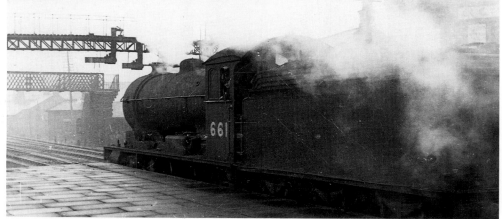

(*above*) As Part 2, all were unlined black and had the number on the cab, with LNER on the tender until after July 1942. This April 1942 photograph shows the wartime blackout.

(*left*) No.659 became 3324 at Tyne Dock shed on Sunday 17th November 1946, the tender having had lettering cut to NE only when ex-works 6th May 1944, and it remained so until its 16th October 1947 withdrawal. Note the cover for the tail rod had been discarded. The tenders of Nos.642, 644, 661, 769, 939 and 1062 never had LNER restored.

No.3301 ex Darlington 1st February 1947 had LNER on the tender again with letters - and figures - in yellow painted and unshaded Gill sans style. Nos.3322 (8th) and 3305 (15th) both March 1947, also got this style.

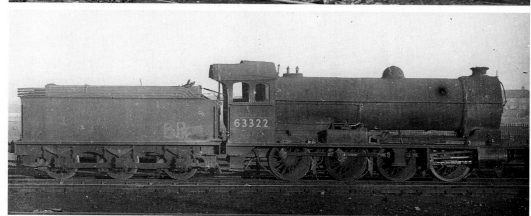

Only one showed any effect of nationalisation, No.63322 being so numbered at a light repair ex-Gateshead works 1st November 1948. Part 2 became extinct when No.3305 was withdrawn on 16th May 1949. Note that No.63322 still had LNER on tender when withdrawn 12th February 1949.

(below) **2117**ᴅ from 18th October 1923 was at Newport and here in 1930 is approaching Ferryhill on a down coal train. On 28th March 1943 it moved to Borough Gardens where on 15th December 1946 they changed it to 3251 and from where it was withdrawn 20th December 1950 still as LNER.

Another twenty engines, Nos.2213 to 2232, were built at Darlington from April to December 1917. These were similar to the previous thirty but the tenders were the improved 4125 gallons self-trimming type although with rails only around the coal space.

Darlington then built a further twenty engines, Nos.2233 to 2252, in two batches, each of ten, between August and December 1918 and May to August 1919. The only modification was to the tender coal rails which now tapered off at the rear similar to the front end.

CLASS Q 6

1247

Darlington.

To traffic 2/1913.

REPAIRS:
Ghd. 6—26/7/23.**L.**
Ghd. 3/11—2/2/24.**G.**
Dar. 6/4—31/8/26.**G.**
Dar. 3/12/26—22/2/27.**L.**
Dar. 31/1—27/3/29.**G.**
Dar. 24/5—24/6/32.**G.**
Dar. 22/5—27/7/36.**G.**
Dar. 16/8—14/9/39.**G.**
Dar. 27/1—25/2/42.**G.**
Dar. 28/11—2/1/43.**N/C.**
Dar. 30/3—22/4/44.**G.**
Ghd. 20/6—11/7/45.**L.**
Dar. 7/12/46—11/1/47.**G.**
Dar. 22/7/48.*Weigh.*
Ghd. 30/8—13/9/48.**L.**
Dar. 15/8—8/9/49.**G.**
Dar. 3—29/12/51.**G.**
Dar. 28/12/53—23/1/54.**H/I.**
Dar. 25—28/1/54.**N/C.**
Dar. 1—4/2/54.**N/C.**
Dar. 25/2—3/3/54.**N/C.**
Dar. 10/8—28/9/55.**C/L.**
Dar. 6—21/10/55.**N/C.**
Dar. 31/5—25/6/56.**G.**
Dar. 10/4—21/5/58.**C/L.**
Dar. 13—24/6/58.**N/C.**
Dar. 2—6/2/59.**N/C.**
Dar. 24/6—20/8/60.**G.**
Dar. 1—27/9/60.**N/C.**

BOILERS:
D162.
D130 *(ex1257)* 31/8/26.
2157 *(new)* 27/3/29.
E4/25 *(exB15 821)* 24/6/32.
E4/25 reno.25 27/7/36.
3023 *(new)* 14/9/39 (50A).
3013 *(ex2223)* 25/2/42 (50A).
2976 *(ex2296)* 22/4/44 (50A).
3004 *(ex3422)* 11/1/47 (50A).
2563 *(ex63419)* 8/9/49.
24279 *(new)* 29/12/51 (50A).
24182 25/6/56 (50A).
24222 20/8/60 (50A).

SHEDS:
Tyne Dock.
York 8/3/24.
Dairycoates 21/2/27.
Newport 18/4/36.
Tyne Dock 29/7/39.
Newport 19/8/39.
Stockton 1/2/43.
Haverton Hill 5/10/47.

Middlesbrough 7/1/51.
Thornaby 1/6/58.
West Auckland 26/10/58.

RENUMBERED:
3340 28/4/46.
63340 13/9/48.

CONDEMNED: 15/7/63.
Into Dar. for cut up 31/7/63.

1248

Darlington.

To traffic 2/1913.

REPAIRS:
Dar. 9/5—27/9/23.**G.**
Dar. 27/10/25—27/1/26.**G.**
Ghd. 3/10—21/11/28.**G.**
Dar. 27/3—17/5/31.**G.**
Dar. 29/5—30/6/34.**G.**
Dar. 28/9—3/12/36.**G.**
Dar. 2/3—19/4/39.**G.**
Dar. 20/4—3/5/39.**N/C.**
Dar. 25/1—29/4/41.**G.**
Dar. 13/4—12/5/43.**G.**
Ghd. 22/5—11/6/45.**L.**
Dar. 22/8—19/9/46.**G.**
Ghd. 12—28/10/47.**L.**
Dar. 18/1—11/2/49.**G.**
Dar. 6/11—1/12/51.**H/I.**
Ghd. 16/9—13/10/52.**C/L.**
Ghd. 8/3—10/4/54.**G.**
Dar. 29/11/55—5/1/56.**C/L.**
Ghd. 29/1—8/3/57.**G.**
Dar. 31/10—15/11/57.**N/C.**
Dar. 14/4—13/5/61.**G.**
Dar. 19—26/5/61.**N/C.**
Dar. 1—9/6/61.**N/C.**
Dar. 25/10—7/12/62.**C/L.**

BOILERS:
D164.
D172 *(ex1252)* 27/9/23.
2394 *(new)* 17/5/31.
AW21 *(ex2285)* 3/12/36.
D1945 *(ex2289)* 19/4/39.
2157 *(ex2262)* 29/4/41.
2384 *(ex1335)* 12/5/43.
3013 *(ex3392)* 19/9/46 (50A).
3852 *(new)* 11/2/49 (50A).
3852 reno.24209 1/12/51.
24167 10/4/54 (50A).
24278 8/3/57 (50A).
24202 13/5/61 (50A).

SHEDS:
Selby.
Newport 25/10/25.

Haverton Hill 10/6/56.
Thornaby 14/6/59.
West Auckland 8/4/62.
West Hartlepool 24/11/63.

RENUMBERED:
3341 14/4/46.
63341 11/2/49.

CONDEMNED: 12/11/64.
Into Dar. for cut up 23/11/64.

1249

Darlington.

To traffic 2/1913.

REPAIRS:
Dar. ?/?—?/7/21.**G.**
Dar. 18/7—12/10/23.**G.**
Dar. 29/1—22/6/26.**G.**
Dar. 30/7—19/9/29.**G.**
Dar. 21/4—23/5/32.**G.**
Dar. 20/6—1/8/34.**G.**
Dar. 16/9—30/10/36.**G.**
Dar. 8/8—9/9/39.**G.**
Dar. 24/2—13/3/42.**L.**
Dar. 28/5—6/7/42.**G.**
Ghd. 19/5—16/6/44.**L.**
Dar. 22/8—21/9/45.**G.**
Ghd. 3—14/12/46.**L.**
Dar. 10/2—5/3/48.**G.**
Dar. 15—22/3/48.**N/C.**
Dar. 25/5—16/6/51.**G.**
Dar. 29/1—25/2/54.**G.**
Dar. 5—11/3/54.**N/C.**
Dar. 7—15/4/54.**N/C.**
Dar. 8—15/5/54.**N/C.**
Ghd. 1/4—3/5/57.**G.**
Dar. 11/3—13/4/60.**G.**
Dar. 26/9—13/11/61.**C/L.**

BOILERS:
D167.
D201 *(ex1280)* 7/21.
2261 *(new)* 19/9/29.
D1941 *(exB15 795)* 1/8/34.
2561 *(ex1250)* 30/10/36.
2565 *(ex2272)* 9/9/39.
2155 *(ex2248)* 21/9/45.
2876 *(ex3370)* 5/3/48.
24180 16/6/51.
24151 25/2/54.
24204 3/5/57 (50A).
24306 13/4/60 (50A).

SHEDS:
Springhead.
Newport 23/5/24.
Borough Gardens 4/12/43.

Consett 14/6/59.
Sunderland 6/5/62.

RENUMBERED:
3342 7/4/46.
E**3342** 5/3/48.
63342 16/6/51.

CONDEMNED: 4/12/63.
Into Dar. for cut up 20/12/63.

1250

Darlington.

To traffic 2/1913.

REPAIRS:
Ghd. ?/?—?/2/21.**G.**
Dar. 26/3—14/8/25.**G.**
Dar. 24/1—29/3/28.**G.**
Dar. 18/11—30/12/30.**G.**
Dar. 28/11/33—9/1/34.**G.**
Dar. 21/8—9/10/36.**G.**
Dar. 14/12/38—25/1/39.**G.**
Dar. 8/1—4/2/41.**G.**
Dar. 26/10—20/11/43.**G.**
Ghd. 25/11—13/12/45.**G.**
Dar. 7/3—2/5/47.**G.**
Dar. 8—13/5/47.**N/C.**
Ghd. 24/6—6/7/48.**L.**
Dar. 6/3—14/4/50.**L/I.**
Dar. 11—29/8/52.**G.**
Dar. 22/10—18/11/54.**G.**
Dar. 23/4—17/5/57.**G.**
Dar. 22—27/10/59.**C/L.**
Dar. 16/11—16/12/60.**G.**
Dar. 6/7—9/8/62.**C/L.**

BOILERS:
D168.
E4/22 *(ex1271)* 30/12/30.
2561 *(new)* 9/1/34.
HL105 *(exB15 782)* 9/10/36.
2999 *(new)* 25/1/39 (50A).
3155 *(ex2231)* 20/11/43 (50A).
24233 29/8/52.
24216 18/11/54.
24296 17/5/57 (50A).
24293 16/12/60 (50A).

SHEDS:
Borough Gardens.
Newport 12/1/23.
Selby 25/10/25.
Newport 19/6/39.
Haverton Hill 10/6/56.
Thornaby 14/6/59.
West Auckland 8/4/62.
Darlington 2/2/64.
West Hartlepool 12/4/64.

Fifty more engines, Nos.2253 to 2302, were then built by Armstrong, Whitworth & Co. Ltd., Scotswood, Newcastle, from November 1919 to March 1921. These were similar to the last twenty built at Darlington. None of the 4125 gallons tenders built with Q6 class were fitted with water pick-up apparatus.

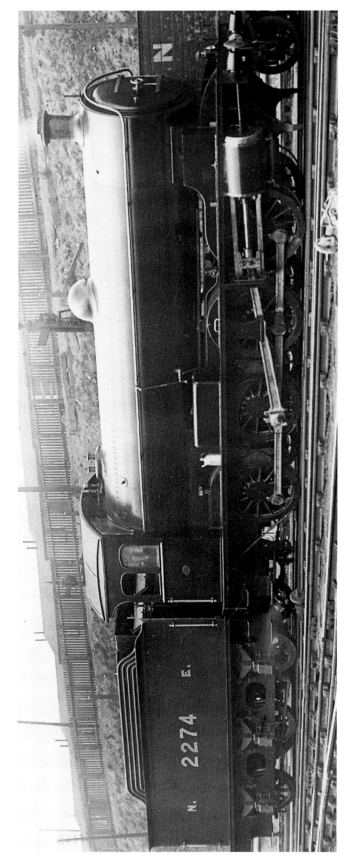

No.2274 seen here 10th May 1920, was in maker's siding ready for delivery. Note that by this one, the works plate was no longer being fitted on the front sandbox.

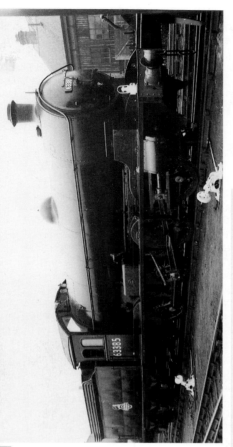

(above) Until 1930, only the first nineteen boilers built had Robinson superheater; all the rest had the Schmidt type. There was no external difference and all had the steam circulating arrangement for protection of elements from burning when steam through them was shut off. Control was by the stop valve on left hand side of the smokebox.

(above, right) Beginning with the boilers built in January 1930, the simpler Gresley anti-vacuum valve on the centre of the header was used for all built thereafter. No.2257 was ex-works 27th March 1930 with a boiler built in February 1930.

(below) Boilers built from October 1938 were to Diagram 50A with 2-ring telescopic barrel. They could be identified because the dome was 1ft 3⅜in. further to the rear and its casing had a flatter top. No.2265 was ex-works 22nd December 1938. Note ARP blacked out windows.

(above) All boilers built to April 1937 were to Diagram 50 and had a butt-jointed 3-ring barrel with dome on the middle ring. The last of this type did not go out of service until June 1966. No.63385's boiler was built February 1937 and came off this engine in July 1959 for cutting up. From 1938 the base cover to the safety valves was discarded but 63449 carried one to November 1949.

1250 cont/.
RENUMBERED:
  3343 14/4/46.
  63343 6/7/48.

CONDEMNED: 7/6/65.
Sold for scrap to Ellis Metals, Swalwell, 7/65

1251

Darlington.

To traffic 2/1913.

REPAIRS:
Ghd. 23/2—23/3/23.**L**.
Ghd. 12—20/6/23.**L**.
Ghd. 26/7—7/8/23.**L**.
Ghd. 7—21/11/23.**L**.
Ghd. 3/6—18/9/25.**G**.
Ghd. 16/10—6/12/28.**G**.
Ghd. 15/5—1/7/31.**G**
Dar. 5/11/34—16/2/35.**G**.
Dar. 15/9/37—5/1/38.**G**.
Dar. 6—24/4/40.**N/C**.
Dar. 16/12/40—16/1/41.**G**.
Dar. 16/4—19/5/43.**G**.
Ghd. 17/6—2/7/45.**L**.
Dar. 20/9—19/10/46.**G**.
Dar. 1—22/10/48.**G**.
Dar. 25/10—3/11/48.**N/C**.
Ghd. 4—16/3/49.**C/L**.
Dar. 8/10—3/11/51.**G**.
Dar. 5/3—8/4/54.**H/I**.
Dar. 3/7—14/8/56.**G**.
Dar. 22/5—19/6/59.**G**.
Dar. 29/6—9/7/59.**N/C**.
Dar. 18/9—12/10/61.**C/L**.
Dar. 24/5—8/7/63.**G**.
Dar. 29—30/7/63.**N/C**.

BOILERS:
  D171.
  D212 *(ex1285)* 18/9/25.
  D616 *(ex1311)* 1/7/31.
  D1944 *(ex1291)* 16/2/35.
  2643 *(exB15 797)* 5/1/38.
  3157 *(new)* 16/1/41 (50A).
  2993 *(ex2283)* 19/10/46 (50A).
  3314 *(ex3415)* 22/10/48 (50A).
  24273 *(new)* 3/11/51 (50A).
  24247 14/8/56.
  24229 19/6/59 (50A).
  24266 8/7/63 (50A).

SHEDS:
Borough Gardens.
Newport 12/4/39.
Haverton Hill 10/6/56.
Thornaby 14/6/59.
Neville Hill 7/6/64.
Normanton 12/6/66.
Tyne Dock 2/10/66.
West Hartlepool 2/7/67.

RENUMBERED:
  3344 14/4/46.
  63344 22/10/48.

CONDEMNED: 9/9/67.
Sold for scrap to T.J.Thompson, Stockton, 10/67.

1252

Darlington.

To traffic 3/1913.

REPAIRS:
Dar. 19/4—24/7/23.**G**.
Ghd. 7/9—17/12/26.**G**.
Dar. 28/1—18/2/27.**L**.
Dar. 13/5—15/7/29.**G**.
Dar. 9/8—26/9/32.**G**.
Dar. 1—29/8/34.**G**.
Dar. 6/8—23/9/36.**G**.
Dar. 28/2—14/4/39.**G**.
Dar. 8/5—13/6/41.**G**.
Dar. 7/8—2/9/43.**G**.
Dar. 11/2—9/3/46.**G**.
Ghd. 21/5—6/6/47.**L**.
Dar. 5/5—11/6/48.**G**.
Dar. 11/12/50—20/1/51.**G**.
Dar. 22—24/1/51.**N/C**.
Dar. 6/3—2/4/53.**G**.
Dar. 14—24/4/53.**N/C**.
Dar. 4—15/6/54.**C/L**.
Dar. 26/2—5/3/55.**C/L**.
Ghd. 7/7—5/8/55.**G**.
Ghd. 18/11—20/12/57.**G**.
Dar. 25/11/60—10/3/61.**G**.

BOILERS:
  D172.
  D222 *(ex1292)* 24/7/23.
  D204 *(ex1257)* 15/7/29.
  2430 *(new)* 26/9/32.
  D1941 *(ex2235)* 14/4/39.
  D2259 *(ex2222)* 13/6/41.
  2435 *(exB15 819)* 2/9/43.
  2157 *(exB15 819)* 9/3/46.
  2871 *(ex3353)* 11/6/48.
  2871 reno.24176 20/1/51.
  24197 2/4/53.
  24246 5/8/55 (50A).
  24202 20/12/57 (50A).
  24331 *(new)* 10/3/61 (50A).

SHEDS:
Newport.
Starbeck 9/4/31.
Neville Hill 28/3/43.
Haverton Hill 19/6/43.
Newport 20/9/44.
Haverton Hill 10/6/56.
Consett 8/5/59.
Sunderland 6/5/62.

RENUMBERED:
  3345 28/4/46.
  63345 11/6/48.

CONDEMNED: 8/6/64.
Into Dar. for cut up 30/6/64.

1253

Darlington.

To traffic 3/1913.

REPAIRS:
Ghd. 13/6—2/9/24.**G**.
Ghd. 6—8/10/24.**N/C**.
Ghd. 11/8—22/11/27.**G**.
Ghd. 12/7—21/8/28.**L**.
Ghd. 2/4—7/5/31.**G**.
Dar. 12/6—18/7/34.**G**.
Dar. 12/11—6/12/34.**L**.
After collision.
Dar. 27/6—7/9/38.**G**.
Dar. 10/12/40—8/1/41.**G**.
Dar. 21/1—12/2/44.**G**.
Ghd. 8—22/1/46.**L**.
Dar. 1/2—3/4/47.**G**.
Dar. 9—17/4/47.**N/C**.
Ghd. 7/7—31/8/48.**L**.
Dar. 21/6—5/8/50.**G**.
Dar. 8—16/8/50.**N/C**.
Dar. 6/2—7/3/53.**G**.
Dar. 9—13/3/53.**N/C**.
Dar. 9/1—3/2/56.**G**.
Dar. 23/9—22/10/58.**G**.
Dar. 12/2—10/3/62.**G**.

BOILERS:
  D175.
  2393 *(new)* 7/5/31.
  AW7 *(ex2222)* 7/9/38.
  2385 *(ex2232)* 8/1/41.
  2258 *(ex2300)* 12/2/44.
  2149 *(ex3442)* 3/4/47.
  2874 *(ex63347)* 5/8/50.
  24252 7/3/53.
  24230 3/2/56.
  24239 22/10/58 (50A).
  24211 10/3/62 (50A).

SHEDS:
Tyne Dock.
Borough Gardens 2/3/27.
Neville Hill 28/3/43.
Haverton Hill 19/6/43.
Newport 29/9/44.
Tyne Dock 14/1/46.
Consett 13/4/47.
Borough Gardens 10/6/56.
Consett 14/6/59.
Sunderland 4/10/64.

RENUMBERED:
  3346 14/4/46.
  63346 31/8/48.

CONDEMNED: 29/5/67.
Sold for scrap to Willoughby's, Choppinghton, 8/67.

1254

Darlington.

To traffic 3/1913.

REPAIRS:
Ghd. 16/2—1/5/25.**G**.
Dar. 21/6—24/8/28.**G**.
Ghd. 24/4—29/5/31.**G**.
Dar. 4/5—14/6/34.**G**.
Dar. 11—28/5/36.**L**.
Dar. 19/10—9/12/37.**G**.
Dar. 17/12/40—25/2/41.**G**.
Dar. 29/4—10/6/43.**G**.
Ghd. 2—23/10/45.**L**.
Dar. 16/1—22/3/47.**G**.
Ghd. 7—16/6/48.**L**.
Dar. 30/5—7/7/50.**G**.
Dar. 30/10/51.*Weigh.*
Dar. 31/3—2/5/53.**G**.
Dar. 26/9—21/10/55.**H/I**.
Dar. 4/5—7/6/56.**C/L**.
Ghd. 15/1—14/2/58.**G**.
Dar. 13—21/3/58.**N/C**.
Dar. 28/8—23/9/61.**G**.
Dar. 10—18/10/61.**N/C**.
Dar. 5—14/6/62.**C/L**.

BOILERS:
  D176.
  D1967 *(new)* 24/8/28.
  D951 *(ex2214)* 14/6/34.
  2429 *(ex2291)* 9/12/37.
  2431 *(ex2289)* 25/2/41.
  2874 *(ex2268)* 22/3/47.
  2566 *(ex3445)* 7/7/50.
  24290 *(new)* 2/5/53 (50A).
  24295 14/2/58 (50A).
  24224 23/9/61 (50A).

SHEDS:
Tyne Dock.
Borough Gardens 8/3/24.
Doncaster 28/12/25.
Borough Gardens 20/6/28.
Newport 12/4/39.
Neville Hill 8/9/44.
Newport 23/7/45.
Haverton Hill 10/6/56.
Thornaby 14/6/59.
West Auckland 1/4/62.
West Hartlepool 12/1/64.

RENUMBERED:
  3347 14/4/46.
  63347 16/6/48.

CONDEMNED: 18/10/65.
Sold for scrap to Willoughby's, Choppington, 11/65.

1257

Darlington.

To traffic 3/1913.

REPAIRS:
Dar. 22/12/22—10/4/23.**G.**
Dar. 9/3—16/7/26.**G.**
Dar. 30/7—12/8/26.**L.**
Dar. 16/4—31/5/29.**G.**
Dar. 29/5—3/7/33.**G.**
Dar. 4/11—18/12/36.**G.**
Dar. 20/4—28/7/39.**G.**
Dar. 7/1—5/2/42.**G.**
Dar. 24/6—3/7/43.**L.**
Dar. 22/5—14/6/44.**G.**
Dar. 25/10/45.*Weigh.*
Dar. 27/8—21/9/46.**G.**
Ghd. 9—27/11/47.**L.**
Ghd. 4—13/7/48.**L.**
Dar. 23/3—14/4/49.**G.**
Ghd. 14/11—11/12/50.**C/L.**
Dar. 4—29/6/51.**G.**
Dar. 5—9/7/51.**N/C.**
Dar. 20/10—15/11/52.**C/L.**
Dar. 9—27/2/54.**G.**
Dar. 1—3/3/54.**N/C.**
Dar. 28/3—4/5/57.**G.**
Dar. 6—9/5/57.**N/C.**
Dar. 11/11—10/12/60.**G.**
Dar. 29/12/60—12/1/61.**N/C.**
Dar. 25/6—11/7/62.**C/L.**

BOILERS:
D180.
D130 *(exB15 813)* 10/4/23.
D204 *(ex1283)* 16/7/26.
D1170 *(ex1288)* 31/5/29.
D863 *(ex1288)* 3/7/33.
2394 *(ex1248)* 18/12/36.
2430 *(ex2254)* 5/2/42.
D1945 *(ex2230)* 14/6/44.
2980 *(ex2246)* 21/9/46 (50A).
2993 *(ex3344)* 14/4/49 (50A).
24192 29/6/51 (50A).
24189 27/2/54 (50A).
24261 4/5/57 (50A).
24333 *(new)* 10/12/60 (50A).

SHEDS:
Neville Hill.
Darlington 8/7/43.
Dairycoates 4/11/44.
West Hartlepool 5/3/45.
Dairycoates 4/9/49.
Selby 20/11/49.
Neville Hill 25/1/53.
Selby 16/6/57.
York 13/9/59.
Neville Hill 6/12/59.

RENUMBERED:
3348 31/3/46.
63348 14/4/49.

CONDEMNED: 17/6/64.
Into Dar. for cut up 14/8/64.

1261

Darlington.

To traffic 4/1913.

REPAIRS:
Dar. 25/8—6/11/24.**G.**
Dar. 16/8—8/11/27.**G.**
Dar. 23/11—2/12/27.**N/C.**
Dar. 9/6—31/7/31.**G.**
Dar. 2/10—3/11/34.**G.**
Dar. 19/1—19/2/38.**G.**
Dar. 3—31/7/40.**G.**
Dar. 13/4—22/5/42.**L.**
Dar. 1/6—8/7/43.**G.**
Dar. 11—29/9/45.**L.**
Dar. 16/10—16/11/46.**G.**
Ghd. 4—27/1/48.**L.**
Dar. 15/7—10/9/48.**L.**
Dar. 14/1—11/2/49.**G.**
Dar. 15—24/2/49.**N/C.**
Dar. 9—28/4/51.**H/I.**
Dar. 6/1—3/2/53.**G.**
Dar. 18—26/2/53.**N/C.**
Dar. 16/5—9/6/55.**H/I.**
Dar. 28/7—3/8/55.**N/C.**
Ghd. 20/8—21/9/56.**C/L.**
Dar. 28/2—18/4/57.**C/L.**
Dar. 7—29/3/58.**G.**
Dar. 12/6—3/7/59.**N/C.**
Dar. 31/7—12/8/59.**N/C.**
Dar. 17/11—16/12/61.**G.**
Dar. 29/12/61—5/1/62.**N/C.**

BOILERS:
D182.
D677 *(ex2228)* 6/11/24.
D817 *(ex2239)* 31/7/31.
3148 *(new)* 31/7/40 (50A).
3152 *(ex2219)* 16/11/46 (50A).
3865 *(new)* 11/2/49 (50A).
3865 reno.24186 28/4/51.
24288 3/2/53 (50A).
24265 29/3/58 (50A).
24287 16/12/61 (50A).

SHEDS:
Neville Hill.
Stockton 21/6/43.
Newport 23/9/44.
Stockton 7/2/48.
Middlesbrough 25/6/50.
Thornaby 1/6/58.

West Hartlepool 23/6/63.

RENUMBERED:
3349 14/4/46.
63349 10/9/48.

CONDEMNED: 5/6/66.
Sold for scrap to Hughes,
Bolckow, Blyth 7/66.

1262

Darlington.

To traffic 4/1913.

REPAIRS:
Ghd. ?/?—?/11/21.**G.**
Ghd. 26/11/25—27/5/26.**G.**
Ghd. 30/7—12/9/28.**L.**
Ghd. 19/12/28—17/1/29.**L.**
Ghd. 13/1—25/2/31.**G.**
Dar. 4/2—18/4/36.**G.**
Dar. 19/8—16/9/39.**G.**
Dar. 19/12/42—20/1/43.**G.**
Ghd. 17/9—8/10/45.**L.**
Dar. 19/11/46—4/1/47.**G.**
Dar. 10—16/1/47.**N/C.**
Ghd. 3—19/5/48.**L.**
Dar. 5—29/4/50.**G.**
Dar. 1—9/5/50.**N/C.**
Dar. 14/10—8/11/52.**G.**
Dar. 15/4—12/5/55.**H/I.**
Dar. 19—26/5/55.**N/C.**
Dar. 22—26/9/55.**N/C.**
Dar. 1—3/10/57.**C/L.**
Ghd. 4/8—5/9/58.**G.**
Dar. 28/12/60—13/2/61.**C/H.**

BOILERS:
D185.
D539 *(ex2213)* 25/2/31.
AW13 *(ex2294)* 18/4/36.
2260 *(ex2248)* 16/9/39.
2862 *(ex2221)* 20/1/43.
HL109 *(ex3395)* 4/1/47.
2423 *(ex63456)* 29/4/50.
24239 8/11/52 (50A).
24214 5/9/58 (50A).

SHEDS:
Tyne Dock.
Annfield Plain 8/3/24.
Tyne Dock 1/25.
Annfield Plain 1/27.
Tyne Dock 14/10/29.
East Hartlepool 18/6/31.
Dairycoates 1/3/37.
York 6/1/40.
Neville Hill 28/3/43.
Darlington 26/6/43.

Neville Hill 24/8/44.
Newport 23/7/45.
Borough Gardens 13/2/48.
Tyne Dock 14/6/59.

RENUMBERED:
3350 28/4/46.
63350 19/5/48.

CONDEMNED: 18/6/63.
Into Dar. for cut up 5/7/63.

1264

Darlington.

To traffic 6/1913.

REPAIRS:
Ghd. 12/5—29/7/24.**G.**
Ghd. 10/2—27/4/28.**G.**
Ghd. 10/7—19/8/31.**G.**
Dar. 27/10—15/12/36.**G.**
Dar. 21/10—15/11/40.**G.**
Dar. 12/3—8/4/43.**G.**
Ghd. 7/7—2/8/44.**L.**
Dar. 16/1—24/2/45.**L.**
Dar. 25/11—19/12/45.**G.**
Dar. 5—12/1/46
Ghd. 31/5—16/6/48.**L.**
Dar. 20/4—14/5/49.**G.**
Dar. 16/4—5/5/51.**G.**
Dar. 1—18/7/53.**G.**
Dar. 4—8/8/53.**N/C.**
Dar. 6/2—1/3/56.**H/I.**
Dar. 9/2—25/3/59.**G.**
Dar. 7/9—12/10/62.**G.**
Dar. 17—25/10/62.**N/C.**

BOILERS:
D192.
D1569 *(new)* 29/7/24.
2433 *(ex2241)* 15/12/36.
3153 *(new)* 15/11/40 (50A).
2985 *(ex2217)* 8/4/43 (50A).
3149 *(ex2217)* 29/12/45 (50A).
3015 *(ex63380)* 14/5/49 (50A).
24184 5/5/51 (50A).
24291 *(new)* 18/7/53 (50A).
24186 25/3/59 (50A).
24257 12/10/62 (50A).

SHEDS:
Tyne Dock.
Annfield Plain 24/6/37.
Consett 9/9/40.
Tyne Dock 29/11/47.
Middlesbrough 13/2/49.
West Auckland 29/8/54.
West Hartlepool 24/11/63.

WORKS CODES:- Cw - Cowlairs. Dar- Darlington. Don - Doncaster. Ghd - Gateshead. Gor - Gorton. Hsi - Hull Springhead. Inv - Inverurie. Str - Stratford.
REPAIR CODES:- **C/H** - Casual Heavy. **C/L** - Casual Light. **G** - General. **H**- Heavy. **H/I** - Heavy Intermediate. **L** - Light. **L/I** - Light Intermediate. **N/C** - Non-Classified.

1264 cont/.
RENUMBERED:
3351 7/4/46.
63351 16/6/48.

CONDEMNED: 18/1/65.
*Sold for scrap M.Baum,
Middlesbrough 3/65.*

1271

Darlington.

To traffic 4/1913.

REPAIRS:
Dar. 30/5—27/9/23.**G.**
Dar. 21/9/25—8/1/26.**G.**
Dar. 22/6—21/8/28.**G.**
Dar. 22/10—27/11/30.**G.**
Dar. 16/2—15/3/34.**G.**
Dar. 13/3—15/5/36.**G.**
Dar. 19—21/5/36.**N/C.**
Dar. 25/3—9/5/38.**G.**
Dar. 30/5—15/8/38.**N/C.**
Dar. 5/8—7/9/40.**G.**
Dar. 11/2—17/3/43.**G.**
Ghd. 23/6—6/7/44.**L.**
Dar. 14/2—14/3/46.**G.**
Ghd. 17/4—1/5/47.**L.**
Dar. 8—31/12/48.**G.**
Dar. 1—24/5/52.**G.**
Dar. 4—29/10/55.**G.**
Dar. 31/10—1/11/55.**N/C.**
Dar. 4—11/10/57.**N/C.**
Dar. 26/11—6/12/57.**C/L.**
Dar. 8/7—13/8/58.**C/H.**
Ghd. 15—26/9/58.**C/L.**
Dar. 5/5—18/6/60.**H/I.**
Dar. 20/6—5/7/60.**N/C.**

BOILERS:
 D190.
 D139 *(exB15 817)* 27/9/23.
 E4/22 *(ex2274)* 21/8/28.
 D610 *(ex2237)* 27/11/30.
 2562 *(new)* 15/3/34.
 2262 *(ex2252)* 7/9/40.
 2425 *(ex2276)* 17/3/43.
 2653 *(ex2286)* 14/3/46.
 3857 *(new)* 31/12/48 *(50A).*
 24225 24/5/52 *(50A).*
 24250 29/10/55.
 24181 13/8/58 *(50A).*

SHEDS:
Darlington.
Selby 1/7/24.
Newport 1/9/25.
Borough Gardens 4/12/43.
Tyne Dock 5/10/47.
Blaydon 8/3/59.
North Blyth 23/9/62.

RENUMBERED:
3352 7/4/46.
63352 31/12/48.

CONDEMNED: 25/2/64.
Into Dar. for cut up 10/3/64.

1276

Darlington.

To traffic 5/1913.

REPAIRS:
Dar. 19/4—23/7/23.**G.**
Dar. 21/8—11/11/25.**G.**
Ghd. 31/7—3/10/28.**G.**
Dar. 10/2—17/3/31.**G.**
Dar. 12/5—16/6/34.**G.**
Dar. 14/12/36—8/2/37.**G.**
Dar. 11—13/12/38.**N/C.**
Dar. 9/4—7/5/40.**G.**
Dar. 1—5/6/40.**N/C.**
Dar. 24/11—24/12/42.**G.**
Dar. 25/4—13/5/44.**L.**
Ghd. 24/7—14/8/44.**L.**
Dar. 15/6—14/7/45.**L.**
Ghd. 16—28/10/46.**L.**
Dar. 15/1—13/2/48.**G.**
Ghd. 1—31/3/49.**L.**
Dar. 28/7—2/9/50.**G.**
Dar. 4—8/9/50.**N/C.**
Ghd. 28/5—19/6/52.**C/H.**
Dar. 20/11—12/12/53.**G.**
Dar. 14—16/12/53.**N/C.**
Dar. 30/12/53—5/1/54.**N/C.**
Ghd. 16/2/55.**C/L.**
Ghd. 1/7—16/8/57.**G.**
Dar. 19/9—28/10/60.**G.**
Dar. 3—7/5/63.*Weigh.*

BOILERS:
 D193.
 D180 *(ex1257)* 23/7/23.
 D241 *(ex1292)* 11/11/25.
 2387 *(new)* 17/3/31.
 D1568 *(ex2264)* 16/6/34.
 2857 *(new)* 8/2/37.
 3320 *(new)* 24/12/42 *(50A).*
 2871 *(ex2221)* 14/7/45.
 2850 *(ex3414)* 13/2/48.
 2850 *reno.24151* 2/9/50.
 24223 12/12/53.
 24155 16/8/57 *(50A).*
 24323 *(new)* 28/10/60 *(50A).*

SHEDS:
Selby.
York 2/4/24.
Dairycoates 2/1/30.
Springhead 18/10/43.
Dairycoates 13/5/44.
Blaydon 20/7/47.
North Blyth 1/7/56.
Newport 29/9/57.

West Auckland 1/6/58.

RENUMBERED:
3353 23/3/46.
E3353 13/2/48.
63353 2/9/50.

CONDEMNED: 15/7/63.
Into Dar. for cut up 6/8/63.

1278

Darlington.

To traffic 5/1913.

REPAIRS:
Ghd. 4/1—23/3/23.**G.**
Dar. 20/8—30/9/25.**L.**
Ghd. 11/6—19/8/26.**L.**
Ghd. 3/1—14/3/28.**G.**
Ghd. 21/8—12/9/28.**L.**
Ghd. 8/10—27/11/29.**L.**
Dar. 9/10—12/11/31.**G.**
Ghd. 19/1—2/2/32.**L.**
Dar. 5/11—5/12/34.**G.**
Dar. 29/6—16/9/37.**G.**
Dar. 27/11/39—11/1/40.**G.**
Dar. 27/1—27/2/42.**G.**
Dar. 4—30/9/43.**G.**
Dar. 1—25/8/45.**L.**
After collision.
Dar. 31/10—1/12/45.**L.**
Dar. 10/12/46—18/1/47.**G.**
Dar. 20/1—4/2/47.**L.**
Dar. 8—28/2/47.**N/C.**
Ghd. 18—29/6/48.**L.**
Dar. 28/11—30/12/49.**G.**
Dar. 12/10—9/11/51.**H/I.**
Ghd. 7/3—4/4/52.**C/L.**
Dar. 29/6—30/7/54.**G.**
Dar. 5/10—11/10/56.**C/L.**
Dar. 21/12/56—19/1/57.**C/L.**
Ghd. 8/7—23/8/57.**G.**
Dar. 1—27/5/61.**G.**
Dar. 27/12/62—30/1/63.**C/L.**
Dar. 15/1/64.*Weigh.*

BOILERS:
 D198.
 D873 *(ex2242)* 12/11/31.
 2394 *(ex1257)* 27/2/42.
 2393 *(ex1363)* 30/9/43.
 2392 *(ex3402)* 18/1/47.
 4036 *(new)* 30/12/49 *(50A).*
 4036 reno.24217 9/11/51.
 24219 30/7/54 *(50A).*
 24310 *(new)* 23/8/57 *(50A).*
 24179 27/5/61 *(50A).*

SHEDS:
Tyne Dock.
Borough Gardens 13/4/26.
Neville Hill 28/3/43.
Darlington 14/7/43.

Neville Hill 9/9/44.
Newport 23/7/45.
Borough Gardens 6/3/48.
Tyne Dock 14/6/59.
Consett 13/12/59.
North Blyth 23/9/62.

RENUMBERED:
3354 14/4/46.
63354 29/6/48.

CONDEMNED: 21/5/65.
*Sold for scrap to M.Baum,
Middlesbrough, 6/65.*

1279

Darlington.

To traffic 5/1913.

REPAIRS:
Ghd. ?/?—?/4/22.**G.**
Ghd. 22/10—17/12/24.**G.**
Ghd. 3/7—4/9/28.**L.**
Ghd. 29/8—25/10/29.**G.**
Ghd. 7—13/11/29.**N/C.**
Ghd. 22—25/11/29.**N/C.**
Ghd. 7—18/1/30.**N/C.**
Ghd. 3/2—21/3/30.**H.**
Ghd. 30/6—17/7/30.**L.**
Dar. 20/12/32—17/1/33.**H.**
Dar. 26/4—29/5/34.**G.**
Dar. 1/3—7/4/37.**G.**
Dar. 9/3—3/5/39.**G.**
Dar. 10/5—13/6/39.**N/C.**
Dar. 2/6—5/7/41.**G.**
Dar. 8/10—4/11/41.**L.**
Dar. 21/8—22/9/43.**G.**
Dar. 19/11—14/12/46.**G.**
Ghd. 20/6—2/7/48.**L.**
Dar. 27/5—7/7/49.**G.**
Dar. 20/5—12/6/52.**G.**
Dar. 12/7—6/8/54.**G.**
Dar. 28/5—14/7/55.**C/L.**
After collision.
Dar. 28/7—12/8/55.**C/L.**
Dar. 3/12/56.*Weigh.*
Dar. 27/2—21/3/57.**H/I.**
Dar. 23/2—25/3/60.**G.**
Dar. 5/4—13/5/60.**N/C.**
Dar. 23/5—3/6/60.**N/C.**

BOILERS:
 D200.
 2434 *(new)* 17/1/33.
 2441 *(ex2299)* 7/4/37.
 2392 *(ex2302)* 3/5/39.
 2640 *(ex2297)* 5/7/41.
 2440 *(ex1284)* 22/9/43.
 2567 *(ex2263)* 14/12/46.
 2441 *(ex63395)* 7/7/49.
 24175 12/6/52.
 24262 6/8/54 *(50A).*
 24275 25/3/60 *(50A).*

Until about April 1920 a pyrometer for measuring superheat temperature was fitted with connection to the cab. By Grouping most had been removed but No.2301 still had the stub (*see* page 68, second from bottom) until January 1927.

(*right*) The 1931 boiler renewal programme included an order for thirteen Diagram 50, two for B15 class and eleven for Q6 class. They were built January to May 1932 and differed from all other boilers used on the class by having five washout plugs on the right hand side of the firebox and four (*see* top page 55) on the left hand side. No.2224 carried one of these boilers from 21st April 1937 to 20th February 1942. Otherwise two plugs on each side was the normal arragement.

(*below*) Throughout, it was standard for the chimney to have a windjabber, which gave a height from rail of 13ft 3in. and no attempt was made to bring this class as a whole within the 13ft 0in. load gauge.

1279 cont/.
SHEDS:
Tyne Dock.
Annfield Plain 8/3/24.
Tyne Dock 14/10/29.
Haverton Hill 23/4/31.
Newport 5/5/31.
West Hartlepool 5/4/48.
Middlesbrough 14/9/52.
Kirkby Stephen 3/4/55.
Middlesbrough 26/6/55.
Thornaby 1/6/58.
West Auckland 3/6/62.

RENUMBERED:
 3355 14/4/46.
63355 2/7/48.

CONDEMNED: 15/7/63.
Into Dar. for cut up 1/8/63.

1280

Darlington.

To traffic 5/1913.

REPAIRS:
Dar. ?/?—?/7/21.**G.**
HSi. ?/?—?/2/24.**G.**
Dar. 15/11/27—17/2/28.**G.**
Dar. 27/11/30—9/1/31.**G.**
Dar. 12/9—17/10/33.**G.**
Dar. 3/4—5/9/36.**G.**
Dar. 2—13/12/38.**N/C.**
Dar. 7/6—7/7/39.**G.**
Dar. 26/5—3/7/42.**G.**
Dar. 27/4—19/5/44.**G.**
Ghd. 24/10—9/11/45.**L.**
Dar. 30/1—22/3/47.**G.**
Dar. 27/4—20/5/50.**G.**
Dar. 22—23/5/50.**N/C.**
Dar. 30—31/5/50.**N/C.**
Dar. 8/10—1/11/52.**G.**
Dar. 3—4/11/52.**N/C.**
Dar. 6—14/11/52.**N/C.**
Dar. 12/11—4/12/53.**N/C.**
Ghd. 23/9—20/10/54.**C/H.**
Dar. 4/5—4/6/56.**G.**
Ghd. 23/12/57—17/1/58.**C/L.**
After collision.
Dar. 21/3—25/4/60.**G.**

BOILERS:
 D201.
 D101 *(exB15 821)* 7/21.
 D167 *(ex1362)* 2/24.
 2392 *(new)* 9/1/31.
 D678 *(ex2244)* 17/10/33.
 2813 *(new)* 5/9/36.
 HL107 *(ex2223)* 7/7/39.
 2570 *(ex2255)* 3/7/42.
 D1941 *(ex1361)* 19/5/44.
 2387 *(ex3434)* 22/3/47.
 HL112 *(ex63416)* 20/5/50.

24241 1/11/52.
24259 4/6/56.
24205 25/4/60 (50A).

SHEDS:
Springhead.
Newport 22/5/24.
Selby 8/11/25.
Newport 10/6/39.
Stockton 4/12/43.
Blaydon 5/10/47.
North Blyth 23/9/62.

RENUMBERED:
 3356 28/4/46.
63356 20/5/50.

CONDEMNED: 3/12/63.
Into Dar. for cut up 12/12/63.

1283

Darlington.

To traffic 5/1913.

REPAIRS:
Dar. 11/4—20/7/23.**G.**
Dar. 12/11/25—25/2/26.**G.**
Dar. 27/8—17/10/28.**G.**
Dar. 6/1—13/2/31.**G.**
Dar. 11/7—16/8/33.**G.**
Dar. 30/8—4/10/35.**G.**
Dar. 23/9—4/12/36.**H.**
Dar. 9/8—4/10/38.**G.**
Dar. 1—22/6/40.**G.**
Dar. 7/3—7/4/41.**L.**
Dar. 31/7—12/9/42.**G.**
Dar. 23/11—16/12/44.**G.**
Ghd. 1—11/5/46.**L.**
Dar. 21/11—?/12/47.**G.**
Ghd. 14/6—12/7/49.**C/L**
Dar. 8/11—23/12/50.**G.**
Dar. 3—20/11/51.**C/L.**
Dar. 14/1—6/2/54.**G.**
Dar. 17—20/2/54.**N/C.**
Dar. 9—13/3/54.**N/C.**
Dar. 16—18/3/54.**N/C.**
Ghd. 14—24/2/55.**C/L.**
Ghd. 21/6—14/8/56.**C/L.**
After collision.
Ghd. 27/5—21/6/57.**G.**
Dar. 26/4—20/5/61.**G.**
Dar. 6/8—6/9/62.**C/L.**
Dar. 15/7—30/8/63.**N/C.**

BOILERS:
 D204.
 E4/25 *(ex2277)* 25/2/26.
 D146 *(ex2226)* 17/10/28.
 2383 *(new)* 13/2/31.
 D1942 *(ex2273)* 4/10/35.
 3150 *(new)* 22/6/40 (50A).
 3311 *(ex2301)* 16/12/44 (50A).
 3317 *(ex3427)* 12/47 (50A).

24167 *(ex3421)* 23/12/50 (50A).
24258 6/2/54 (50A).
24308 *(new)* 22/6/57 (50A).
24286 20/5/61 (50A).

SHEDS:
Selby.
Newport 8/11/25.
Consett 4/12/43.

RENUMBERED:
 3357 7/4/46.
63357 11/7/49.

CONDEMNED: 17/5/65.
Sold for scrap to M.Baum,
Middlesbrough, 6/65.

1284

Darlington.

To traffic 6/1913.

REPAIRS:
Ghd. 14/5—19/8/24.**G.**
Ghd. 28/12/27—21/1/28.**L.**
Ghd. 10/8—20/9/28.**L.**
Ghd. 19/8—10/12/29.**G.**
Ghd. 18—23/6/31.**N/C.**
Dar. 24/1—27/2/33.**G.**
Dar. 9/9—4/11/35.**H.**
Dar. 26/5—19/8/38.**G.**
Dar. 21/2—8/3/40.**L.**
Dar. 9/5—12/6/41.**G.**
Dar. 22/6—3/9/43.**G.**
Dar. 13/7—24/8/46.**G.**
Dar. 19/10—5/11/48.**G.**
Dar. 4—27/10/51.**G.**
Ghd. 8—14/11/51.**C/L.**
Dar. 4/5—6/6/53.**C/L.**
Dar. 8—10/6/53.**N/C.**
Dar. 5/11—2/12/54.**H/I.**
Dar. 27/3—23/4/56.**C/L.**
After collision.
Dar. 2—30/8/57.**G.**
Dar. 13/3—23/6/61.**G.**

BOILERS:
 D208.
 E4/41 *(ex2293)* 10/12/29.
 E4/4 *(2219)* 27/2/33.
 E4/4 reno.4 4/11/35.
 2393 *(ex1253)* 19/8/38.
 2440 *(ex2266)* 12/6/41.
 D1568 *(ex2220)* 3/9/43.
 2657 *(exB15 817)* 24/8/46.
 2429 *(ex3426)* 5/11/48.
 24207 27/10/51 (50A).
 24289 30/8/57 (50A).
 24330 *(new)* 23/6/61 (50A).

SHEDS:
Tyne Dock.
Annfield Plain 8/3/24.

Tyne Dock 14/10/29.
East Hartlepool 18/6/31.
West Hartlepool 17/4/39.
Springhead 10/5/40.
Neville Hill 28/3/43.
Darlington 10/7/43.
Newport 20/9/44.
Dairycoates 4/9/49.
Borough Gardens 11/12/49.
Tyne Dock 14/6/59.

RENUMBERED:
 3358 12/5/46.
63358 5/11/48.

CONDEMNED: 9/3/64.
Into Dar. for cut up 16/3/64.

1285

Darlington.

To traffic 6/1913.

REPAIRS:
Ghd. ?/?—?/10/20.**G.**
Ghd. 10/3—25/5/25.**G.**
Ghd. 11/5—12/7/28.**G.**
Ghd. 19/12/28—15/1/29.**L.**
Ghd. 16/5—25/7/30.**H.**
Ghd. 8—30/1/31.**N/C.**
Ghd. 4—24/3/31.**L.**
Ghd. 21/7—23/8/32.**G.**
Dar. 28/10—20/12/35.**G.**
Dar. 1—25/6/40.**G.**
Dar. 20/6—2/7/41.**N/C.**
Dar. 21/4—23/5/42.**G.**
Dar. 8/9—7/10/44.**G.**
Ghd. 20/2—7/3/46.**L.**
Dar. 7/11—5/12/47.**G.**
Ghd. 24/12/49—19/1/50.**C/L.**
Dar. 23/11/50—6/1/51.**G.**
Dar. 21/1—20/2/54.**G.**
Dar. 7/3—3/4/57.**G.**
Dar. 10—15/4/57.**N/C.**
Dar. 14/12/59—29/1/60.**C/H.**
Dar. 30/8—30/9/61.**G.**
Dar. 12/10—1/11/61.**N/C.**
Dar. 7—28/11/61.**N/C.**

BOILERS:
 D212.
 D156 *(ex2231)* 25/5/25.
 HL990 *(new)* 25/7/30.
 2423 *(ex2266)* 20/12/35.
 AW28 *(ex2227)* 25/6/40.
 2569 *(ex2238)* 23/5/42.
 2813 *(ex2229)* 7/10/44.
 HL107 *(ex3435)* 5/12/47.
 24169 6/1/51 (50A).
 24204 20/2/54 (50A).
 24217 3/4/57 (50A).
 24192 30/9/61 (50A).

In March 1934 it was announced that as Nos.2254, 2257 and 2259 had moved from London Road (ex NER) to Canal (ex NBR) shed at Carlisle, their windjabber would be removed, cutting the height to 13ft 1in., enabling them to work over the Waverley route to Edinburgh if required. No.2259 lost its windjabber at a general repair 5th December 1934, as did No.2254 ex-works 21st November 1935 and No.2257 also out from general repair on 22nd November 1935.

(below) From new until September 1936, standard whistle gear was an organ pipe on the right hand side and a bell shape on left hand side, on a twin mounting.

(below) Starting in September 1936, on the last batch of Diagram 50 boilers built, there was a change to a single bell shape mounted above an isolating valve on the firebox. As they went for repair, the earlier boilers were changed to this style, which was also used for all Diagram 50A boilers (*see* page 49, bottom).

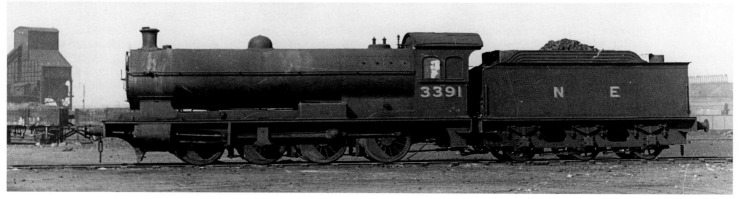

1285 cont/.

SHEDS:
Tyne Dock.
Annfield Plain 1/27.
Tyne Dock 14/10/29.
Annfield Plain 24/6/37.
Consett 21/12/39.
West Hartlepool 1/1/51.
Tyne Dock 6/7/52.
Consett 27/2/55.
North Blyth 23/9/62.

RENUMBERED:
3359 7/4/46.
63359 6/1/51.

CONDEMNED: 27/4/65.
Sold for scrap to Ellis Metals, Swalwell, 6/65.

1288

Darlington.

To traffic 6/1913.

REPAIRS:
Dar. ?/?—?/7/22.**G.**
Dar. 21/5—20/8/24.**G.**
Dar. 11/10—29/12/27.**G.**
Dar. 25/1—15/2/29.**G.**
Dar. 13/5—8/8/30.**G.**
Dar. 23/3—27/4/33.**G.**
Dar. 25/9—25/10/35.**G.**
Dar. 11/5—9/7/38.**G.**
Dar. 17/9—17/10/40.**G.**
Dar. 18/9—1/10/41
Tender only.
Dar. 8/6—6/7/43.**G.**
Ghd. 27/9—15/10/45.**L.**
Dar. 27/12/46—1/3/47.**G.**
Dar. 4—11/3/47.**N/C.**
Ghd. 17/10—3/11/48.**L.**
Ghd. 30/11—15/12/48.**L.**
Dar. 8/5—17/6/50.**G.**
Dar. 19/6—22/6/50.**N/C.**
Dar. 26/6—5/7/50.**N/C.**
Dar. 14—25/8/50.**N/C.**
Dar. 18/12/52—20/1/53.**G.**
Dar. 29/4—28/5/55.**G.**
Dar. 31/5—2/6/55.**N/C.**
Dar. 16/10/57.*Weigh.*
Ghd. 5/11—6/12/57.**G.**
Ghd. 17—26/2/58.**N/C.**
Dar. 20/8—2/9/59.**C/L.**
Dar. 1—12/2/60.**N/C.**
Dar. 12/3—13/4/62.**G.**
Dar. 10/2/64.*Weigh.*

BOILERS:
D213.
D1170 *(new)* 7/22.
D863 *(ex2239)* 15/2/29.
2437 *(new)* 27/4/33.
AW30 *(ex2248)* 25/10/35.

AW4 *(ex1284)* 9/7/38.
2387 *(ex2301)* 17/10/40.
HL106 *(ex2268)* 6/7/43.
2820 *(ex63367)* 17/6/50.
24249 20/1/53 (50A).
24206 28/5/55.
24232 6/12/57.
24216 13/4/62.

SHEDS:
Selby.
Newport 16/8/39.
Thornaby 1/6/58.
Tyne Dock 2/12/62.

RENUMBERED:
3360 28/4/46.
63360 3/11/48.

CONDEMNED: 26/6/66.
Sold for scrap to Hughes, Bolckow, Blyth, 8/66.

1291

Darlington.

To traffic 6/1913.

REPAIRS:
Ghd. 7/3—23/5/23.**G.**
Ghd. 8/2—23/5/27.**G.**
Ghd. 30/5—16/7/29.**N/C.**
Ghd. 14/4—27/5/30.**G.**
Ghd. 6/6—18/7/32.**L.**
Dar. 27/12/34—8/2/35.**G.**
Dar. 9/10—24/11/39.**G.**
Dar. 24/11—1/12/39.**N/C.**
Dar. 4/5—13/6/42.**G.**
Ghd. 13/5—9/6/44.**L.**
Dar. 18/9—20/10/45.**G.**
Ghd. 5—30/5/47.**L.**
Dar. 8/7—26/8/48.**G.**
Dar. 1—17/9/48.**N/C.**
Dar. 30/4—26/5/51.**G.**
Dar. 28—30/5/51.**N/C.**
Ghd. 8/8—3/9/51.**C/L.**
Dar. 26/6/52.*Weigh.*
Ghd. 4—11/2/53.**N/C.**
Dar. 13—28/11/53.**G.**
Ghd. 3/12/56—4/1/57.**G.**
Dar. 8/5—3/6/61.**G.**
Dar. 6—15/6/61.**N/C.**
Dar. 14/8—12/9/63.**C/L.**

BOILERS:
D217.
D1944 *(new)* 23/5/27.
2637 *(new)* 8/2/35.
3321 *(ex2227)* 20/10/45 (50A).
3019 *(ex3375)* 26/8/48 (50A).
24188 26/5/51.
24162 28/11/53.
24196 4/1/57.
24307 3/6/61 (50A).

SHEDS:
Tyne Dock *at* 22/5/23.
Dairycoates ?/??
Tyne Dock 2/3/27.
Annfield Plain 24/6/37.
Consett 9/9/40.
Tyne Dock 11/5/58.
Stockton 8/6/58.
Haverton Hill 12/10/58.
Thornaby 14/6/59.
West Auckland 1/4/62.
Thornaby 2/2/64.
West Hartlepool 17/5/64.

RENUMBERED:
3361 7/4/46.
63361 26/8/48.

CONDEMNED: 7/6/65.
Sold for scrap to Ellis Metals, Swalwell 7/65.

1292

Darlington.

To traffic 6/1913.

REPAIRS:
Dar. 7/12/22—27/2/23.**G.**
Dar. 11/5—31/8/25.**G.**
Dar. 21/12/26—28/3/27.**G.**
Ghd. 11/7—17/9/28.**G.**
Ghd. 22/4—29/5/31.**G.**
Dar. 13/6—2/8/34.**G.**
Dar. 12/10—26/11/38.**G.**
Dar. 4/4—10/5/41.**G.**
Dar. 30/9—17/10/42.**L.**
Dar. 11/8—10/9/43.**G.**
Dar. 15/3—3/5/47.**G.**
Dar. 6—12/5/47.**N/C.**
Ghd. 16—27/8/48.**L.**
Dar. 4—27/1/50.**G.**
Ghd. 5/11—6/12/51.**C/L.**
Dar. 24/3—19/4/52.**G.**
Dar. 28/5—26/6/54.**G.**
Dar. 28—29/6/54.**N/C.**
Dar. 31/7—11/8/56.**C/L.**
After collision.
Ghd. 23/9—25/10/57.**G.**
Dar. 24/11—2/12/59.**N/C**
Dar. 9—21/5/60.**C/L.**
Dar. 27/2—12/4/61.**C/L.**
Dar. 22/10—23/11/62.**G.**
Dar. 24/2/65.*Weigh.*

BOILERS:
D222.
D241 *(ex1363)* 27/2/23.
D142 *(exB15 823)* 31/8/25.
2390 *(new)* 29/5/31.
2656 *(exB15 825)* 10/5/41.
2259 *(ex1252)* 10/9/43.
2385 *(ex3387)* 3/5/47.
2392 *(ex63354)* 27/1/50.

24219 19/4/52 (50A).
24192 26/6/54 (50A).
24258 25/10/57 (50A).
24254 23/11/62 (50A).

SHEDS:
Selby.
Springhead 27/8/24.
Borough Gardens 24/5/27.
Tyne Dock 1/3/40.
Borough Gardens 28/3/43.
Tyne Dock 5/10/47.
Neville Hill 7/11/48.
Selby 3/12/50.
Tyne Dock 13/6/54.
Blaydon 8/3/59.
North Blyth 16/6/63.

RENUMBERED:
3362 7/4/46.
63362 27/8/48.

CONDEMNED: 14/11/65.
Sold for scrap to Hughes, Bolckow, Blyth 12/65.

1293

Darlington.

To traffic 6/1913.

REPAIRS:
Ghd. 25/1—12/4/23.**G.**
Ghd. 5/2—28/4/26.**G.**
Ghd. 7—9/2/27.**L.**
Ghd. 28/4—7/6/27.**H.**
Ghd. 4/6—25/7/30.**G.**
Dar. 4/11/35—14/1/36.**G.**
Dar. 29/8—28/9/39.**G.**
Dar. 25/11—5/12/40.**N/C.**
Dar. 15/12/41—17/1/42.**G.**
Dar. 24/3—22/4/44.**G.**
Ghd. 1—21/7/45.**L.**
Dar. 18/6—12/7/47.**G.**
Dar. 24/7—13/8/47.**N/C.**
Ghd. 5—22/2/49.**L/I.**
Ghd. 3/7—11/8/50.**L/I.**
Dar. 3/7—8/8/51.**C/H.**
Dar. 30/11—22/1/52.**C/H.**
Dar. 23/12/52—24/1/53.**G.**
Dar. 26—28/1/53.**N/C.**
Dar. 13/2—17/3/54.**C/L.**
Dar. 29/8—24/9/55.**G.**
Ghd. 22/11/56—11/1/57.**C/L.**
After collision.
Ghd. 8/9—17/10/58.**G.**
Dar. 11—17/8/59 **C/L.**
Dar. 4/1—1/2/63.**G.**
Dar. 21/2/63.*Weigh.*
Dar. 2/12/63—2/1/64.**C/L.**

BOILERS:
D225.
D234 *(ex1335)* 28/4/26.

1293 cont/.
D1939 (new) 7/6/27.
HL111 (ex1285) 14/1/36.
  2875 (exB15 820) 28/9/39.
  2888 (ex2253) 17/1/42.
  2576 (exB15 825) 22/4/44.
  2638 (ex3428) 12/7/47.
  24197 8/8/51.
  24250 24/1/53.
  24254 24/9/55 (50A).
  24201 17/10/58 (50A).
  24258 1/2/63 (50A).

SHEDS:
Tyne Dock.
Borough Gardens 28/3/43.
Tyne Dock 5/10/47.
Selby 26/11/50.
Blaydon 27/9/53.
Tyne Dock 2/12/62.

RENUMBERED:
  3363 7/4/46.
  63363 22/2/49.

CONDEMNED: 4/9/66.
Sold for scrap to Hughes,
Bolckow, Blyth, 10/66.

1294

Darlington.

To traffic 7/1913.

REPAIRS:
Ghd. 9/4—23/6/23.**G.**
Ghd. 7/7—6/10/25.**G.**
Ghd. 3/7—18/9/28.**G.**
Ghd. 18—30/10/28.**L.**
Ghd. 19/10/31—5/1/32.**H.**
Ghd. 16—19/2/32.**L.**
Dar. 6/6—1/8/34.**G.**
Dar. 17/2—22/4/37.**L.**
Dar. 17/7—23/8/39.**G.**
Dar. 5/11—6/12/41.**G.**
Dar. 4/2—11/9/44.**G.**
Dar. 4/1—2/2/46.**L.**
Dar. 8/3—3/5/47.**G.**
Ghd. 20—28/9/48.**L.**
Dar. 25/5—25/6/49.**G.**
Dar. 27—29/6/49.**N/C.**
Dar. 24/8—20/9/51.**G.**
Dar. 19/8—11/9/53.**H/I.**
Dar. 21—22/9/53.**N/C.**
Dar. 15/3—23/4/54.**C/L.**
Dar. 2/11/55—5/1/56.**G.**
Ghd. 23/6—3/10/58.**G.**
Dar. 17/8—3/9/59.**N/C.**

BOILERS:
D231.
D154 (exB15 824) 7/22.
D616 (ex2220) 27/10/24.
  2386 (new) 28/5/31.

BOILERS:
D226.
E4/16 (ex2268) 18/9/28.
AW23 (ex2276) 1/8/34.
  3021 (new) 23/8/39 (50A).
  3002 (ex2244) 6/12/41 (50A).
  3021 (ex2223) 11/9/44 (50A).
  3149 (ex63351) 25/6/49 (50A).
  24272 (new) 20/9/51 (50A).
  24236 5/1/56 (50A).
  24174 3/10/58 (50A).

SHEDS:
Tyne Dock.
Annfield Plain 24/6/37.
Neville Hill 15/7/39.
Darlington 10/7/43.
West Hartlepool 5/3/45.
Middlesbrough 5/10/47.
Thornaby 1/6/58

RENUMBERED:
  3364 31/3/46.
  63364 28/9/48.

CONDEMNED: 29/4/63.
Into Dar. for cut up 14/5/63.

1311

Darlington.

To traffic 7/19113.

REPAIRS:
Dar. ?/?—?/7/22.**G.**
Dar. 22/8—27/10/24.**G.**
Ghd. 4/5—23/9/27.**G.**
Ghd. 23/4—28/5/31.**G.**
Dar. 22/8—20/9/34.**G.**
Dar. 13/9—30/12/38.**G.**
Dar. 14/7—18/8/41.**G.**
Dar. 21/8—28/9/43.**G.**
Dar. 16/1—22/3/47.**G.**
Dar. 4/9—1/10/47.**N/C.**
Dar. 10/6—1/7/48.**L.**
Dar. 29/6—23/8/50.**G.**
Dar. 27—30/12/50.**C/L.**
Dar. 31/10—3/11/51.**C/L.**
Dar. 12/3—17/4/53.**G.**
Dar. 28/9/53.*Weigh.*
Dar. 8/8—6/9/56.**H/I.**
Dar. 10/7—29/8/57.**C/L.**
Dar. 25/6—10/7/59.**C/L.**
Dar. 7/4—3/6/60.**G.**

BOILERS:
D234.
D171 (ex1251) 17/11/25.
D930 (ex2247) 6/11/29.
E4/39 (ex2291) 7/7/32.
  2384 (ex2253) 6/5/37.
  2441 (ex2287) 2/4/43.

AW17 (ex2269) 20/9/34.
  2992 (new) 30/12/38 (50A).
  3007 (ex2215) 18/8/41 (50A).
  24222 17/4/53 (50A).
  24262 3/6/60 (50A).

SHEDS:
Springhead.
Borough Gardens 1/2/27.
Blaydon 29/3/41.
Newport 28/3/43.
Neville Hill 9/9/44.
Consett 23/7/45.
Sunderland 6/5/62.

RENUMBERED:
  3365 20/1/46.
  63365 1/7/48.

CONDEMNED: 10/6/63.
Into Dar. for cut up 26/6/63.

1335

Darlington.

To traffic 7/1913.

REPAIRS:
Ghd. ?/?—?/11/21.**?.**
Ghd. 24/11—19/12/23.**L.**
Ghd. 7/9—17/11/25.**G.**
Ghd. 28/5—9/7/26.**L.**
Ghd. 18/2—22/4/27.**L.**
Ghd. 12/7—6/11/29.**G.**
Ghd. 30/5—7/7/32.**G.**
Dar. 2/4—6/5/37.**G.**
Dar. 22/11—30/12/39.**G.**
Dar. 24/2—2/4/43.**G.**
Dar. 27/1—5/3/45.**L.**
Ghd. 30/5—15/6/45.**L.**
Dar. 3/10—2/11/46.**G.**
Ghd. 8—30/1/48.**L.**
Ghd. 27/7—11/8/48.**L.**
Dar. 18/10—12/11/49.**G.**
Dar. 14—16/11/49.**N/C.**
Dar. 3—30/11/51.**H/I.**
Dar. 3/8—11/9/54.**G.**
Dar. 13—14/9/54.**N/C.**
Ghd. 3/9—6/11/56.**C/H.**
Dar. 10/12—16/1/59.**G.**
Dar. 23/2—14/3/61.**C/L.**
Dar. 11/2—18/3/63.**G.**

BOILERS:
D234.

2810 (ex1362) 2/11/46.
  4019 (new) 12/11/49 (50A).
  4019 re-no.24210 30/11/51.
  24294 (new) 11/9/54 (50A).
  24167 16/1/59 (50A).
  24189 18/3/63 (50A).

SHEDS:
Borough Gardens.
Stockton 28/3/43.
Newport 20/9/44.
Borough Gardens 15/2/48.
Blaydon 14/6/59.
Tyne Dock 2/12/62.

RENUMBERED:
  3366 28/4/46.
  63366 12/11/49.

CONDEMNED: 16/5/67.
Sold for scrap to A. Draper,
Hull, 21/7/67. Cut up 11/9/67.

1361

Darlington.

To traffic 8/1913.

REPAIRS:
Ghd. 19/11/23—2/2/24.**G.**
Ghd. 20/6—21/10/27.**G.**
Dar. 11/6—28/8/30.**G.**
Dar. 5/7—14/8/33.**G.**
Dar. 14/4—22/9/36.**G.**
Dar. 9—28/11/38.**N/C.**
Dar. 23/1—7/3/39.**G.**
Dar. 28/5—3/7/41.**G.**
Dar. 4—31/5/43.**L.**
Dar. 28/2—20/3/44.**G.**
Dar. 9/3—6/4/46.**L.**
Dar. 27/12/46—8/3/47.**G.**
Ghd. 10—25/11/48.**L.**
Dar. 28/12/49—19/1/50.**G.**
Dar. 26/1—1/2/50.**N/C.**
Dar. 23/6—12/7/52.**G.**
Dar. 14—16/7/52.**N/C.**
Ghd. 2/9—1/10/53.**C/L.**
Dar. 28/10—25/11/54.**G.**
Dar. 13/5—1/6/57.**G.**
Dar. 3/6—5/6/57.**N/C.**
Dar. 14—24/6/57.**N/C.**
Dar. 1/12/58—12/1/59.**C/L.**
Derailment damage.
Dar. 3—5/11/59.**C/L.**
Dar. 26/5—6/7/60.**C/H.**
Dar. 22/6—12/8/61.**G.**

BOILERS:
D238.
E4/20 (ex2277) 21/10/27.

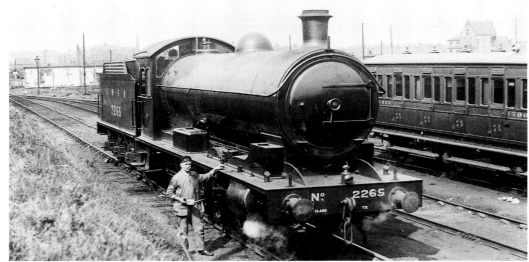

Until into the 1930's it was usual for smokebox door fastening to be by a wheel and a handle.

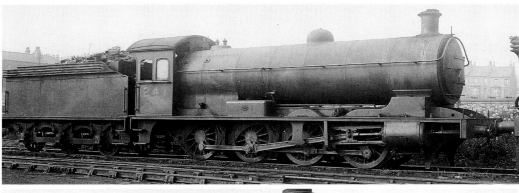

During the 1930's, the wheel was superseded by a second handle, and by 1938 it was no longer to be seen on Q6. This change had actually started before Grouping (*see* page 78, second from bottom).

The smokebox door had a flat flange which fitted flush with a sealing ring in the front plate and this type was used until 1945. It could still be seen to September 1955 on No.63377.

Starting on No.2286, ex-works 1st December 1945, a change began to a more dished door with a pressed joint ring for sealing, and most had this type by withdrawal.

1361 cont/.
D918 *(exB15 822)* 28/8/30.
E4/10 *(ex2293)* 14/8/33.
2817 *(new)* 22/9/36.
D1941 *(ex1252)* 3/7/41.
2639 *(exB15 787)* 20/3/44.
2820 *(ex3451)* 8/3/47.
2639 *(ex63447)* 19/1/50.
24232 12/7/52.
24210 25/11/54 (50A).
24260 1/6/57 (50A).
24326 *(new)* 12/8/61 (50A).

SHEDS:
Tyne Dock.
York 8/3/24.
Dairycoates 2/1/30.
West Hartlepool 5/3/45.
Stockton 2/11/47.
Haverton Hill 6/2/49.
Thornaby 14/6/59.
Sunderland 7/7/63.

RENUMBERED:
3367 6/4/46.
63367 25/11/48.

CONDEMNED: 31/8/64.
Sold for scrap to G. Cohen Cargo Fleet, 1/65.

1362

Darlington.

To traffic 8/1913.

REPAIRS:
Dar. ?/?—?/10/21.**G.**
Dar. 28/8—16/11/23.**G.**
Dar. 7/7—23/11/26.**G.**
Dar. 20/6—16/8/29.**G.**
Dar. 6/7—15/8/32.**G.**
Dar. 4/6—2/8/35.**G.**
Dar. 15/2—14/4/37.**H.**
Dar. 3/12/38—23/1/39.**G.**
Dar. 10/4—2/5/40.**H.**
Dar. 21/7—20/8/41.**G.**
Dar. 2—6/9/41.**N/C.**
Dar. 10/2—7/3/44.**G.**
Ghd. 13/6—28/6/45.**L.**
Dar. 2/8—6/9/46.**G.**
Dar. 12—18/9/46.**N/C.**
Ghd. 16/10—10/11/47.**L.**
Dar. 31/12/48—2/2/49.**G.**
Dar. 20/2—17/3/51.**G.**
Dar. 19—21/3/51.**N/C.**
Dar. 28/5—20/6/53.**H/I.**
Dar. 22—25/6/53.**N/C.**
Dar. 30/6—2/7/53.**N/C.**
Dar. 2/9—1/10/55.**G.**
Dar. 3—4/10/55.**N/C.**
Ghd. 10/4—16/5/58.**G.**
Dar. 10—12/11/59.**N/C.**
Dar. 16/4—19/5/62.**G.**

Dar. 1/6—6/7/62.**N/C.**
Dar. 10/7—7/8/62.**N/C.**
Dar. 9—15/8/62.**N/C.**
Dar. 14/10/64.Weigh.

BOILERS:
D239.
D167 *(ex1249)* ?/10/21.
D164 *(ex1248)* 16/11/23.
2262 *(new)* 16/8/29.
E4/28 *(ex2273)* 15/8/32.
HL106 *(ex2256)* 2/8/35.
2862 *(new)* 14/4/37.
2815 *(ex2283)* 20/8/41.
2810 *(exB15 822)* 7/3/44.
3162 *(ex2244)* 6/9/46 (50A).
3157 *(ex3438)* 2/2/49 (50A).
24270 17/3/51 (50A).
24240 1/10/55 (50A).
24300 16/5/58 (50A).
24281 19/5/62 (50A).

SHEDS:
Selby.
Dairycoates 18/11/29.
York 18/5/40.
Neville Hill 28/3/43.
Darlington 8/7/43.
Neville Hill 2/10/44.
West Hartlepool 23/7/45.
Middlesbrough 5/10/47.
Thornaby 1/6/58.
Blaydon 8/11/59.
Consett 20/8/61.
West Hartlepool 23/5/65.

RENUMBERED:
3368 6/9/46.
63368 2/2/49.

CONDEMNED: 31/12/66.
Sold for scrap to A. Draper, Hull. Cut up 15/5/67.

1363

Darlington.

To traffic 9/1913.

REPAIRS:
Ghd. ?/?—?/10/22.**G.**
Ghd. 12/4—4/8/26.**G.**
Ghd. 5/10—1/11/28.**L.**
Ghd. 31/7—3/8/29.**N/C.**
Ghd. 25/4—6/6/30.**G.**
Ghd. 7—18/8/30.**N/C.**
Ghd. 18/5—9/6/31.**L.**
Dar. 22/10—28/12/34.**G.**
Dar. 26/5—17/8/38.**G.**
Dar. 9/6—11/7/41.**G.**
Dar. 14/7—26/8/43.**G.**
Ghd. 8—24/8/45.**L.**
Dar. 19/12/46—22/2/47.**G.**
Dar. 24/10—12/11/49.**G.**

Dar. 20/11—15/12/51.**G.**
Dar. 17—21/12/51.**N/C.**
Dar. 12/11—5/12/53.**H/I.**
Dar. 7—8/12/53.**N/C.**
Dar. 19/4—31/5/56.**G.**
Dar. 29/5—24/6/59.**G.**
Dar. 30/6—29/7/59.**N/C.**
Dar. 19—23/10/59.**N/C.**
Dar. 29/2—19/4/60.**C/L.**

BOLIERS:
D241.
D213 *(ex1288)* 10/22.
HL989 *(new)* 6/6/30.
HL989 reno.HL110 28/12/34.
AW24 *(ex2294)* 17/8/38.
2393 *(ex1284)* 11/7/41.
2161 *(ex2292)* 26/8/43.
2976 *(ex63393)* 12/11/49 (50A).
24275 *(new)* 15/12/51 (50A).
24243 31/5/56 (50A).
24303 24/6/59 (50A).

SHEDS:
Tyne Dock.
Newport 28/3/43.
Neville Hill 8/9/44.
West Hartlepool 23/7/45.
Stockton 2/11/47.
Middlesbrough 25/6/50.
Thornaby 1/6/58.

RENUMBERED:
3369 1/9/46.
63369 12/11/49.

CONDEMNED: 15/7/63.
Into Dar. for cut up 23/8/63.

2213

Darlington.

To traffic 4/1917.

REPAIRS:
Ghd. ?/?—24/8/22.**G.**
Ghd. 14/10—21/1/26.**G.**
Dar. 4—15/2/26.**L.**
Ghd. 24/8—18/10/28.**G.**
Dar. 12/12/29—9/1/30.**H.**
Dar. 5/1—11/2/31.**G.**
Dar. 5/4—2/5/34.**G.**
Dar. 17/6—8/8/36.**G.**
Dar. 1/5—9/6/39.**G.**
Dar. 5—30/1/42.**G.**
Dar. 26/11—4/12/43.**L.**
Dar. 19/6—14/7/45.**G.**
Dar. 10/7—12/8/46.**L.**
Ghd. 21—31/8/46.**N/C.**
Dar. 15/1—20/2/48.**G.**
Ghd. 22/11/49—6/1/50.**C/L.**
Dar. 17—23/1/50.**N/C.**
Dar. 9/11—16/12/50.**G.**
Dar. 2/2—7/3/53.**G.**

Dar. 27/3—1/4/53.**N/C.**
Dar. 4—30/4/55.**H/I.**
Dar. 23/5—21/6/57.**G.**
Dar. 2—8/7/57.**N/C.**
Dar. 14/3—10/4/58.**C/L.**
Dar. 5—15/10/59.**C/L.**
Dar. 25—29/4/60.**N/C.**
Dar. 19/11—17/12/60.**G.**

BOILERS:
D539.
D558 *(ex2215)* 11/2/31.
2155 *(ex2224)* 2/5/34.
2383 *(ex2220)* 9/6/39.
D1963 *(exB15 815)* 30/1/42.
2876 *(ex2278)* 14/7/45.
3320 *(ex3384)* 20/2/48.
24165 *(ex63441)* 16/12/50.
24289 *(new)* 7/3/53 (50A).
24307 21/6/57 (50A).
24256 17/12/60 (50A).

SHEDS:
Tyne Dock.
Borough Gardens 26/4/26(T).
Borough Gardens 2/3/27 (P).
Neville Hill 28/3/43.
Stockton 21/6/43.
Newport 13/4/47.
Thornaby 1/6/58.
Neville Hill 11/11/62.

RENUMBERED:
3370 9/8/46.
ᴇ**3370** 20/2/48.
63370 6/1/50.

CONDEMNED: 1/6/64.
Into Dar. for cut up 30/6/64.

2214

Darlington.

To traffic 5/1917.

REPAIRS:
Dar. 29/7—24/10/23.**G.**
Dar. 27/5—24/9/26.**G.**
Dar. 11/7—20/9/28.**G.**
Dar. 25/6—11/8/31.**G.**
Dar. 22/3—21/4/34.**G.**
Dar. 23—26/4/34.**N/C.**
Dar. 19/12/38—7/2/39.**G.**
Dar. 11/3—16/4/41.**G.**
Dar. 26/10—20/11/43.**G.**
Dar. 21/8—18/9/45.**L.**
Dar. 8/1—5/2/46.**N/C.**
Ghd. 24/2—14/3/46.**N/C.**
Dar. 3/6—5/7/47.**G.**
Dar. 11/4—6/5/50.**G.**
Dar. 8/5—11/5/50.**N/C.**
Dar. 22/10—15/11/52.**H/I.**
Dar. 17—19/11/52.**N/C.**
Ghd. 17/6—23/7/54.**C/L.**

RegisterRegisterRegisterRegisterRegisterRegisterRegisterRegisterRegisterRegisterRegisterRegisterRegisterRegisterRegisterRegisterRegisterRegister
RegRegRegReg

2214 cont/.
Dar. 13/6—2/7/55.**G.**
Dar. 4—5/7/55.**N/C.**
Dar. 11—14/7/55.**N/C.**
Ghd. 25/11—27/12/57.**G.**
Dar. 8—13/2/60.**N/C.**
Dar. 18/9—4/11/61.**G.**

BOILERS:
D656.
D190 *(ex1271)* 24/10/23.
D139 *(ex1271)* 20/9/28.
D951 *(ex2226)* 11/8/31.
2566 *(new)* 21/4/34.
2394 *(ex1278)* 20/11/43.
2890 *(ex3385)* 5/7/47.
2984 *(ex63394)* 6/5/50 (50A).
2984 reno.24246 15/11/52.
24154 2/7/55 (50A).
24274 27/12/57 (50A).
24295 4/11/61 (50A).

SHEDS:
Selby.
Sunderland 5/7/34.
Borough Gardens 15/1/38.
Blaydon 15/2/41.
Newport 28/3/43.
Thornaby 1/6/58.
Tyne Dock 7/7/63.

RENUMBERED:
3371 14/3/46.
63371 6/5/50.

CONDEMNED: 7/11/65.
Sold for scrap to Hughes,
Bolckow, Blyth, 12/65.

2215

Darlington.

To traffic 6/1917.

REPAIRS:
Ghd. 13/12/24—3/3/25.**G.**
Ghd. 29/8/27—9/1/28.**G.**
Ghd. 20—29/11/28.**L.**
Ghd. 7—18/1/30.**N/C.**
Ghd. 28/10—5/12/30.**G.**
Dar. 29/10/34—11/1/35.**G.**
Dar. 25/1—3/3/39.**G.**
Dar. 11/7—15/8/41.**G.**
Dar. 8/10—18/11/42.**G.**
Dar. 3—25/3/44.**G.**
Ghd. 6—21/6/45.**L.**
Dar. 12/5—21/6/47.**G.**
Dar. 19/1—28/2/50.**G.**
Dar. 25/9—18/10/52.**G.**
Dar. 20—25/10/52.**N/C.**
Ghd. 15/5—10/6/53.**C/L.**
Dar. 11—16/1/54.**N/C.**
Dar. 13/5—9/6/55.**G.**
Ghd. 30/12/57—31/1/58.**G.**

Dar. 12/2—26/3/59.**C/L.**
Dar. 22/3/60. *Not repaired after*
derailment.

BOILERS:
D558.
E4/43 *(ex2300)* 5/12/30.
D703 *(ex2259)* 11/1/35.
3007 *(new)* 3/3/39 (50A).
3008 *(ex2217)* 15/8/41 (50A).
3002 *(ex1294)* 25/3/44 (50A).
3138 *(ex63386)* 28/2/50 (50A).
24284 *(new)* 18/10/52 (50A).
24286 9/6/55 (50A).
24207 31/1/58 (50A).

SHEDS:
Tyne Dock.
Annfield Plain 1/3/40.
Consett 9/9/40.

RENUMBERED:
3372 25/8/46.
63372 28/2/50.

CONDEMNED: 16/5/60.
Cut up at Darlington.

2216

Darlington.

To traffic 6/1917.

REPAIRS:
Dar. 17/4—30/6/24.**G.**
Dar. 28/9—14/12/27.**G.**
Dar. 3/3—10/4/30.**G.**
Dar. 11/5—21/6/33.**G.**
Dar. 5/7—20/8/35.**G.**
Dar. 29/9—22/12/38.**G.**
Dar. 30/12/40—3/2/41.**G.**
Dar. 10—24/3/41.**N/C.**
Dar. 15/9—1/10/41.
Tender only.
Dar. 19/1—16/2/43.**G.**
Ghd. 30/5—19/6/44.**L.**
Dar. 10/8—8/9/45.**G.**
Dar. 17/10—1/11/46.**L.**
Dar. 7/1—6/2/48.**G.**
Ghd. 1—15/7/49.**C/L.**
Dar. 16/8—21/9/50.**G.**
Dar. 8—16/11/50.**N/C.**
Dar. 29/5—28/6/52.**G.**
Dar. 30/6—4/7/52.**N/C.**
Dar. 15/10—11/11/54.**H/I.**
Dar. 6/6—6/7/55.**C/L.**
Derailment damage.
Dar. 6—29/6/57.**G.**
Dar. 1—2/7/57.**N/C.**
Dar. 19—26/8/59.**C/L.**
Dar. 3—9/5/60.**N/C.**
Dar. 19/10—25/11/60.**G.**

BOILERS:
D598.
D940 *(ex2249)* 14/12/27.
2260 *(exB15 813)* 21/6/33.
D906 *(ex2277)* 20/8/35.
2988 *(new)* 22/12/38 (50A).
3335 *(new)* 16/2/43 (50A).
3017 *(ex2257)* 8/9/45 (50A).
3846 *(new)* 6/2/48 (50A).
3846 reno.24154 21/9/50.
24281 *(new)* 28/6/52 (50A).
24151 29/6/57.
24305 25/11/60 (50A).

SHEDS:
Newport.
Haverton Hill 4/12/43.
Newport 18/10/44.
West Hartlepool 13/11/49.
Middlesbrough 16/7/50.
Kirkby Stephen 3/4/55.
Middlesbrough 26/6/55.
Thornaby 1/6/58.
West Auckland 3/6/62.

RENUMBERED:
3373 1/11/46.
ᴇ**3373** 6/2/48.
63373 21/9/50.

CONDEMNED: 15/7/63.
Into Dar. for cut up 1/8/63.

2217

Darlington.

To traffic 6/1917.

REPAIRS:
Dar. 1/12/22—29/3/23.**G.**
Dar. 25/9/25—20/1/26.**G.**
Dar. 6/3—3/5/28.**G.**
Dar. 9/7—12/8/29.**G.**
Dar. 15/1—24/2/31.**G.**
Dar. 2—31/10/33.**G.**
Dar. 5/5—4/7/36.**G.**
Dar. 31/1—21/3/39.**G.**
Dar. 10/6—16/7/41.**G.**
Dar. 2/3—5/4/43.**G.**
Ghd. 3—26/6/44.**L.**
Dar. 28/9—9/11/45.**G.**
Ghd. 24/12/46—9/1/47.**L.**
Dar. 25/4—24/5/47.**L.**
Dar. 28/4—21/5/48.**G.**
Dar. 22/1—17/2/51.**G.**
Ghd. 7—30/5/52.**C/L.**
Dar. 9/6—2/7/53.**G.**
Ghd. 5/12/55—6/1/56.**H/I.**
Dar. 8/10—6/11/56.**C/L.**
After collision.
Dar. 30/11—4/12/56.**N/C.**
Dar. 24/10—12/12/57.**C/H.**
Dar. 9—24/2/59.**C/L.**
Dar. 13/5—12/6/59.**G.**

Dar. 5—10/10/59.**N/C.**
Dar. 30/11/60—9/1/61.**C/L.**
Dar. 17—23/2/61.**N/C.**

BOILERS:
D610.
D180 *(ex1276)* 20/1/26.
2385 *(new)* 24/2/31.
E4/33 *(ex2278)* 31/10/33.
E4/33 reno.33 4/7/36.
3008 *(new)* 21/3/39 (50A).
2985 *(ex2279)* 16/7/41 (50A).
3149 *(ex2219)* 5/4/43 (50A).
D1940 *(ex2258)* 9/11/45.
2561 *(ex3409)* 21/5/48.
24179 *(ex63415)* 17/2/51 (50A).
24150 2/7/53 (50A).
24242 12/6/59 (50A).

SHEDS:
Dairycoates.
Springhead 20/1/40.
Neville Hill 28/3/43.
Stockton 23/6/43.
Haverton Hill 5/10/47.
Thornaby 14/6/59.
West Auckland 25/11/62.

RENUMBERED:
3374 25/8/46.
63374 21/5/48.

CONDEMNED: 29/4/63.
Into Dar. for cut up 20/6/63.

2218

Darlington.

To traffic 6/1917.

REPAIRS:
Dar. 24/10/24—21/1/25.**G.**
Dar. 22/5—31/8/27.**G.**
Dar. 24/9—8/11/29.**G.**
Dar. 20/1—24/2/32.**G.**
Dar. 21/5—2/7/35.**G.**
Dar. 11/6—11/11/38.**G.**
Dar. 26/6—3/7/41.**N/C.**
Dar. 11/11—9/12/41.**G.**
Dar. 9/2—10/3/44.**G.**
Ghd. 14/8—5/9/45.**L.**
Dar. 24/9—26/10/46.**G.**
Dar. 7/2—5/3/48.**G.**
Dar. 2/5—1/6/50.**G.**
Dar. 11—15/7/50.**N/C.**
Dar. 25/4—16/5/52.**G.**
Dar. 27/10/52.*Weigh.*
Dar. 13—19/11/52.**N/C.**
Dar. 18/3—8/5/54.**C/L.**
Dar. 1—25/3/55.**G.**
Dar. 29/3—1/4/55.**N/C.**
Dar. 25/11—20/12/57.**G.**
Dar. 21—28/3/60.**N/C.**
Dar. 10/8—9/9/61.**G.**

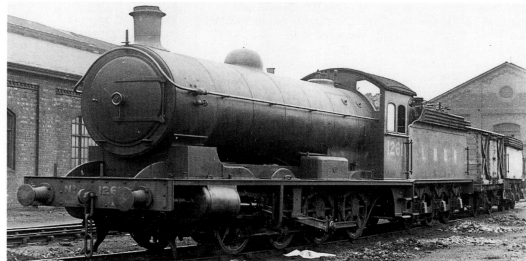

All originally had NER design drawhook and taper buffers with circular flange. The first fifty built at Darlington, to No.2232 had wood sandwich buffer beam.

Ex-works 10th May 1928, No.2284 had been fitted with 'Turplat no-weld' buffers made by Turton Platts & Co., Sheffield. These had hollow spindle, parallel shank and square flange, which developed into the Group Standard type. Note GS drawhook has already been fitted.

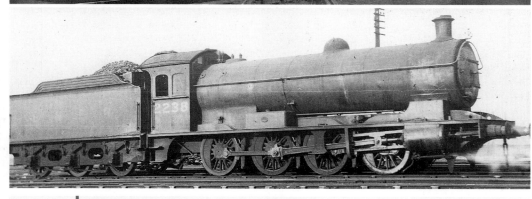

From No.2233 only single plate front buffer beam was fitted and by December 1928, the stepped shank GS buffers were being put on. By 14th September 1939 when No.1247 was so fitted, it seems the whole class then had them.

Of the last three in stock, Nos.63344 and 63387 still had the sandwich type buffer beam. The other one, 63395 always had single plate type.

2218 cont/.
BOILERS:
 D613.
 D673 *(ex2226)* 31/8/27.
 D598 *(ex2285)* 2/7/35.
 2976 *(new)* 11/11/38 (50A).
 2984 *(ex2257)* 9/12/41 (50A).
 3019 *(ex2266)* 26/10/46 (50A).
 3847 *(new)* 5/3/48 (50A).
 2819 *(ex63413)* 1/6/50.
 24206 16/5/52.
 24297 *(new)* 25/3/55 (50A).
 24287 20/12/57 (50A).
 24210 9/9/61 (50A).

SHEDS:
Dairycoates.
Heaton 27/11/33.
Blaydon 9/10/34.
Newport 28/3/43.
Middlesbrough 25/5/48.
Thornaby 1/6/58.
West Auckland 10/3/63.

RENUMBERED:
 3375 26/10/46.
 E3375 5/3/48.
 63375 1/6/50.

CONDEMNED: 19/8/63.
Into Dar. for cut up 19/9/63.

2219

Darlington.

To traffic 6/17.

REPAIRS:
Dar. 23/4—30/6/24.**G.**
Dar. 30/5—7/9/27.**G.**
Dar. 15/3—2/5/30.**G.**
Dar. 29/11/32—5/1/33.**G.**
Dar. 12/2—13/3/35.**G.**
Dar. 18/5—5/8/38.**G.**
Dar. 2—26/10/40.**G.**
Dar. 6/2—17/3/43.**G.**
Ghd. 10—25/6/45.**L.**
Dar. 2/10—2/11/46.**G.**
Dar. 11/1—2/2/50.**G.**
Dar. 21/2—14/3/52.**G.**
Dar. 2—25/2/55.**G.**
Dar. 24/3—24/4/59.**G.**
Dar. 30/9—19/10/60.**C/L.**
Dar. 4—17/1/63.**C/L.**

BOILERS:
 D619.
 E4/49 *(ex2301)* 7/9/27.
 E4/4 *(ex2256)* 2/5/30.
 D613 *(ex2223)* 5/1/33.
 2640 *(new)* 13/3/35.
 HL110 *(ex1363)* 5/8/38.
 3149 *(new)* 26/10/40 (50A).
 3152 *(ex2261)* 17/3/43 (50A).

2383 *(ex2266)* 2/11/46.
2999 *(ex63436)* 2/2/50 (50A).
24218 14/3/52 (50A).
24208 25/2/55 (50A).
24272 24/4/59 (50A).

SHEDS:
Selby.
Dairycoates 7/8/39.
Springhead 18/10/43.
Dairycoates 13/5/44.
Blaydon 20/7/47.
Sunderland 9/9/62.

RENUMBERED:
 3376 2/11/46.
 63376 2/2/50.

CONDEMNED: 1/7/63.
Into Dar. for cut up 8/63.

2220

Darlington.

To traffic 6/1917.

REPAIRS:
Dar. 5/6—26/9/24.**G.**
Dar. 16/2—8/7/27.**G.**
Dar. 20/11/29—10/1/30.**G.**
Dar. 11/4—22/5/33.**G.**
Dar. 19/9—21/10/35.**G.**
Dar. 27/4—26/5/39.**G.**
Dar. 10/5—13/6/41.**G.**
Dar. 18—26/6/41.**N/C.**
Dar. 29/6—5/8/43.**G.**
Dar. 6/9—12/10/46.**G.**
Ghd. 6—14/6/48.**L.**
Dar. 1—24/9/49.**G.**
Dar. 3—20/9/52.**L/I.**
Dar. 26/9—26/10/55.**G.**
Dar. 3—14/1/57.**C/L.**
Dar. 11/9—18/10/57.**C/H.**
Dar. 8/9—3/10/58.**G.**
Dar. 15/10—15/11/62.**G.**
Dar. 6—11/12/62.**N/C.**

BOILERS:
 D616.
 D670 *(ex2224)* 26/9/24.
 D872 *(ex2297)* 10/1/30.
 HL987 *(ex2272)* 22/5/33.
 2383 *(ex1283)* 21/10/35.
 2441 *(ex1279)* 26/5/39.
 D1568 *(ex2299)* 13/6/41.
 AW19 *(ex2252)* 5/8/43.
 2857 *(exB15 1695)* 12/10/46.
 3021 *(ex63364)* 24/9/49 (50A).
 3021 reno.24238 20/9/52.
 24270 26/10/55 (50A).
 24251 3/10/58 (50A).
 24297 15/11/62 (50A).

SHEDS:
Dairycoates.
Springhead 20/1/40.
Neville Hill 28/3/43.
Darlington 14/7/43.
Neville Hill 4/9/44.
Consett 23/7/45.
Borough Gardens 29/11/47.
Blaydon 14/6/59.
Tyne Dock 20/8/61.

RENUMBERED:
 3377 12/10/46.
 63377 14/6/48.

CONDEMNED: 10/11/66.
Sold for scrap to Arnott Young, Dinsdale, 1/67.

2221

Darlington.

To traffic 6/1917.

REPAIRS:
Dar. ?/?—?/7/22.**G.**
Dar. 14/5—13/8/24.**G.**
Dar. 9/6—29/9/27.**G.**
Dar. 8/10—26/11/29.**G.**
Dar. 1/6—1/7/32.**G.**
Dar. 1/12/36—13/1/37.**G.**
Dar. 19/12/38—10/1/39.**N/C.**
Dar. 27/10—2/12/39.**G.**
Dar. 2/9—3/10/41.**G.**
Dar. 11/11—7/12/42.**G.**
Dar. 14/2—14/3/45.**G.**
Ghd. 11—22/6/46.**L.**
Dar. 17/9—10/10/47.**G.**
Dar. 2/5—9/6/50.**G.**
Dar. 13/11—5/12/52.**G.**
Dar. 8/3—2/4/55.**G.**
Dar. 4—6/4/55.**N/C.**
Dar. 13—19/4/55.**N/C.**
Dar. 21/2—14/3/57.**G.**
Dar. 19—25/3/57.**N/C.**
Dar. 19/9—29/10/60.**G.**
Dar. 4/11—6/12/60.**N/C.**
Dar. 31/1/64.*Weigh.*

BOILERS:
 D636.
 2157 *(ex1247)* 1/7/32.
 2855 *(new)* 13/1/37.
 2862 *(ex1362)* 3/10/41.
 2871 *(ex2246)* 7/12/42.
 3310 *(ex2280)* 14/3/45 (50A).
 3298 *(ex3437)* 10/10/47 (50A).
 HL109 *(ex63350)* 9/6/50.
 24286 *(new)* 5/12/52 (50A).
 24296 *(new)* 2/4/55 (50A).
 24305 *(new)* 14/3/57 (50A).
 24182 29/10/60 (50A).

SHEDS:
Dairycoates.
Selby 7/10/39.
Normanton 14/11/48.
Selby 26/12/48.
Whitby 3/5/53.
Selby 1/11/53.
Tyne Dock 16/6/57.
Blaydon 14/9/58.
North Blyth 23/9/62.
Tyne Dock 2/12/62.

RENUMBERED:
 3378 14/7/46.
 63378 9/6/50.

CONDEMNED: 5/4/65.
Sold for scrap to G.Cohen, Cargo Fleet 5/65.

2222

Darlington.

To traffic 6/1917.

REPAIRS:
Ghd. 27/3—6/8/25.**G.**
Ghd. 21/5—17/7/30.**G.**
Ghd. 19/11—30/12/30.**L.**
Ghd. 27/10—5/11/31.**N/C.**
Dar. 31/8/34—22/1/35.**G.**
Dar. 25/7—16/9/38.**G.**
Dar. 5/3—4/4/41.**G.**
Dar. 20—24/6/41.**N/C.**
Dar. 23—25/9/41.**N/C.**
Dar. 26/1—20/2/42.**L.**
Dar. 29/4—20/5/43.**L.**
Dar. 15/11—11/12/43.**G.**
Dar. 26/3—10/5/47.**G.**
Ghd. 1—16/12/48.**L.**
Dar. 30/5—29/6/50.**L/I.**
Ghd. 7—13/12/51.**C/L.**
Dar. 3—21/6/52.**G.**
Dar. 23—26/6/52.**N/C.**
Ghd. 21/8—15/9/53.**C/L.**
Ghd. 27/10—19/11/53.**C/L.**
Dar. 24/2—19/3/55.**G.**
Dar. 21—22/3/55.**N/C.**
Ghd. 5/2—29/3/57.**C/L.**
Dar. 10—16/10/57.**C/L.**
Dar. 14/4—23/5/58.**G.**
Dar. 29/3—3/6/61.**C/L.**
Dar. 4/2—7/3/63.**G.**

BOILERS:
 D645.
 AW7 *(ex2258)* 22/1/35.
 2259 *(ex2266)* 16/9/38.
 2149 *(ex2294)* 4/4/41.
 2643 *(ex2262)* 11/12/43.
 2562 *(ex3381)* 10/5/47.
 24231 21/6/52 (50A).
 24218 19/3/55 (50A).
 24269 *(new)* 23/5/58 (50A).

2222 *cont/.*
24316 7/3/63 (50A).

SHEDS:
Blaydon.
Darlington 14/6/41.
Stockton 28/3/43.
Newport 22/9/44.
Tyne Dock 14/1/46.
Consett 13/4/47.
Tyne Dock 23/5/65.

RENUMBERED:
3379 12/10/46.
63379 16/12/48.

CONDEMNED: 4/9/66.
Sold for scrap to Hughes,
Bolckow, Blyth 10/66.

2223

Darlington.

To traffic 7/1917.

REPAIRS:
Ghd. 22/10/23—9/1/24.**G.**
Dar. 24/6—8/10/27.**G.**
Dar. 9/12/29—29/1/30.**G.**
Dar. 25/10—23/11/32.**G.**
Dar. 23/11/32—15/12/33
In store at paint shop
Dar. 20/10—11/12/35.**G.**
Dar. 3—28/1/38.**N/C.**
Dar. 24/4—7/6/39.**G.**
Dar. 26/9—7/10/39.**N/C.**
Dar. 25/8—19/9/40.**N/C.**
Dar. 1/12/41—7/1/42.**G.**
Dar. 21/11—3/12/42.**N/C.**
Dar. 12—21/12/42.**N/C.**
Dar. 27/7—19/8/44.**G.**
Dar. 5/9—5/10/46.**G.**
Ghd. 27/6—12/7/48.**L.**
Dar. 19/3—8/4/49.**G.**
Dar. 11—12/4/49.**N/C.**
Dar. 24/9—18/10/51.**G.**
Dar. 6—24/10/53.**G.**
Ghd. 28/7—12/8/55.**C/L.**
Dar. 3/7—14/8/56.**G.**
Dar. 29/7—3/9/59.**G.**

BOILERS:
D658.
D613 *(ex2218)* 8/10/27.
E4/47 *(ex2280)* 23/11/32.
HL107 *(ex2257)* 11/12/35.
3013 *(new)* 7/6/39 (50A).
3021 *(ex1294)* 7/1/42 (50A).
3019 *(ex2237)* 19/8/44 (50A).
3015 *(ex3426)* 5/10/46 (50A).
3152 *(ex63349)* 8/4/49 (50A).
24205 18/10/51 (50A).
24179 24/10/53 (50A).
24241 14/8/56.

24320 *(new)* 3/9/59 (50A).

SHEDS:
Tyne Dock.
York 8/3/24.
Dairycoates 21/2/27.
Mexborough 18/12/33.
Newport 6/5/37.
Haverton Hill 27/5/37.
West Hartlepool 26/11/38.
Stockton 16/10/39.
Middlesbrough 4/6/50.
Thornaby 1/6/58.
West Hartlepool 8/4/62.

RENUMBERED:
3380 5/10/46.
63380 12/7/48.

CONDEMNED: 15/7/63.
Into Dar. for cut up 16/8/63.

2224

Darlington.

To traffic 8/1917.

REPAIRS:
Dar. 5/2—9/4/24.**G.**
Dar. 8/6—30/11/26.**G.**
Dar. 25/1—13/3/29.**G.**
Dar. 11/9—16/10/31.**G.**
Dar. 6/3—5/4/34.**G.**
Dar. 11/3—21/4/37.**G.**
Dar. 17/10—24/11/39.**G.**
Dar. 24/11—5/12/39.**N/C.**
Dar. 20/2—21/3/42.**G.**
Dar. 11/11—4/12/43.**G.**
Dar. 26/3—21/4/45.**L.**
Dar. 11/2—3/4/47.**G.**
Ghd. 21/9—4/11/47.**L.**
After collision.
Ghd. 5—25/5/49.**C/L.**
Dar. 15/11—23/12/50.**G.**
Dar. 22/9—17/10/53.**G.**
Dar. 19—20/10/53.**N/C.**
Ghd. 20/5—15/6/54.**C/L.**
Dar. 27/6—9/8/57.**G.**
Dar. 12—13/8/57.**N/C.**
Dar. 1—4/9/59.**C/L.**
Dar. 29/11/61—26/1/62.**G.**
Dar. 22/1/64.*Weigh.*
Dar. 8/7—24/8/65.**C/L.**

BOILERS:
D670.
D872 *(ex2241)* 9/4/24.
D162 *(ex1247)* 30/11/26.
2155 *(new)* 13/3/29.
D1956 *(exB15 791)* 5/4/34.
2434 *(ex1279)* 21/4/37.
D873 *(ex1278)* 21/3/42.
2562 *(exB15 795)* 4/12/43.
2855 *(ex3386)* 3/4/47.

2855 *reno.* 24170 23/12/50.
24159 17/10/53.
24216 9/8/57.
24290 26/1/62 (50A).

SHEDS:
Selby.
Dairycoates 18/11/29.
Newport 18/4/36.
Darlington 29/9/44.
West Hartlepool 5/3/45.
Blaydon 5/10/47.
North Blyth 23/9/62.
Tyne Dock 9/1/66.

RENUMBERED:
3381 8/9/46.
63381 25/5/49.

CONDEMNED: 8/12/66.
Sold for scrap to Willoughby's,
Choppington, 16/2/67.

2225

Darlington.

To traffic 8/1917.

REPAIRS:
Ghd. 24/5—12/7/23.**L.**
Ghd. 14/8—16/10/24.**G.**
Dar. 12/1—4/3/27.**L.**
Dar. 17/1—23/3/28.**G.**
Dar. 19/8—24/9/31.**G.**
Dar. 12/3—7/4/34.**G.**
Dar. 31/10—31/12/36.**L.**
Dar. 18/7—31/8/39.**G.**
Dar. 31/8—11/9/39.**N/C.**
Dar. 2/4—6/5/40.**N/C.**
Dar. 31/12/41—9/2/42.**G.**
Dar. 14—30/9/43.**L.**
Dar. 30/3—24/4/44.**G.**
Dar. 22/2—12/4/45.**L.**
Ghd. 2—19/10/46.**L.**
Dar. 13—16/11/46.**L.**
Dar. 20/11—3/12/46.**N/C.**
Dar. 10/10—14/11/47.**G.**
Dair. 12/6—8/7/50.**G.**
Dar. 10—14/7/50.**N/C.**
Dar. 23/1—7/2/52.**C/L**
Dar. 4—31/12/52.**G.**
Ghd. 23/9—11/10/54.**C/L.**
Dar. 24/6—16/7/55.**G.**
Dar. 18—20/7/55.**N/C.**
Dar. 23/10—16/11/57.**G.**
Dar. 25/11—10/12/57.**N/C.**
Dar. 25/5—24/6/61.**G.**

BOILERS:
D671.
D677 *(ex1261)* 24/9/31.
D610 *(ex1271)* 7/4/34.
3015 *(new)* 31/8/39 (50A).
3008 *(ex2215)* 24/4/44 (50A).

3310 *(ex3378)* 14/11/47 (50A).
3298 *(ex3378)* 8/7/50 (50A).
3298 *reno.*24222 7/2/52.
24244 31/12/52.
24287 16/7/55 (50A).
24192 16/11/57 (50A).
24289 24/6/61 (50A).

SHEDS:
Tyne Dock.
Stockton 20/12/24.
Selby 3/7/30.
Annfield Plain 7/6/34.
Blaydon 15/7/39.
Newport 28/3/43.
Selby 4/12/43.
Stockton 8/6/58.
Haverton Hill 12/10/58.
Thornaby 14/6/59.
West Hartlepool 8/4/62.

RENUMBERED:
3382 14/7/46.
63382 8/7/50.

CONDEMNED: 18/9/64.
Sold for scrap to T.J.Thompson,
Stockton on Tees, 1/65.

2226

Darlington.

To traffic 9/1917.

REPAIRS:
Dar. 21/12/22—21/4/23.**G.**
Dar. 21/5—7/9/25.**G.**
Dar. 7/12/26—14/1/27.**G.**
Dar. 9/7—19/9/28.**G.**
Dar. 22/5—30/6/31.**G.**
Dar. 19/4—18/5/34.**G.**
Dar. 15/2—16/3/37.**G.**
Dar. 12—24/10/38.**N/C.**
Dar. 23/11/39—11/1/40.**G.**
Dar. 9/2—12/3/42.**G.**
Dar. 18/5—10/6/44.**G.**
Dar. 27/11/46—25/1/47.**G.**
Dar. 5—14/2/47.**N/C.**
Ghd. 23/5—1/6/48.**L.**
Dar. 28/9—22/10/49.**G.**
Dar. 24—27/10/49.**N/C.**
Dar. 10/12/52—16/1/53.**G.**
Dar. 22—27/1/53.**N/C.**
Dar. 27/9—21/10/55.**H/I.**
Dar. 29/10—3/11/55.**N/C.**
Dar. 15/5—11/6/58.**C/L.**
Dar. 26/3—30/4/59.**G.**

BOILERS:
D673.
D146 *(exB15 799)* 14/1/27.
D951 *(ex2251)* 19/9/28.
D916 *(ex2251)* 30/6/31.
D699 *(ex2274)* 18/5/34.

2226 cont/.
2876 *(new)* 16/3/37.
2818 *(ex2249)* 12/3/42.
D1965 *(ex2263)* 10/6/44.
2652 *(exB15 782)* 25/1/47.
HL111 *(ex3457)* 22/10/49.
24242 16/1/53 (50A).
24160 30/4/59 (50A).

SHEDS:
Selby.
Dairycoates 18/11/29.
West Hartlepool 5/3/45.

RENUMBERED:
3383 8/9/46.
63383 1/6/48.

CONDEMNED: 13/4/64.
Sold for scrap to Arnott Young, Dinsdale 6/64.

2227

Darlington.

To traffic 10/1917.

REPAIRS:
Ghd. 15/9—19/10/23.**L.**
Ghd. 5/4—6/6/24.**G.**
Ghd. 25—28/8/24.**L.**
Dar. 28/3—9/6/28.**G.**
Ghd. 7/7—13/8/31.**G.**
Dar. 9/3—2/9/34.**H.**
Dar. 3/8—4/11/37.**G.**
Dar. 29/5—20/6/40.**G.**
Dar. 9/4—14/5/41.**G.**
Dar. 3/12/42—7/1/43.**G.**
Ghd. 23/8—1/9/44.**L.**
Dar. 25/8—28/9/45.**G.**
Ghd. 24/9—12/10/46.**L.**
Dar. 24/12/47—23/1/48.**G.**
Dar. 6/12/50—13/1/51.**L/I.**
Dar. 26/11—19/12/52.**G.**
Ghd. 31/5—1/7/55.**G.**
Ghd. 25/8—3/10/58.**G.**
Dar. 12/2—9/3/59.**C/L.**
Dar. 15/12/60—10/2/61.**C/L.**
Dar. 24/12/62—25/1/63.**G.**

BOILERS:
D678.
E4/31 *(ex2283)* 9/6/28.
AW16 *(ex1294)* 2/9/34.
AW28 *(ex2288)* 4/11/37.
3147 *(new)* 20/6/40 (50A).
3321 *(new)* 7/1/43 (50A).
3320 *(ex1276)* 28/9/45 (50A).
3845 *(new)* 23/1/48 (50A).
3845 reno.24174 13/1/51.
24287 *(new)* 19/12/52 (50A).
24231 1/7/55 (50A).
24240 3/10/58 (50A).
24267 25/1/63 (50A.

SHEDS:
Borough Gardens.
Doncaster 27/12/25.
Borough Gardens 28/3/28.
West Hartlepool 10/1/40.
Springhead 6/5/40.
Neville Hill 28/3/43.
Haverton Hill 19/6/43.
Newport 18/10/44.
Borough Gardens 15/2/48.
Blaydon 14/6/59.
Tyne Dock 19/3/61.

RENUMBERED:
3384 15/9/46.
63384 13/1/51.

CONDEMNED: 2/1/66.
Sold for scrap to Arnott Young, Dinsdale 2/66.

2228

Darlington.

To traffic 10/1917.

REPAIRS:
Dar. 27/5—27/8/24.**G.**
Ghd. 26/7—1/10/28.**G.**
Dar. 4/11/31—8/1/32.**G.**
Dar. 9/8—22/10/34.**G.**
Dar. 9—19/11/34.**N/C.**
Dar. 25/3—14/5/37.**G.**
Dar. 8—28/12/38.**N/C.**
Dar. 22/8—20/9/39.**G.**
Dar. 6/11—5/12/41.**G.**
Dar. 2—13/2/43.**N/C.**
Dar. 24/5—17/6/44.**G.**
Ghd. 15—31/12/45.**L.**
Dar. 14/5—28/6/47.**G.**
Dar. 25/10—2/12/50.**G.**
Dar. 14/8—5/9/53.**G.**
Dar. 14—17/9/53.**N/C.**
Ghd. 19/11—17/12/54.**C/L.**
Dar. 14—24/1/55.**C/L.**
Dar. 27/9—19/10/56.**G.**
Dar. 25/10/56.**N/C.**
Ghd. 15/1—6/2/59.**C/L.**
Dar. 6/7—21/8/59.**G.**
Dar. 28/8—15/9/59.**N/C.**

BOILERS:
D677.
D131 *(exB15 815)* 27/8/24.
D226 *(ex1294)* 1/10/28.
D697 *(exB15 824)* 8/1/32.
AW34 *(ex2286)* 22/10/34.
2890 *(new)* 14/5/37.
2855 *(ex2221)* 5/12/41.
2890 *(ex2253)* 17/6/44.
2643 *(ex3379)* 28/6/47.
2643 reno.24166 2/12/50.
24196 5/9/53.
24195 19/10/56.
24318 *(new)* 21/8/59 (50A).

SHEDS:
Selby.
Scarborough 17/2/25.
York 6/7/25.
Scarborough 4/1/26.
York 14/5/28.
Neville Hill 17/6/39.
Darlington 14/7/43.
Dairycoates 4/11/44.
Blaydon 20/7/47.
Sunderland 24/2/63.

RENUMBERED:
3385 15/9/46.
63385 2/12/50.

CONDEMNED: 16/10/63.
Into Dar. for cut up 26/11/63.

2229

Darlington.

To traffic 10/1917.

REPAIRS:
Ghd. 18/9—23/11/23.**G.**
Ghd. 24/8—17/112/26.**G.**
Dar. 12/6—14/8/29.**G.**
Dar. 17/8—22/9/32.**G.**
Dar. 24/12/36—10/2/37.**G.**
Dar. 11—18/2/37.**N/C.**
Dar. 9—28/12/38.**N/C.**
Dar. 23/4—25/5/40.**G.**
Dar. 7—15/6/40.**N/C.**
Dar. 4/4—6/5/42.**G.**
Dar. 19/6—12/7/44.**G.**
Ghd. 20/10—6/11/45.**L.**
Dar. 22/1—23/2/46.**L.**
Dar. 8/1—1/3/47.**G.**
Ghd. 25/8—7/9/48.**L.**
Dar. 7/11—7/12/49.**G.**
Dar. 8/8—1/9/51.**H/I.**
Dar. 26/3—23/4/54.**G.**
Ghd. 6/6—10/7/56.**C/L.**
Dar. 29/10—22/11/57.**G.**
Dar. 29/8—21/10/61.**G.**
Dar. 12/10/64.*Weigh.*

BOILERS:
D690.
E4/37 *(ex2289)* 14/8/29.
2262 *(ex1362)* 22/9/32.
2871 *(new)* 10/2/37.
2850 *(ex2269)* 25/5/40.
2813 *(ex2278)* 6/5/42.
2855 *(ex2228)* 12/7/44.
3138 *(ex3406)* 1/3/47 (50A).
4028 *(new)* 7/12/49 (50A).
4028 reno.24202 1/9/51.
24169 23/4/54 (50A).
24312 *(new)* 22/11/57 (50A).
24304 21/10/61 (50A).

SHEDS:
Tyne Dock.
Borough Gardens 8/3/24.
Dairycoates 25/8/27.
Springhead 20/1/40.
Neville Hill 28/3/43.
Haverton Hill 19/6/43.
Newport 18/10/44.
Borough Gardens 15/2/48.
Blaydon 14/6/59.
North Blyth 23/9/62.

RENUMBERED:
3386 15/9/46.
63386 7/9/48.

CONDEMNED: 5/12/65.
Sold for scrap to Hughes, Bolckow, Blyth 2/66.

2230

Darlington.

To traffic 11/1917.

REPAIRS:
Dar. ?/?—?/7/22.**G.**
Dar. 3/9—12/12/24.**G.**
Ghd. 15/11/29—20/1/30.**G.**
Ghd. 26/3—5/4/30.**L.**
Ghd. 25/4—4/6/30.**H.**
Dar. 5—27/4/34.**G.**
Dar. 3/9—13/10/37.**G.**
Dar. 14/5—12/6/40.**H.**
Dar. 8/3—9/4/41.**G.**
Dar. 14/7—15/8/42.**L.**
Dar. 3—28/4/44.**G.**
Ghd. 9—26/9/45.**L.**
Dar. 15/3—26/4/47.**G.**
Dar. 14—21/5/47.**N/C.**
Ghd. 12—21/9/48.**L.**
Dar. 15/9—18/10/49.**G.**
Dar. 20/10—1/11/50.**C/L.**
Dar. 18/12/51—18/1/52.**G.**
Dar. 24—30/1/52.**N/C.**

WORKS CODES:- Cw - Cowlairs. Dar- Darlington. Don - Doncaster. Ghd - Gateshead. Gor - Gorton. Hsi - Hull Springhead. Inv - Inverurie. Str - Stratford.
REPAIR CODES:- **C/H** - Casual Heavy. **C/L** - Casual Light. **G** - General. **H**- Heavy. **H/I** - Heavy Intermediate. **L** - Light. **L/I** - Light Intermediate. **N/C** - Non-Classified.

2230 cont/.
Dar. 29/6—11/7/53.**N/C.**
Dar. 8/2—4/3/55.**G.**
Dar. 10—15/3/55.**N/C.**
Ghd. 20/2—5/4/57.**C/L.**
Ghd. 24/3—25/4/58.**G.**
Dar. 4/3—4/4/63.**G.**
Dar. 29/12/65—25/1/66.**C/L.**

BOILERS:
 D697.
 D154 *(ex1311)* 12/12/24.
HL982 *(new)* 20/1/30.
 2582 *(new)* 27/4/34.
D1945 *(ex1248)* 9/4/41.
 2385 *(ex1253)* 28/4/44.
 2656 *(ex3397)* 26/4/47.
 3004 *(ex63340)* 18/10/49 (50A).
 24214 18/1/52 (50A).
 24211 4/3/55 (50A).
 24266 *(new)* 25/4/58 (50A).
 24163 4/4/63 (50A).

SHEDS:
Springhead.
East Hartlepool 26/1/27.
West Hartlepool 17/4/39.
Selby 6/9/41.
Tyne Dock 17/8/52.
Consett 1/11/59.
Blaydon 11/9/60.
Sunderland 24/2/63.
Neville Hill 3/10/65.
Normanton 12/6/66.
Tyne Dock 2/10/66.
West Hartlepool 2/7/67.

RENUMBERED:
 3387 28/7/46.
63387 21/9/48.

CONDEMNED: 9/9/67.
*Sold for scrap to T.J.Thompson,
Stockton, 10/67.*

All originally had tail rods to the cylinder pistons and these were still fitted until after BR took over. No.63365 had them at least to March 1953. Note that it had a Q5 chimney with inner rim and no windjabber.

Starting from late in 1949, the tail rods and their covers were removed, all eventually losing them. An end cover for the cylinder was provided but in the last year or so, even this was discarded (*see* page 71, bottom).

(below) **Being superheated, all were equipped with NER design mechanical lubricator for cylinders and valves. To No.2242 this was mounted on the top edge of the right hand frame (*see* page 53, centre) but No.2243 onward had it on the running plate, and some earlier ones (*see* page 58, second from top) had it moved to that position. In both cases drive from the motion decreased oil flow when notched up.**

2231

Darlington

To traffic 12/1917.

REPAIRS:
Ghd. ?/?—?/12/22.**G.**
Ghd. 29/9—3/12/24.**G.**
Ghd. 12/12/27—28/3/28.**G.**
Ghd. 9/2—17/3/31.**G.**
Dar. 20/3—1/5/35.**G.**
Dar. 19/1—25/3/38.**G.**
Dar. 13—29/3/40.**N/C.**
Dar. 11/12/40—9/1/41.**G.**
Dar. 13/10/43—3/2/44.**G.**
Dar. 28/2—3/5/47.**G.**
Dar. 6—31/5/47.**L.**
Ghd. 6—20/12/48.**L.**
Dar. 1/2—15/4/50.**G.**
Dar. 23/11—20/12/51.**C/L.**
Dar. 10/1—7/2/53.**H/I.**
Dar. 10—17/2/53.**N/C.**
Dar. 14/7—6/8/55.**G.**
Dar. 8—9/8/55.**N/C.**
Dar. 2/4—1/5/58.**G.**
Dar. 13—20/5/58.**N/C.**
Dar. 13—17/8/59.**N/C.**
Dar. 8—21/9/59.**C/L.**
Dar. 7—8/12/59.**C/L.**
Dar. 13/2—17/3/62.**G.**

BOILERS:
D699.
D156 *(exB15 825)* 12/22.
D192 *(ex1264)* 3/12/24.
2384 *(new)* 17/3/31.
2652 *(new)* 1/5/35.
3155 *(new)* 9/1/41 (50A).
2989 *(ex2279)* 3/2/44 (50A).
4052 *(new)* 15/4/50 (50A).
4052 reno.24213 20/12/51.
24181 6/8/55 (50A).
24268 *(new)* 1/5/58 (50A).
24220 17/3/62 (50A).

SHEDS:
Tyne Dock.
Springhead 31/1/25.
Blaydon 31/3/27.
Heaton 28/10/39.
Tyne Dock 2/3/40.
Borough Gardens 28/3/43.
Newport 6/2/49.
Thornaby 1/6/58.
West Auckland 23/6/63.
Sunderland 6/10/63.

RENUMBERED:
3388 15/9/46.
63388 20/12/48.

CONDEMNED: 16/3/64.
Into Dar. for cut up, 15/4/64.

2232

Darlington

To traffic 12/1917.

REPAIRS:
Ghd. ?/?—?/12/22.**G.**
Ghd. 12/6—25/9/25.**G.**
Ghd. 11/5—10/7/28.**G.**
Ghd. 18/3—26/4/32.**L.**
Dar. 3/8—8/9/33.**G.**
Dar. 11/5—23/6/37.**G.**
Dar. 19/11—19/12/40.**G.**
Dar. 24/2—23/4/41.**N/C.**
Dar. 1—24/12/42.**G.**
Ghd. 27/7—19/8/44.**L.**
Dar. 6—30/12/44.**L.**
Dar. 20/11—15/12/45.**G.**
Ghd. 7—15/3/47.**L.**
Dar. 20/5—11/6/48.**G.**
Dar.15—24/6/48.**N/C.**
Dar. 29/12/50—20/1/51.**G.**
Dar. 22—23/1/51.**N/C.**
Dar. 6—28/11/53.**H/I.**
Dar. 30/11—2/12/53.**N/C.**
Dar. 4—7/12/53.**N/C.**
Dar. 11—14/7/55.**C/L.**
Dar. 2/12/55—8/2/56.**G.**
Dar. 16/12/58—21/1/59.**G.**
Dar. 13—21/11/59.**N/C.**
Dar. 5/6—13/7/62.**G.**

BOILERS:
D703.
E4/48 *(ex2300)* 10/7/28.
D918 *(ex1361)* 8/9/33.
2385 *(ex2234)* 23/6/37.
2433 *(ex1264)* 19/12/40.
2561 *(ex2295)* 24/12/42.
2426 *(ex2242)* 15/12/45.
2388 *(ex3404)* 11/6/48.
24164 *(ex63427)* 20/1/51 (50A).
24272 8/2/56 (50A).
24273 21/1/59 (50A).
24239 13/7/62 (50A).

SHEDS:
Tyne Dock.
Annfield Plain 24/6/37.
Consett 9/9/40.
Tyne Dock 2/5/41.
Newport 28/3/43.
Stockton 4/12/43.
Newport 13/4/47.
Thornaby 1/6/58.
Tyne Dock 2/12/62.

RENUMBERED:
3389 15/9/46.
63389 11/6/48.

CONDEMNED: 27/12/65.
*Sold for scrap to Hughes,
Bolckow, Blyth, 2/66.*

2233

Darlington

To traffic 8/1918

REPAIRS:
Dar. 23/6—12/9/23.**G.**
Dar. 25/5—14/9/25.**G.**
Dar. 30/9—16/10/25.**L.**
Dar. 10/7—13/9/28.**L.**
Dar. 18/2—2/4/31.**G.**
Dar. 1—23/3/34.**G.**
Dar. 21/12/36—12/2/37.**G.**
Dar. 17/10—29/11/39.**G.**
Dar. 8/4—6/5/42.**G.**
Dar. 4/7—5/8/44.**G.**
Dar. 5/12/46—25/1/47.**G.**
Ghd. 25/10—5/11/48.**L.**
Dar. 8—30/9/50.**G.**
Dar. 23/2—28/3/53.**G.**
Dar. 30/3—2/4/53.**N/C.**
Dar. 9—11/4/53.**N/C.**
Dar. 17/4—7/5/53.**N/C.**
Ghd. 10/4—9/5/56.**C/H.**
Ghd. 22/1—12/2/57.**C/L.**
Ghd. 11/2—21/3/58.**G.**
Ghd. 21/11/58—25/2/59.**C/H.**
Dar. 10/7—21/8/59.**C/L.**
After collision.

BOILERS:
D796.
D911 *(ex2244)* 13/9/28.
2388 *(new)* 2/4/31.
E4/22 *(ex1250)* 23/3/34.
HL103 *(ex2267)* 12/2/37.
2653 *(exB15 823)* 6/5/42.
HL111 *(ex2256)* 5/8/44.
2440 *(ex3355)* 25/1/47.
24158 *(ex3412)* 30/9/50.
24255 28/3/53.
24199 21/3/58 (50A).

SHEDS:
Dairycoates.
York 22/3/24.
Dairycoates 3/26.
Newport 22/2/36.
Stockton 4/12/43.
Blaydon 5/10/47.
Tyne Dock 24/2/63.

RENUMBERED:
3390 3/11/46.
63390 5/11/48.

CONDEMNED: 8/8/63.
Into Dar. for cut up, 2/9/63.

2234

Darlington

To traffic 9/1918

REPAIRS:
Hsi. ?/?—?/2/24.**G.**
Dar. 15/12/25—30/3/26.**G.**
Dar. 18/5—6/7/28.**G.**
Dar. 3/10—14/11/30.**G.**
Dar. 11/10—24/11/33.**G.**
Dar. 7/4—18/5/37.**G.**
Dar. 2/8—1/9/37.**N/C.**
Dar. 12/3—9/4/40.**G.**
Dar. 21/4—9/6/42.**G.**
Dar. 19/4—9/6/45.**G.**
Ghd. ?/?—22/11/46.**L.**
Dar. 30/8—17/9/48.**G.**
Dar. 10—29/9/51.**G.**
Dar. 9—13/10/51.**N/C.**
Dar. 21/7—2/9/55.**G.**
Ghd. 29/7—11/9/57.**C/L.**
Dar. 22/8—18/9/58.**G.**
Dar. 31/3—11/5/60.**C/L.**
Dar. 31/8—25/9/62.**C/L.**
Dar. 30/10/62.*Weigh.*
Dar. 18/3—24/4/63.**G.**
Dar. 30/4—7/5/63.**N/C.**

BOILERS:
D806.
E4/38 *(ex2290)* 6/7/28.
2385 *(ex2217)* 24/11/33.
D1956 *(ex2224)* 18/5/37.
AW28 *(ex1285)* 9/6/42.
2433 *(ex2289)* 9/6/45.
2637 *(ex3443)* 17/9/48.
24201 29/9/51 (50A).
24244 2/9/55.
24236 18/9/58 (50A).
24240 24/4/63 (50A).

SHEDS:
Dairycoates.
Springhead 12/5/23.
Dairycoates 1/7/24.
Springhead 6/7/40.
Dairycoates 28/3/43.
Blaydon 20/7/47.
North Blyth 1/7/56.
Haverton Hill 16/6/57.
West Hartlepool 8/6/58.

RENUMBERED:
3391 15/9/46.
63391 17/9/48.

CONDEMNED: 12/4/65.
*Into Dar. for cut up, 12/4/65,
then sold for scrap to G.Cohen,
Cargo Fleet, 3/6/65 with boiler
No.24217.*

Starting with No.63368, ex-works 2nd February 1949, what was termed 'positive drive' was adopted. Drive was now taken from the right hand crank pin and flat bar linkage, but the lubricator position was unchanged.

By 7th December 1949 some thirty-one had positive drive with flat bar link, but on the next eleven through the works no alteration to lubrication was made. Change to positive drive was resumed with 63372 ex-works 28th February 1950 but with a rod instead of the flat bar. About January 1952, the linkage was reduced by moving the lubricator to the rear of the second splasher and all duly got that arrangement.

The whole one hundred and twenty Q6's were fitted with steam brake on the engine and remained so. Tender wheels were braked but only operated through a connecting link from the engine brake.

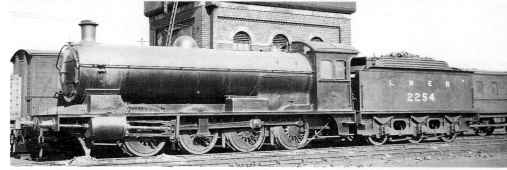

Only from about 1965 were any fitted to carry the small type of snowplough, with the buffer beam drilled for that purpose.

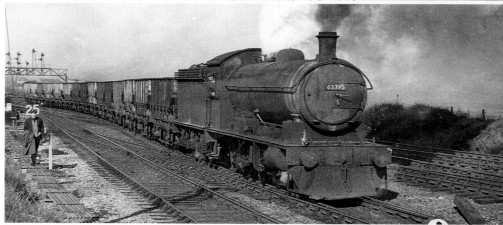

Ex-works 4th August 1932, No.2273 had been fitted with rail washing gear, to clear sand which might interfere with track circuits. This was the purpose of the extra pipe under the cab. No others were so fitted but 2273 still had the gear when it went for repair on 9th August 1938.

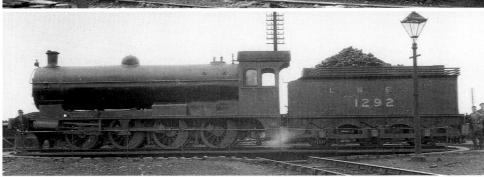

The 1913 built engines were coupled with the then standard 5 tons and 3940 gallons capacity tender which had three coal rails all round with a fourth just around the coal space. No type changes took place prior to January 1938, and some of these non-self-trimming tenders were with Q6 class to their 1967 withdrawal. Note striker for Raven fog signal apparatus under the cab.

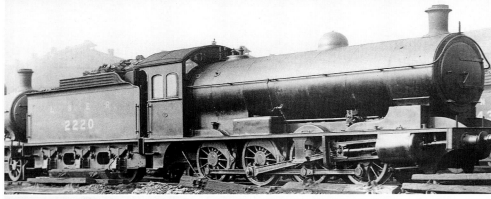

Nos.2213 to 2232 had the 4125 gallons self-trimming type tender, but in 1932-34 ten of them were taken to be used to better effect coupled to Class C7 passenger engines.

The remaining seventy also had 4125 gallons self-trimming type until 1932-34 when twenty of them also went to C7 class, and in 1938 seven more self-trimming type went to D49 class.

In replacement of the self-trimming type, Q6 got 4125 gallons tender built in 1911 and 1914 for C7 class but which were not self-trimming. The 1911 builds had two large, almost semi-circular frame slots and similar smaller ones at each end of the frame. This tender was with C7 No.706 to 18th August 1932 and began on Q6 No.2280 from 19th October 1932.

CLASS Q 6

2235

Darlington

To traffic 10/1918.

REPAIRS:
Dar. 28/6—26/9/23.**G.**
Dar. 20/1—22/4/26.**G.**
Str. 23/9—15/10/26.**L.**
Lifted for heating.
Dar. 10/9—30/10/28.**G.**
Dar. 26/8—26/9/29.**G.**
Dar. 1/12/31—22/1/32.**G.**
Dar. 8/3—4/4/34.**G.**
Dar. 23/9—13/11/36.**G.**
Dar. 23/1—24/2/39.**G.**
Dar. 8/8—18/9/39.**H.**
Dar. 21/9—7/10/39.**N/C.**
Dar. 24/9—21/10/40.**L.**
Dar. 19/6—17/7/42.**G.**
Dar. 17/4—9/5/44.**G.**
Ghd. 4/7—1/8/45.**L.**
Dar. 28/5—11/6/46.*Exam.*
Dar. 24/6—20/7/46.**G.**
Ghd. 24/11—12/12/47.**L.**
Dar. 14—30/4/48.**L.**
Dar. 10/3—1/4/49.**G.**
Dar. 26/5—14/6/52.**G.**
Dar. 16—17/6/52.**N/C.**
Dar. 15/6—8/7/55.**H/I.**
Dar. 27/12/56—24/1/57.**C/L.**
Dar. 16/1—12/3/58.**C/L.**
Dar. 10/2—6/3/59.**G.**
Dar. 17—24/3/59.**N/C.**
Dar. 6/10—29/11/60.**C/H.**

BOILERS:
D817.
D190 *(ex2214)* 30/10/28.
E4/45 *(ex2273)* 26/9/29.
E4/21 *(ex2290)* 4/4/34.
D1941 *(ex1249)* 13/11/36.
HL105 *(ex1250)* 24/2/39.
3138 *(ex2269)* 17/7/42 (50A).
3013 *(ex1247)* 9/5/44 (50A).
2425 *(ex1271)* 20/7/46.
2569 *(ex3423)* 1/4/49.
24280 *(new)* 14/6/52 (50A).
24294 6/3/59 (50A).

SHEDS:
Stockton.
Newport 9/6/30.
West Hartlepool 17/11/36.
Stockton 16/10/39.
West Hartlepool 1/4/40.
Newport 3/9/42.
Darlington 4/12/43.
Dairycoates 4/11/44.
West Hartlepool 5/3/45.

RENUMBERED:
3392 22/6/46.
63392 30/4/48.

CONDEMNED: 18/11/63.
Into Dar. for cut up, 28/11/63.

2236

Darlington

To traffic 10/1918.

REPAIRS:
Ghd. 10/10—13/12/23.**G.**
Ghd. 8/3—29/6/26.**G.**
Ghd. 12/7—25/9/29.**G.**
Ghd. 19/6—20/7/31.**L.**
Ghd. 9/9—19/10/32.**G.**
Dar. 9/12/35—5/2/36.**G.**
Dar. 10/7—17/8/39.**G.**
Dar. 22/1—26/3/40.**L.**
After collision.
Dar. 14/1—7/2/42.**G.**
Dar. 6/6—1/7/44.**G.**
Ghd. 7—22/12/45.**L.**
Dar. 19/12/46—20/2/47.**G.**
Dar. 29/3—12/4/47.**L.**
Ghd. 2—10/8/48.**L.**
Dar. 27/9—15/10/49.**G.**
Dar. 17—21/10/49.**N/C.**
Dar. 9/4—3/5/52.**H/I.**
Dar. 5—10/5/52.**N/C.**
Ghd. 27/7—8/9/54.**C/H.**
Ghd. 8/8—30/9/55.**G.**
Ghd. 22/4—30/5/58.**G.**
Dar. 17—23/2/59.**C/L.**
Dar. 28/8—2/10/59.**C/L.**
Dar. 27/11/61—5/1/62.**G.**
Dar. 23/1—6/2/62.**N/C.**

BOILERS:
D833.
E4/42 *(ex2294)* 19/10/32.
AW47 *(ex2223)* 5/2/36.
AW26 *(ex2241)* 17/8/39.
2819 *(ex2296)* 7/2/42.
2439 *(exB15 813)* 1/7/44.
2976 *(ex3340)* 20/2/47 (50A).
2862 *(ex63406)* 15/10/49.
2862 *reno.24230* 3/5/52.
24174 30/9/55 (50A).
24211 30/5/58 (50A).
24324 *(new)* 5/1/62 (50A).

SHEDS:
Borough Gardens.
Stockton 28/3/43.
Middlesbrough 4/6/50.
Thornaby 1/6/58.
Tyne Dock 2/12/62.

RENUMBERED:
3393 15/9/46.
63393 10/8/48.

CONDEMNED: 17/6/64.
Into Dar. for cut up, 4/9/64.

2237

Darlington

To traffic 11/1918.

REPAIRS:
Dar. 30/9/22—25/1/23.**G.**
Dar. 22/12/25—26/3/26.**G.**
Ghd. 16/8—17/10/28.**G.**
Dar. 15/9—17/10/30.**G.**
Dar. 7/7—14/8/31.**H.**
Dar. 11/1—9/2/34.**G.**
Dar. 9/9—4/11/36.**G.**
Dar. 8/8—13/9/39.**G.**
Dar. 2/3—8/4/40.**L.**
After collision.
Dar. 2/5—10/6/41.**G.**
Dar. 28/6—31/7/44.**G.**
Dar. 3/9—2/10/45.**L.**
Dar. 25/10—23/11/46.**G.**
Ghd. 11—28/5/48.**L.**
Dar. 14/12/49—20/1/50.**G.**
Dar. 16/5—7/6/52.**G.**
Dar. 23/3—16/4/55.**G.**
Ghd. 26/4—15/5/56.**N/C.**
Ghd. 6/5—13/6/58.**G.**
Dar. 15—24/12/59.**N/C.**
Dar. 22/5—22/6/62.**G.**
Dar. 23/6/65.*Weigh.*

BOILERS:
D845.
D610 *(ex2217)* 26/3/26.
D855 *(ex2265)* 17/10/30.
E4/26 *(exB15 782)* 9/2/34.
D916 *(ex2296)* 4/11/36.
3019 *(new)* 13/9/39 (50A).
3145 *(ex2260)* 31/7/44 (50A).
2984 *(ex2218)* 23/11/46 (50A).
2652 *(ex63383)* 20/1/50.
24198 7/6/52.
24214 16/4/55 (50A).
24276 13/6/58 (50A).
24225 22/6/62 (50A).

SHEDS:
Springhead.
Newport 26/5/24.
Darlington 4/12/43.
West Hartlepool 5/3/45.
Blaydon 5/10/47.
Percy Main 12/5/63.
Consett 19/1/64.
West Hartlepool 23/5/65.

RENUMBERED:
3394 15/9/46.
63394 28/5/48.

CONDEMNED: 7/6/67.
Sold for scrap to Hughes, Bolckow, Blyth, 8/67.

2238

Darlington

To traffic 12/1918.

REPAIRS:
Ghd. 29/7—1/10/24.**G.**
Ghd. 11/4—13/6/28.**G.**
Ghd. 7/11—10/12/29.**H.**
Ghd. 22/4—12/5/31.**N/C.**
Ghd. 29/8—6/10/32.**G.**
Dar. 2/1—27/2/36.**G.**
Dar. 17/8—16/9/39.**G.**
Dar. 10/4—12/5/42.**G.**
Dar. 11/11—7/12/44.**G.**
Dar. 16/10—15/11/46.**G.**
Dar. 2—18/4/47.**L.**
Ghd. 14/5—18/6/48.**H.**
Dar. 29/4—21/5/49.**G.**
Dar. 23—28/5/49.**N/C.**
Dar. 7/12/51—11/1/52.**G.**
Dar. 26/10—20/11/53.**H/I.**
Dar. 16/11—9/12/55.**G.**
Dar. 18/2—21/3/58.**G.**
Dar. 28/9—5/10/59.**C/L.**
Dar. 5/1—8/3/61.**G.**
Dar. 29/11/61.**N/C.**
Dar. 8/2/63.*Weigh.*
Dar. 12/8—30/9/65.**H/I.**

BOILERS:
D855.
E4/14 13/6/28.
E4/35 *(ex2287)* 6/10/32.
D1939 *(ex1293)* 27/2/36.
2569 *(ex2295)* 16/9/39.
2388 *(ex2267)* 12/5/42.
HL109 *(exB15 815)* 7/12/44.
2441 *(ex3366)* 15/11/46.
2817 *(ex3430)* 21/5/49.
24277 *(new)* 11/1/52 (50A).
24255 9/12/55 (50A).
24286 21/3/58 (50A).
24332 *(new)* 8/3/61 (50A).
24251 30/9/65 (50A).

SHEDS:
Blaydon.
Newport 28/3/43.
Darlington 4/12/43.
West Hartlepool 5/3/45.
Dairycoates 4/9/49.
Selby 1/12/49.
Darlington 14/6/59.
Sunderland ?/5/65.

RENUMBERED:
3395 15/9/46.
63395 18/6/48.

WITHDRAWN: 9/9/67.
Sold for preservation 29/10/67.

69

This was No.2229's original tender and it remained with that engine until 19th June 1944, getting tender number 8742 from 25th May 1940. It then served Nos.1291 (from 27th July 1944), 63342 (from 16th June 1951), 63402 (from 28th August 1953), 63358 (from 2nd December 1954) and 63400 (from 6th June 1957). After this collision it was in Darlington from 18th October to 5th December 1957. Note that NER design tenders had no footsteps on the back plate.

On 5th December 1957 tender No.8742 returned to traffic with engine 63400, having been rebuilt with straight-sided body from withdrawn D20 class No.62387. Note that it now had two access steps on the back plate. On 2nd September 1958 Borough Gardens shed transferred this tender to 63377 which had it to 18th February 1965. Before it was sent for scrap, it also served 63384 (18th February to 26th November 1965) (*see* below; and 63389 (26th November to 27 December 1965). Then *see* bottom illustration.

After its long spell with No.63377 - which had moved to Tyne Dock shed - that shed used the straight-sided tender for engines they were trying to keep in traffic. No.63384 had it and then 63389 when that engine was withdrawn.

On No.63389's demise, the rebuilt tender went to 63445 which was in service for another six months to 26th June 1966 when it too was withdrawn.

From January 1949 seven tenders from withdrawn Q5 class engines were transferred to replace Q6 tenders in poor condition. This was a reversion to 3940 gallons for some of them. From 14th March to 1st April 1965 and again from 30th September 1965 to 9th September 1967 withdrawal, 63395 used the Q5 tender which was built in 1911 for No.771.

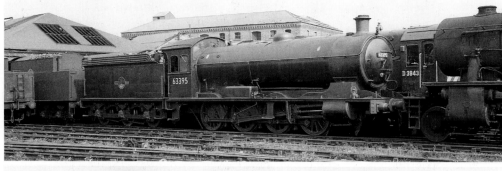

From 1932 tender changing was a frequent occurrence with Q6 class especially after tenders were given individual numbers from March 1938. All varieties were used indiscriminately.

No.2250 (which became 63407) kept its original tender to 18th October 1932 and then had the tender off C7 class 2164 to 5th August 1947. That tender was re-plated 2250 from 2164 in 1932 and was renumbered 8763 on 6th January 1939. After losing that tender, no less than thirteen other tenders were subsequently coupled to 63407.

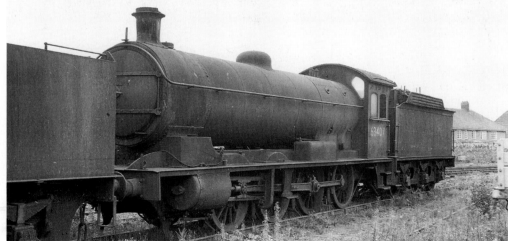

This was No.2270's original tender and it remained with that engine until 30th October 1951. It was then coupled to four other engines before being withdrawn for scrap 2nd January 1966. In this 8th July 1956 photograph note that cylinder end casings have been discarded.

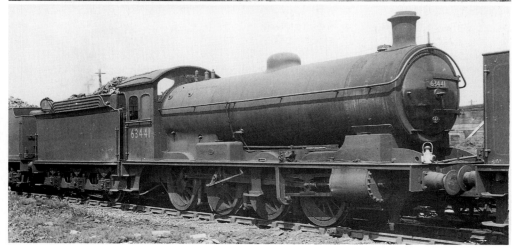

2239

Darlington

To traffic 12/1918.

REPAIRS:
Dar. 28/3—15/6/23.**G.**
Dar. 15/12/25—31/3/26.**G.**
Dar. 24/10—30/11/28.**G.**
Dar. 20/5—29/6/31.**G.**
Dar. 30/10—5/12/33.**G.**
Dar. 18/1—17/2/37.**G.**
Dar. 26/9—6/10/38.**N/C.**
Dar. 3/3—16/4/41.**G.**
Dar. 31/3—3/5/43.**G.**
Dar. 19/1—8/2/45.**L.**
Dar. 8/12/45—24/1/46.**G**
Ghd. 1—16/4/47.**L.**
Dar. 28/1—27/2/48.**G.**
Dar. 10/10—18/11/50.**G.**
Dar. 20—22/11/50.**N/C.**
Dar. 12—30/5/53.**G.**
Dar. 3—6/6/53.**N/C.**
Dar. 8—16/7/54.**C/L.**
Dar. 14/3—16/4/56.**G.**
Dar. 22/4—20/5/59.**G.**
Dar. 21/9—2/10/59.**N/C.**

BOILERS:
 D863.
 D817 *(ex2235)* 30/11/28.
 D1165 *(exB15 799)* 29/6/31.
 HL983 *(ex2263)* 5/12/33.
 2874 *(new)* 17/2/37.
 2262 *(ex1271)* 3/5/43.
 HL110 *(exB15 796)* 24/1/46.
 3141 *(ex3439)* 27/2/48 (50A).
 3141 reno.24163 18/11/50.
 24203 30/5/53.
 24226 16/4/56 (50A).
 24208 20/5/59 (50A).

SHEDS:
Dairycoates.
East Hartlepool 17/2/37.
West Hartlepool 17/4/39.
Springhead 23/5/40.
Neville Hill 28/3/43.
Stockton 21/6/43.
Newport 20/9/44.
West Hartlepool 1/6/48.
Middlesbrough 14/8/55.
Thornaby 1/6/58.

RENUMBERED:
 3396 20/10/46.
 ᴇ**3396** 27/2/48.
 63396 18/11/50.

CONDEMNED: 29/4/63.
Into Dar. for cut up, 15/5/63.

2240

Darlington

To traffic 12/1918.

REPAIRS:
Dar. 5—12/1/23.**L.**
Ghd. 2/10—4/12/24.**G.**
Ghd. 12/12/27—20/3/28.**G.**
Ghd. 13—20/4/28.**L.**
Ghd. 18/3—4/6/29.**H.**
Ghd. 14/12/31—12/2/32.**G.**
Dar. 31/3—5/9/36.**G.**
Dar. 7—15/9/36.**N/C.**
Dar. 28/11—8/12/38.**N/C.**
Dar. 12/4—11/5/40.**G.**
Dar. 15—16/5/41.**N/C.**
Dar. 19/1—3/3/42.**G.**
Dar. 18/10—13/11/43.**G.**
Ghd. 28/1—14/2/46.**L.**
Dar. 15/2—29/3/47.**G.**
Dar. 1—11/4/47.**N/C.**
Dar. 12—19/5/48.**L.**
Ghd. 5—17/9/48.**L.**
Dar. 23/11—20/12/49.**G.**
Dar. 28/10—22/11/52.**G.**
Dar. 1—26/11/55.**G.**
Dar. 25/11/58—2/1/59.**G.**
Dar. 22/10—17/11/62.**G.**

BOILERS:
 D867.
 2812 *(new)* 5/9/36.
 2656 *(ex1292)* 13/11/43.
 2437 *(ex3445)* 29/3/47.
 2810 *(ex3366)* 20/12/49.
 24285 *(new)* 22/11/52 (50A).
 24186 26/11/55 (50A).
 24154 2/1/59 (50A).
 24276 17/11/62 (50A).

SHEDS:
Tyne Dock.
Blaydon 3/26.
Newport 28/3/43.
West Hartlepool 12/5/48.

RENUMBERED:
 3397 15/9/46.
 63397 19/5/48.

CONDEMNED: 31/5/67.
*Sold for scrap to Arnott Young,
Dinsdale, 8/67.*

2241

Darlington

To traffic 12/1918.

REPAIRS:
Dar. 29/9—14/12/23.**G.**
Dar. 4—17/1/24.**L.**
Dar. 19/3—4/4/24.**L.**
Dar. 16/5—24/8/27.**G.**
Dar. 31/12/29—12/2/30.**G.**
Dar. 12/12/32—18/1/33.**G.**
Dar. 18/1/33—18/1/34
In store at paint shop.
Dar. 15/10—28/11/36.**G.**
Dar. 16/11/37—31/1/38.**H.**
Dar. 4/5—4/8/39.**G.**
Dar. 10—27/10/41.**N/C.**
Dar. 8/1—8/2/43.**G.**
Ghd. 2—21/6/44.**L.**
Dar. 6/10—24/11/45.**G.**
Ghd. 21/3—3/4/47.**L.**
Ghd. 12/9—22/10/47.**L.**
Dar. 18/9—15/10/48.**G.**
Ghd.25/9—2/11/50.**L.**
Dar. 7/4—2/5/51.**G.**
Ghd. 1/7—19/8/53.**C/L.**
Ghd. 15—29/4/54.**C/L.**
After collision.
Dar. 15/11—8/12/54.**G.**
Dar. 27/4—11/5/56.**N/C.**
Ghd. 14/10—27/11/57.**C/L.**
Dar. 23—27/1/58.*Weigh.*
Dar. 6/3—8/4/59.**G.**
Dar. 24/4—13/5/59.**N/C.**
Dar. 12/7/61.*Weigh.*
Dar. 4/12/62—4/1/63.**G.**
Dar. 12/8/65. *Not repaired.*

BOILERS:
 D872.
 D656 *(ex2214)* 14/12/23.
 D670 *(ex2220)* 12/2/30.
 2433 *(new)* 18/1/33.
 AW26 *(ex2237)* 28/11/36.
 HL108 *(ex2254)* 4/8/39.
 2857 *(ex1276)* 8/2/43.
 2565 *(ex1249)* 24/11/45.
 2434 *(ex3406)* 15/10/48.
 24183 2/5/51.
 24233 8/12/54.
 24163 8/4/59 (50A).
 24251 4/1/63 (50A).
 24332 *allocated* 12/8/65 (50A).

SHEDS:
Dairycoates.
Springhead 18/10/43.
Dairycoates 13/5/44.
Blaydon 20/7/47.
North Blyth 1/7/56.
Newport 29/9/57.
West Auckland 1/6/58.
Thornaby 2/2/64.
Tyne Dock 21/6/64.

RENUMBERED:
 3398 20/10/46.
 63398 15/10/48.

CONDEMNED: 11/10/65.
*Sold for scrap to W.Willoughby,
Choppington, 11/65.*

2242

Darligton

To traffic 12/1918.

REPAIRS:
Ghd. 27/7—21/9/23.**G.**
Ghd. 17/6—9/9/25.**G.**
Ghd. 17/8—25/10/28.**G.**
Ghd. 6/5—11/6/31.**G.**
Dar. 23/1—21/2/35.**G.**
Dar. 23/8—23/9/39.**G.**
Dar. 21/8—21/9/42.**G.**
Dar. 7—28/9/43.**L.**
Ghd. 26/6—10/7/44.**L.**
Dar. 20/9—27/10/45.**G.**
Ghd. 7—15/11/45.**N/C.**
Ghd. 6—20/3/47.**L.**
Dar. 22/11—17/12/48.**G.**
Dar. 16/7—25/8/51.**G.**
Ghd. 21/1—26/2/53.**C/L.**
Ghd. 25/5—26/6/54.**G.**
Ghd. 22/12/55—20/1/56.**N/C.**
Ghd. 9/9—1/11/57.**G.**
Dar. 8/9—12/11/59.**C/H.**
After derailment.
Dar. 16/3—4/5/61.**C/L.**
Dar. 16/1—10/2/62.**G.**
Dar. 20/3—4/4/62.**C/L.**

BOILERS:
 D873.
 E4/32 *(ex2290)* 11/6/31.
 2638 *(new)* 21/2/35.
 2426 *(ex2282)* 21/9/42.
 HL108 *(exB15 798)* 27/10/45.
 2433 *(ex3391)* 17/12/48.
 24199 25/8/51 (50A).
 24202 26/6/54 (50A).
 24212 1/11/57 (50A).
 24219 10/2/62 (50A).

SHEDS:
Tyne Dock.
East Hartlepool 18/6/31.
Blaydon 8/3/37.
Newport 28/3/43.
Darlington 4/12/43.
Dairycoates 4/11/44.
Blaydon 27/7/47.
North Blyth 1/7/56.
Blaydon 30/6/57.
Thornaby 8/11/59.

WORKS CODES:- Cw - Cowlairs. Dar- Darlington. Don - Doncaster. Ghd - Gateshead. Gor - Gorton. Hsi - Hull Springhead. Inv - Inverurie. Str - Stratford.
REPAIR CODES:- **C/H** - Casual Heavy. **C/L** - Casual Light. **G** - General. **H**- Heavy. **H/I** - Heavy Intermediate. **L** - Light. **L/I** - Light Intermediate. **N/C** - Non-Classified.

2242 cont/.
Tyne Dock 2/12/62.

RENUMBERED:
3399 20/10/46.
63399 17/12/48.

CONDEMNED: 16/3/64.
Into Dar. for cut up, 15/4/64.

2243

Darlington

To traffic 5/1919.

REPAIRS:
Ghd. 13/3—22/5/24.**G.**
Dar. 23/6—4/8/25.**L.**
Ghd. 22/4—17/10/27.**G.**
Dar. 5/10—15/11/28.**L.**
Ghd. 8—23/7/29.**L.**
Ghd. 20/9—29/10/29.**L.**
Ghd. 9/12/29—18/2/30.**H.**
Ghd. 25/1—29/2/32.**L.**
Ghd. 5/12/32—20/1/33.**G.**
Dar. 8—19/7/35.**N/C.**
Dar. 17/2—29/4/37.**G.**
Dar. 3/4—2/5/40.**G.**
Dar. 6—8/5/40.**N/C.**
Dar. 3/7—2/9/42.**G.**
Dar. 11/1—9/2/45.**G.**
Dar. 5/4—15/5/46.**L.**
Dar. 1/9—3/10/47.**G.**
Dar. 8/3—3/4/51.**G.**
Ghd. 18/8—10/9/52.**C/L.**
Dar. 11/3—2/4/53.**G.**
Dar. 13—16/4/53.**N/C.**
Dar. 1—27/3/56.**G.**
Dar. 25/4—4/5/56.**N/C.**
Ghd. 10/7—2/8/56.**C/L.**
Ghd. 12/6—12/7/57.**C/L.**
Dar. 18/10—5/12/57.**C/H.**
After collision.
Ghd. 7/10—28/11/58.**G.**
Dar. 11/10—2/11/61.**C/L.**

BOILERS:
D906.
E4/11 *(ex2263)* 18/2/30.
E4/14 *(ex2238)* 20/1/33.
AW50 *(exB15 820)* 29/4/37.
3298 *(new)* 2/9/42 (50A).
3297 *(ex2245)* 9/2/45 (50A).
3150 *(ex3407)* 3/10/47 (50A).
24181 *(ex63404)* 3/4/51 (50A).
24256 2/4/53 (50A).
24301 *(new)* 27/3/56 (50A).
24231 28/11/58 (50A).

SHEDS:
Tyne Dock.
Springhead 31/1/25.
Tyne Dock 1/2/27.
Borough Gardens 28/3/43.

Blaydon 14/6/59.
Sunderland 17/2/63.

RENUMBERED:
3400 15/9/46.
63400 3/4/51.

CONDEMNED: 12/8/63.
Into Dar. for cut up, 8/63.

2244

Darlington

To traffic 5/1919.

REPAIRS:
Dar. 19/8—30/10/25.**G.**
Dar. 21/6—17/8/28.**G.**
Dar. 16/1—2/3/31.**G.**
Dar. 7/9—7/10/33.**G.**
Dar. 19/8—1/10/36.**G.**
Dar. 11/1—16/2/39.**G.**
Dar. 25/10/40—25/2/41.**H.**
Dar. 2—30/9/41.**G.**
Dar. 2/2—6/3/44.**G.**
Ghd. 23/8—12/9/45.**L.**
Dar. 27/6—15/8/46.**G.**
Ghd. 2—17/9/47.**L.**
Dar. 24/11—21/12/48.**G.**
Dar. 22/10—15/11/51.**G.**
Dar. 28/6—23/7/54.**H/I.**
Dar. 28—31/7/54.**N/C.**
Dar. 29/9—12/11/55.**C/L.**
Dar. 15/9—18/10/56.**C/H.**
Ghd. 8/10—8/11/57.**G.**
Dar. 1—7/4/60.**N/C.**
Dar. 19/6—29/7/61.**G.**

BOILERS:
D911.
D678 *(ex2227)* 17/8/28.
D946 *(ex2284)* 7/10/33.
AW41 *(ex2283)* 1/10/36.
3002 *(new)* 16/2/39 (50A).
3162 *(new)* 30/9/41 (50A).
2815 *(ex2296)* 15/8/46.
3143 *(ex3431)* 21/12/48 (50A).
24274 *(new)* 15/11/51 (50A).
24311 *(new)* 8/11/57 (50A).
24308 29/7/61 (50A).

SHEDS:
Dairycoates 18/12/22.
Springhead 20/1/40.
West Hartlepool 2/3/40.
Springhead 8/5/40.
Neville Hill 28/3/43.
Haverton Hill 19/6/43.
Newport 18/10/44.
West Hartlepool 5/12/48.
Middlesbrough 31/8/52.
Thornaby 1/6/58.
Tyne Dock 18/8/63.

RENUMBERED:
3401 12/10/46.
63401 21/12/48.

CONDEMNED: 6/4/64.
Sold for scrap to Hughes, Bolckow, Blyth, 8/64.

2245

Darlington

To traffic 5/1919.

REPAIRS:
Dar. 22/8—27/10/23.**G.**
Ghd. 16/4—16/7/26.**G.**
Dar. 13/6—7/8/28.**G.**
Dar. 19/5—5/8/30.**G.**
Dar. 29/5—28/6/33.**G.**
Dar. 7/10—13/11/35.**G.**
Dar. 15/2—18/3/37.**H.**
Dar. 22/10—2/12/37.**G.**
Dar. 20/2—19/3/40.**G.**
Dar. 11/7—29/8/42.**G.**
Dar. 29/12/44—27/1/45.**G.**
Dar. 8—15/2/45.**N/C.**
Ghd. 1—18/4/46.**L.**
Dar. 26/11/46—4/1/47.**G.**
Dar. 18—28/1/47.**N/C.**
Ghd. 9—31/5/48.**L.**
Dar. 9/3—13/4/50.**L/I.**
Dar. 27/2—21/3/52.**G.**
Dar. 9—30/10/54.**G.**
Dar. 18/10—16/11/57.**G.**
Dar. 7/11—17/12/58.**C/L.**
After derailment.
Dar. 21/2—30/3/61.**G.**
Dar. 4—7/4/61.**N/C.**

BOILERS:
D916.
D806 *(ex2234)* 7/8/28.
E4/49 *(ex2219)* 5/8/30.
2440 *(new)* 28/6/33.
2437 *(ex1288)* 13/11/35.
D1944 *(ex1251)* 2/12/37.
3297 *(new)* 29/8/42 (50A).
2392 *(exB15 821)* 27/1/45.
3145 *(ex3394)* 4/1/47 (50A).
24221 21/3/52 (50A).
24220 30/10/54 (50A).
24309 *(new)* 16/11/57 (50A).
24261 30/3/61 (50A).

SHEDS:
Tyne Dock.
Stockton ?/25.
Selby 3/7/30.
Newport 19/6/39.
Tyne Dock 14/1/46.
Borough Gardens 13/4/47.
Blaydon 14/6/59.
North Blyth 24/2/63.

RENUMBERED:
3402 15/9/46.
63402 31/5/48.

CONDEMNED: 16/9/64.
Sold for scrap to G.Cohen, Cargo Fleet, 1/65.

2246

Darlington

To traffic 5/1919.

REPAIRS:
Dar. 11/6—29/8/24.**G.**
Dar. 10/8—29/10/27.**G.**
Dar. 11/2—27/3/30.**G.**
Dar. 16/5—17/6/30.**L.**
Dar. 20/12/32—20/1/33.**G.**
Dar. 20/1/33—18/1/34
In store at Paint Shop.
Dar. 18/1—15/2/37.**G.**
Dar. 14/5—6/6/40.**G.**
Dar. 18/9—17/10/42.**G.**
Ghd. 4/7—3/8/44.**L.**
Dar. 25/6—10/8/46.**G.**
Dar. 8/7—12/8/49.**G.**
Dar. 13/11—7/12/51.**H/I.**
Dar. 30/12/54—22/1/55.**G.**
Dar. 24—28/1/55.**N/C.**
Dar. 31/12/57—25/1/58.**G.**
Dar. 27—29/1/58.**N/C.**
Dar. 8—20/1/60.**C/L.**
Dar. 4/12/61—4/1/62.**G.**
Dar. 30/7/62.*Weigh.*

BOILERS:
D918.
D658 *(ex2223)* 29/10/27.
HL985 *(new)* 27/3/30.
D833 *(ex2236)* 20/1/33.
2261 *(ex2286)* 15/2/37.
2871 *(ex2229)* 6/6/40.
2980 *(ex2259)* 17/10/42 (50A).
2640 *(exB15 795)* 10/8/46.
2980 *(ex3348)* 12/8/49 (50A).
2980 reno.24268 7/12/51.
24276 22/1/55 (50A).
24198 25/1/58.
24325 *(new)* 4/1/62 (50A).

SHEDS:
Dairycoates.
Cudworth 13/5/44.
Dairycoates 29/7/46.
Blaydon 20/7/47.
North Blyth 1/7/56.
Newport 29/9/57.
Thornaby 1/6/58.
West Auckland 26/10/58.
West Hartlepool 24/11/63.

(left) **BR made early trials of this Nathan visual water level indicator and one tender each in classes B12, O4 and Q6 were chosen to be so fitted. At the rear end of the left hand side of the tender, these glasses were fitted, so that the internal level could be seen, with the object of avoiding waste of water through spillage by over-filling. Q6 tender No.8786 was the one fitted and was ex-works 2nd February 1949 with engine 63368. It stayed so coupled to 19th August 1951 and then moved to twelve other engines before its 16th November 1964 withdrawal.**

(below) **The Nathan idea, although laudable, had not been thought through enough from a practical aspect. It required one man to climb on the tender, and remain there, if he was to observe the rising level and tell a colleague when to shut off the supply. Nor, as here, was the water column on the same side as the indicator in some cases. So it is evident why only one was fitted and why no shed hung on to that tender.**

(below) **The problem of windjabber corrosion was perennial. No.2245 was ex-works 28th June 1933 and in two years (the photograph was taken 30th June 1935) there is only a ragged edge at the top of the chimney.**

No.63411 in September 1949 has a rough edge to the rim of its chimney although only ex-works 21st March 1949 from general repair. As No.2254 it was one of three Carlisle engines from which the windjabber was removed in 1934/5 but all three returned to the NE Area in March 1939.

(above) The problem was never solved; No.63357 was out 20th May 1961 from a general repair and by July 1963 this was its chimney top condition.

(right) The steam reversing gear was the original two-handle control type. From 1929, other classes had single handle control substituted, e.g. Q5 Part 2 which eliminated the lever pivoted on the boiler handrail, and the rod to the operating valve. Class Q6 was not altered.

2246 cont/.

RENUMBERED:
3403 10/8/46.
63403 12/8/49.

CONDEMNED: 27/7/64.
Into Dar. for cut up, 17/8/64.

2247

Darlington

To traffic 6/1919.

REPAIRS:
Ghd. 7/10—10/12/24.**G.**
Dar. 28/5—27/10/26.**G.**
Ghd. 21/6—23/8/29.**G.**
Ghd. 3—16/10/29.**N/C.**
Ghd. 6/11—16/12/31.**G.**
Dar. 2/9—24/10/34.**G.**
Dar. 20/4—2/6/37.**G.**
Dar. 20/5—11/6/40.**G.**
Dar. 12/6—11/7/42.**G.**
Dar. 22/4—13/5/43.**L.**
Dar. 29/11/44—6/1/45.**G.**
Dar. 20/7—15/9/45.**L.**
Ghd. 6—18/10/46.**L.**
Dar. 26/1—27/2/48.**G.**
Dar. 8—22/3/48.**N/C.**
Ghd. 27/3—11/5/50.**C/L.**
Dar. 8/2—6/3/51.**G.**
Ghd. 18—27/11/52.**C/L.**
Dar. 15/10—14/11/53.**L/I.**
Dar. 16/11/53.**N/C.**
Ghd. 14/9—14/10/55.**C/L.**
After derailment.
Dar. 21/11—14/12/56.**G.**
Dar. 17/10—18/11/60.**G.**
Dar. 29/9/64.*Weigh.*

BOILERS:
D930.
E4/19 *(ex2271)* 23/8/29.
2386 *(ex1311)* 24/10/34.
AW44 *(ex2255)* 2/6/37.
AW34 *(ex2255)* 11/6/40.
HL107 *(ex1280)* 11/7/42.
2388 *(ex2238)* 6/1/45.
3335 *(ex3408)* 27/2/48 (50A).
24168 *(ex63370)* 6/3/51 (50A).
24235 *(new)* 14/12/56 (50A).
24329 *(new)* 18/11/60 (50A).

SHEDS:
Borough Gardens.
Springhead 16/2/25.
Borough Gardens 1/2/27.
Heaton 21/11/34.
Blaydon 8/6/37.
Heaton 17/7/39.
Tyne Dock 2/3/40.
Blaydon 15/2/41.
Newport 28/3/43.
Consett 14/1/46.

Sunderland 6/5/62.

RENUMBERED:
3404 25/8/46.
E**3404** 27/2/48.
63404 11/5/50.

CONDEMNED: 17/5/65.
*Sold for scrap to M.Baum,
Middlesbrough, 6/65.*

2248

Darlington

To traffic 6/1919.

REPAIRS:
Dar. 26/9—30/11/23.**G.**
Ghd. 1/7—29/9/26.**G.**
Dar. 17/9—2/11/28.**G.**
Dar. 3/12/28—10/1/29.**L.**
Dar. 1/4—5/5/32.**G.**
Dar. 15/8—19/9/35.**G.**
Dar. 15/1—1/3/37.**L.**
Dar. 6/7—12/8/39.**G.**
Dar. 6/7—27/8/42.**G.**
Ghd. 13/5—3/6/44.**L.**
Dar. 11/5—28/6/45.**G.**
Ghd. 18/10—2/11/46.**L.**
Dar. 23/2—31/3/48.**G.**
Dar. 29/1—17/2/51.**H/I.**
Dar. 29/12/52—28/1/53.**G.**
Dar. 5—25/2/53.**N/C.**
Ghd. 28/5—12/6/53.**N/C.**
Dar. 19/7—13/8/55.**G.**
Dar. 29/8—1/9/55.**N/C.**
Dar. 10—17/10/57.**C/L.**
Dar. 18/4—15/5/58.**G.**
Dar. 7—12/1/60.**N/C.**
Dar. 12/2—1/4/60.**C/H.**
Dar. 15—21/6/61.**C/L.**
Dar. 21/10—24/11/61.**G.**
Dar. 8/4/65.*Weigh.*

BOILERS:
D935.
E4/30 *(ex2282)* 5/5/32.
2260 *(ex2216)* 19/9/35.
2155 *(ex2213)* 12/8/39.
2434 *(ex2267)* 28/6/45.
3849 *(new)* 31/3/48 (50A).
24174 28/1/53 (50A).
24227 13/8/55 (50A).
24225 15/5/58 (50A).
24246 24/11/61 (50A).

SHEDS:
Stockton.
Springhead 27/11/30.
Dairycoates 4/12/30.
Newport 24/6/39.
West Hartlepool 27/6/48.
Haverton Hill 7/11/48.
Middlesbrough 7/1/51.

Thornaby 1/6/58.
Sunderland 21/7/63.

RENUMBERED:
3405 17/8/46.
E**3405** 31/3/48.
63405 17/2/51.

CONDEMNED: 14/12/66.
*Sold for scrap to W.Willoughby,
Choppington, 16/2/67.*

2249

Darlington

To traffic 6/1919.

REPAIRS:
Dar. 4/4—28/6/24.**G.**
Dar. 13/7—28/10/27.**G.**
Dar. 9/1—15/2/30.**G.**
Dar. 9/6—18/7/32.**G.**
Dar. 15/1—15/4/36.**G.**
Dar. 5/7—9/8/39.**G.**
Dar. 4/1—12/3/40.**G.**
Dar. 25—30/1/41.**N/C.**
Dar. 21/1—17/2/42.**G.**
Dar. 10/7—6/8/42.**N/C.**
Dar. 8—29/6/44.**G.**
Dar. 13/12/46—8/2/47.**G.**
Ghd. 31/10—16/11/48.**L**
Dar. 29/6—10/8/49.**G.**
Dar. 15—18/8/49.**N/C.**
Dar. 25/1—16/2/52.**G.**
Dar. 18—20/2/52.**N/C.**
Ghd. 6—26/3/52.**C/L.**
After derailment.
Dar. 23/3—18/4/53.**C/L.**
Dar. 21/7—13/8/54.**G.**
Dar. 12/2—1/3/57.**G.**
Dar. 4—7/3/57.**N/C.**
Dar. 14—21/3/57.**N/C.**
Dar. 8/2—10/3/60.**G.**
Dar. 20/11—16/12/61.**G.**
Dar. 21/12—3/1/62.**N/C.**
Dar. 19/1—6/2/62.**N/C.**
Dar. 12/8—2/9/63.**N/C.**
Dar. 3/2/64.*Weigh.*
Dar. 20/5/64.*Weigh.*
Dar. 23/3/65.*Weigh.*

BOILERS:
D940.
D619 *(ex2219)* 28/10/27.
D671 *(exB15 824)* 15/4/36.
2813 *(ex1280)* 9/8/39.
2818 *(ex2278)* 12/3/40.
2875 *(ex1293)* 17/2/42.
3138 *(ex2235)* 29/6/44 (50A).
2862 *(ex3350)* 8/2/47.
2888 *(ex3440)* 10/8/49.
24215 16/2/52.
24261 13/8/54 (50A).
24205 1/3/57 (50A).

24187 10/3/60 (50A).
24274 16/12/61 (50A).

SHEDS:
Dairycoates.
Mexborough 15/12/33.
Dairycoates at 1/1/35.
Selby 2/10/35.
Mexborough ?/12/35.
Dairycoates 28/6/36.
Newport 5/5/37.
Haverton Hill 27/5/37.
West Hartlepool 26/11/38.
Dairycoates 1/7/39.
Selby 7/10/39.
Tyne Dock 16/6/57.
Consett 18/1/59.
Sunderland 8/9/63.

RENUMBERED:
3406 27/10/46.
63406 16/11/48.

CONDEMNED: 31/7/66.
*Sold for scrap to Hughes,
Bolckow, Blyth, 9/66.*

2250

Darlington

To traffic 7/1919.

REPAIRS:
Dar. 21/6—19/9/24.**G.**
Dar. 13/9—30/11/27.**G.**
Dar. 8/3—22/4/30.**G.**
Dar. 4/7—1/8/30.**N/C.**
Dar. 18/10—16/11/32.**G.**
Dar. 30/1—21/3/36.**G.**
Dar. 23/11/38—6/1/39.**G.**
Dar. 18/3—20/4/43.**G.**
Dar. 9/1—9/2/45.**G.**
Ghd. 9—25/4/46.**L.**
Dar. 11—16/1/47.
Not repaired.
Ghd. 16/1—1/2/47.**L.**
Dar. 5/8—6/9/47.**G.**
Dar. 13/6—12/7/50.**H/I.**
Dar. 6—28/8/52.**G.**
Dar. 12/1—5/2/55.**G.**
Dar. 7—10/2/55.**N/C.**
Dar. 2/7/56.*Weigh.*
Dar. 25/6—2/8/57.**G.**
Dar. 6—9/8/57.**N/C.**
Dar. 19—22/8/57.**N/C.**
Dar. 30/8—9/9/57.**N/C.**
Dar. 29/10—6/11/57.**N/C.**
Dar. 13/3/58.**C/L.**
Dar. 5/2—12/3/60.**C/L.**
Dar. 21—25/3/60.**N/C.**
Dar. 4/5—2/6/61.**G.**
Dar. 12/5—14/6/65.**C/L.**

2250 cont/.

BOILERS:
D946.
D217 *(ex1291)* 30/11/27.
HL988 *(new)* 22/4/30.
2431 *(new)* 16/11/32.
2993 *(new)* 6/1/39 (50A).
3153 *(ex1264)* 20/4/43 (50A).
3150 *(ex1283)* 9/2/45 (50A).
3305 *(ex3416)* 6/9/47 (50A).
24234 28/8/52.
24232 5/2/55.
24210 2/8/57 (50A).
24235 2/6/61 (50A).

SHEDS:
Dairycoates.
Cudworth 25/3/40.
Neville Hill 28/3/43.
Stockton 19/6/43.
Haverton Hill 6/2/49.
West Auckland 14/6/59.
Darlington 2/2/64.
West Hartlepool 12/4/64.

RENUMBERED:
3407 25/4/46.
63407 12/7/50.

CONDEMNED: 1/7/67.
*Sold for scrap to Clayton &
Davie, Dunston, 9/67.*

2251

Darlington

To traffic 7/1919.

REPAIRS:
Dar. 19/10/23—8/1/24.**G**.
Dar. 25/3—18/8/25.**G**.
Dar. 28/9—27/10/25.**L**.
Dar. 25/6—30/8/28.**G**.
Dar. 13/3—29/4/31.**G**.
Dar. 16/3—17/4/34.**G**.
Dar. 6/10—4/12/36.**G**.
Dar. 28/12/39—9/3/40.**G**.
Dar. 29/9—29/10/42.**G**.
Dar. 14/9—11/10/45.**G**.
Ghd. 10—23/8/46.**L**.
Dar. 11/12/47—9/1/48.**G**.
Dar. 18/4—11/5/50.**G**.
Dar. 12—27/12/50.**C/L**.
Dar. 1—25/10/52.**G**.
Ghd. 15/10—3/12/54.**C/L**.
After collision.
Dar. 4/8—10/9/55.**G**.
Ghd. 7/10—4/11/55.**C/L**.
After collision.
Dar. 9/5—3/7/57.**C/L**.
Dar. 8/4—7/5/59.**G**.
Dar. 12—21/9/61.**N/C**.
Dar. 24/4/63.*Weigh.*

BOILERS:
D951.
D916 *(ex2245)* 30/8/28.
E4/12 *(ex2264)* 29/4/31.
2388 *(ex2233)* 17/4/34.
D1940 *(exB15 796)* 4/12/36.
3314 *(new)* 29/10/42 (50A).
3335 *(ex2216)* 11/10/45 (50A).
3311 *(ex3357)* 9/1/48 (50A).
2989 *(ex63388)* 11/5/50
(50A).
24240 25/10/52 (50A).
24213 10/9/55 (50A).
24191 7/5/59 (50A).

SHEDS:
Selby.
Dairycoates 18/11/29.
Cudworth 20/3/44.
Dairycoates 29/9/46.
Selby 5/10/47.
Borough Gardens 27/1/52.
Blaydon 14/6/53.
Tyne Dock 24/2/63.

RENUMBERED:
3408 23/8/46.
63408 11/5/50.

CONDEMNED: 2/7/63.
Into Dar. for cut up, 7/63.

2252

Darlington

To traffic 8/1919.

REPAIRS:
Dar. 6/11/23—30/1/24.**G**.
Dar. 15/12/25—22/3/26.**G**.
Ghd. 7/12/28—23/1/29.**G**.
Dar. 16/6—31/7/33.**G**.
Dar. 8/3—21/6/34.**H**.
Dar. 5/3—16/4/37.**G**.
Dar. 15/7—12/8/40.**G**.
Dar. 12—19/8/40.**N/C**.
Dar. 4/11—10/12/41.**H**.
Dar. 20/5—1/7/43.**G**.
Dar. 16/2—16/3/46.**G**.
Dar. 6/4—6/5/48.**G**.
Dar. 22/6—12/7/49.**C/L**.
Ghd. 5/6—13/7/50.**L/I**.
Dar. 3—28/9/51.**G**.
Dar. 25/3—16/4/53.**H/I**.
Dar. 3/12/53—5/1/54.**H/I**.
Dar. 24/2—26/3/56.**G**.
Dar. 14/10—11/11/58.**G**.
Dar. 19—26/11/58.**N/C**.
Dar. 9/12/58—5/1/59.**N/C**.
Dar. 3/3—2/4/59.**C/L**.
After collision.
Dar. 3—5/11/59.**N/C**.
Dar. 30/1—3/2/61.**C/L**.
Dar. 25/6—22/8/62.**G**.

Dar. 30/8—13/9/62.**N/C**.
Dar. 18—25/9/62.**N/C**.

BOILERS:
D957.
E4/29 *(ex2281)* 23/1/29.
E4/1 *(ex2253)* 31/7/33.
2262 *(ex2229)* 16/4/37.
AW19 *(ex2273)* 12/8/40.
2817 *(ex2283)* 1/7/43.
2561 *(ex2232)* 16/3/46.
2658 *(exB15 1696)* 6/5/48.
24203 28/9/51.
24253 16/4/53.
24164 26/3/56 (50A).
24254 11/11/58 (50A).
24270 22/8/62 (50A).

SHEDS:
Dairycoates.
Springhead 8/12/24.
Blaydon 31/3/27.
Borough Gardens 7/11/31.
Blaydon 26/11/31.
Darlington 14/5/41.
Newport 14/9/42.
Middlesbrough 15/5/48.
Thornaby 1/6/58.
Tyne Dock 2/12/62.

RENUMBERED:
3409 16/3/46.
63409 6/5/48.

CONDEMNED: 11/9/66.
*Sold for scrap to A.Draper,
Hull, 10/66. Cut up 12/12/66*

2253

Armstrong Whitworth 1.

To traffic 11/1919.

REPAIRS:
Dar. 7/1—15/4/25.**G**.
Ghd. 4/6—23/8/27.**G**.
Dar. 3/2—22/3/30.**G**.
Dar. 3/12/31—6/1/32.**L**.
Dar. 1/6—4/7/33.**G**.
Dar. 12/4—17/5/35.**G**.
Dar. 22/3—23/4/37.**G**.
Dar. 29/12/38—10/1/39.**N/C**.
Dar. 11/1—13/2/40.**G**.
Dar. 1/12/41—6/1/42.**G**.
Dar. 22/4—12/5/44.**G**
Ghd. 19—29/8/45.**L**.
Dar. 19/7—31/8/46.**N/C**.
Dar. 12—14/9/46.**N/C**.
Ghd. 3—14/5/48.**L**.
Dar. 29/3—30/6/49.**G**.
Dar. 30/6—19/7/52.**G**.
Dar. 24/5—18/6/55.**G**.
Dar. 23/12/57—25/1/58.**G**.
Dar. 30/9—8/11/60.**C/H**.

Dar. 8/6—10/8/62.**G**.
Dar. 7/5/64.*Weigh.*

BOILERS:
E4/1.
D504 *(ex2285)* 4/7/33.
2384 *(ex2231)* 17/5/35.
2888 *(new)* 23/4/37.
2890 *(ex2228)* 6/1/42.
2888 *(ex1293)* 12/5/44.
2386 *(exB15 824)* 31/8/46.
3013 *(ex3341)* 30/6/49 (50A).
24154 19/7/52 (50A).
24249 18/6/55 (50A).
24297 25/1/58 (50A).
24268 10/8/62 (50A).

SHEDS:
Stockton.
Thornton Jct. 3/5/23.
Stockton 31/10/23.
Newport 9/6/30.
Starbeck 9/4/31.
Neville Hill 18/1/37.
Darlington 26/6/43.
Neville Hill 2/10/44.
West Hartlepool 4/5/47.

RENUMBERED:
3410 30/8/46.
63410 14/5/48.

CONDEMNED: 5/6/66.
*Sold for scrap to Hughes,
Bolckow, Blyth, 7/66.*

2254

Armstrong Whitworth 2.

To traffic 12/1919.

REPAIRS:
Ghd. ?/?—27/7/22.**G**.
Ghd. 1/12/24—18/2/25.**G**.
Ghd. 23/11/26—24/2/27.**G**.
Ghd. 16/5—31/7/29.**G**.
Ghd. 10/6—18/7/32.**G**.
Dar. 8/10—21/11/35.**G**.
Dar. 14/1—5/3/36.**L**.
Dar. 29/4—16/7/36.**H**.
Dar. 31/3—16/5/39.**G**.
Dar. 26/11—26/12/41.**G**.
Dar. 17/8—7/9/44.**G**.
Ghd. 2—16/1/46.**L**.
Dar. 26/11—28/12/46.**G**.
Dar. 28/2—21/3/49.**G**.
Dar. 31/3—12/4/49.**N/C**.
Dar. 29/6—9/7/49.**N/C**.
Dar. 11—12/7/49.**N/C**.
Dar. 12—30/6/51.**H/I**.
Dar. 5—9/7/51.**N/C**.
Ghd. 30/12/52—29/1/53.**C/L**.
After collision.
Dar. 25/5—20/6/53.**G**.

Whatever may have been the advantage of change to other classes, on Q6 it was clearly not needed. The 1913 design and application of two-handle steam reverse served one hundred and twenty Class Q6 through to the 1960's, a class with a popular and reliable reputation. This is an August 1964 photograph. Note hole still in buffer beam - now partly obscured by GS buffer flange - which enabled the tail rod to be drawn forward for ring examination of the piston head.

Until 1932 there were no lifting holes in the front end of the main frames.

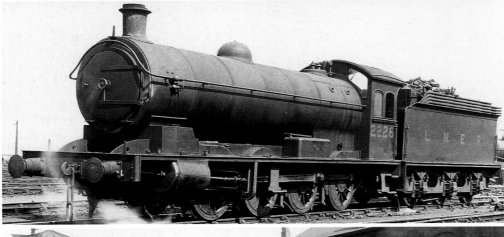

During 1932 Darlington works put in improved lifting facilities, and as engines went through for repair, lifting holes were drilled in the frames.

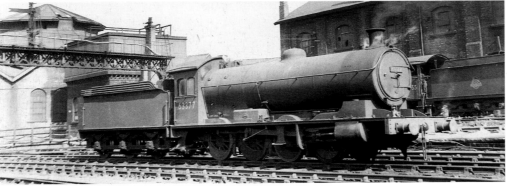

Some smoke boxes of the original type with flat flange door proved quite durable and No.63377 had one until it went for repair in September 1955, as seen here on 18th May 1954.

Normal axle box lubrication was from oil boxes, of which there were two on each side, both having two feeds. That to the rear of the front splasher fed the 1st and 2nd axles and the one by the side of the firebox dealt with the 3rd and 4th axles. During the 1920's a few of the class also had a sight feed lubricator in the cab, but none so fitted have been noted after the number moved to the cab.

Whilst tail rods were fitted there was an oil cup serving them fitted just in front of the leading sandbox. When the rods went, these cups were also taken off.

In BR days it was distinctly unusual to see a Q6 still with mechanical lubricator in the original position, but in addition to No.3371, No.63363 also had same siting, probably to July 1951. The combination of LNER number with a BRITISH RAILWAYS lettered tender was very rare. No.3371 was so numbered ex-works 14th March 1946 but in November 1949 its tender was damaged and had to be replaced at Newport shed by a spare sent from the works.

Only the thirty built in 1913 acquired large brass number plate and N.E.R. on tender, and from 1917 all were in No.2272's style showing them as taken over by the LNER. It seems likely they were in unlined black.

2254 cont/.
Dar. 22/7/53.*Weigh.*
Dar. 11/10—10/11/55.**H/I.**
Dar. 2/5—7/6/57.**C/L.**
Dar. 29/9—30/10/58.**G.**
Dar. 9—15/12/59.**N/C.**
Dar. 2/4—4/5/62.**G.**
Dar. 16—23/5/62.**N/C.**

BOILERS:
  E4/2.
  D225 (*ex1293*) 24/2/27.
  2259 (*new*) 31/7/29.
  HL108 (*ex2220*) 21/11/35.
  2430 (*ex1252*) 16/5/39.
  2152 (*ex2284*) 26/12/41.
  2826 (*ex2275*) 7/9/44.
  2816 (*exB15 821*) 28/12/46.
  2657 (*ex3358*) 21/3/49.
  2657 reno.24196 30/6/51.
  24292 (*new*) 20/6/53 (50A).
  24270 30/10/58 (50A).
  24279 4/5/62 (50A).

SHEDS:
Carlisle.
West Hartlepool 29/3/39.
Stockton 16/10/39.
West Hartlepool 1/4/40.
Springhead 18/5/40.
Neville Hill 28/3/43.
Haverton Hill 19/6/43.
Newport 18/10/44.
Middlesbrough 7/11/48.
Thornaby 1/6/58.
Tyne Dock 2/12/62.

RENUMBERED:
  3411 15/9/46.
  63411 21/3/49.

CONDEMNED: 6/4/65.
Sold for scrap to G.Cohen,
Cargo Fleet, 6/65.

2255

Armstrong Whitworth 3.

To traffic 12/1919.

REPAIRS:
Ghd. 24/5—19/7/23.**G.**
Ghd. 29/7—26/10/26.**G.**
Dar. 7/11—22/12/28.**G.**
Dar. 19/8—6/10/31.**G.**
Dar. 30/5—27/6/34.**G.**
Dar. 20/4—25/5/37.**G.**
Dar. 1—25/5/40.**G.**
Dar. 28—30/5/40.**N/C.**
Dar. 14—24/7/41.**N/C.**
Dar. 11/5—24/6/42.**G.**
Dar. 1—24/8/44.**G.**
Dar. 6/3—26/4/47.**G.**
Dar. 13/7—5/9/50.**G.**

Dar. 4/3—11/4/53.**H/I.**
Dar. 27/6—12/9/56.**G.**
Dar. 29/1—3/3/62.**G.**
Dar. 9/12/63—16/1/64.**C/H.**

BOILERS:
  E4/3.
  AW44 (*ex2296*) 27/6/34.
  AW34 (*ex2228*) 25/5/37.
  2570 (*ex2290*) 25/5/40.
  HL103 (*ex2233*) 24/6/42.
  2430 (*ex1257*) 24/8/44.
  24152 (*ex3424*) 5/9/50 (50A).
  24279 12/9/56 (50A).
  24265 3/3/62 (50A).
  24167 16/1/64 (50A).

SHEDS:
Tyne Dock.
Stockton 24/12/24.
Springhead 27/11/30.
Dairycoates 4/12/30.
Blaydon 20/7/47.
Haverton Hill 16/6/57.
West Hartlepool 8/6/58.

RENUMBERED:
  3412 15/9/46.
  63412 5/9/50.

CONDEMNED: 11/7/66.
Sold for scrap to W. Willoughby,
Choppington, 8/66.

2256

Armstrong Whitworth 4.

To traffic 2/1920.

REPAIRS:
Dar. 1/10—18/12/24.**G.**
Dar. 23/8—15/11/27.**G.**
Dar. 11/2—28/3/30.**G.**
Dar. 14/1—10/2/33.**G.**
Dar. 29/5—11/7/35.**G.**
Dar. 21/6—28/10/37.**G.**
Dar. 28/8—17/10/39.**G.**
Dar. 28/5—30/6/42.**G.**
Dar. 6—24/6/44.**G.**
Ghd. 29/11—17/12/45.**L.**
Dar. 10/1—22/2/47.**G.**
Ghd. 17/11—3/12/48.**L.**
Dar. 30/3—28/4/50.**G.**
Ghd. 10/5—6/6/51.**C/H.**
Ghd. 7/4—1/5/52.**C/L.**
Dar. 16/12/52—17/1/53.**H/I.**
Ghd. 5—29/7/55.**N/C.**
Dar. 28/11—23/12/55.**G.**
Dar. 18/2—19/3/60.**G.**
Dar. 27/8—10/10/63.**H/I.**
Dar. 22—23/10/63.**N/C.**
Dar. 2/6/65.*Weigh.*

BOILERS:
  E4/4.
  D656 (*ex2241*) 28/3/30.
  HL985 (*ex2246*) 10/2/33.
  D935 (*exB15 823*) 11/7/35.
  HL112 (*exB15 788*) 28/10/37.
  HL111 (*ex1293*) 17/10/39.
  2570 (*ex1280*) 24/6/44.
  2819 (*ex3432*) 22/2/47.
  4059 (*new*) 28/4/50 (50A).
  4059 reno.24191 6/6/51.
  24285 23/12/55 (50A).
  24168 19/3/60 (50A).

SHEDS:
Darlington.
Newport ?/24.
Selby ?/25.
Newport 19/6/39.
Stockton 1/2/43.
Blaydon 5/10/47.
North Blyth 23/9/62.
Tyne Dock 9/1/66.

RENUMBERED:
  3413 15/9/46.
  63413 3/12/48.

CONDEMNED: 23/1/67.
Sold for scrap to Clayton &
Davie, Dunston, 17/3/67.

2257

Armstrong Whitworth 5.

To traffic 2/1920.

REPAIRS:
Ghd. ?/?—26/7/22.**G.**
Ghd. 20/2—29/5/25.**G.**
Ghd. 14/1—12/2/26.**L.**
Ghd. 9/6—9/7/26.**L.**
Ghd. 12/7—25/10/27.**G.**
Ghd. 19/2—27/3/30.**G.**
Ghd. 19—27/3/31.**N/C.**
Dar. 10/7—22/8/33.**G.**
Dar. 8/10—22/11/35.**G.**
Dar. 26/8—6/12/38.**G.**
Dar. 7—19/12/38.**N/C.**
Dar. 15/2—21/3/41.**N/C.**
Dar. 22/9—28/10/41.**G.**
Dar. 13/4—10/6/43.**G.**
Dar. 6/6—6/7/45.**G.**
Dar. 27/11—21/12/45.**L.**
Dar. 25/9—23/10/47.**G.**
Ghd. 31/5—3/7/50.**L/I.**
After derailment.
Dar. 17/11—6/12/52.**G.**
Dar. 9—16/12/52.**N/C.**
Dar. 18—22/12/52.**N/C.**
Dar. 23/2—20/3/56.**G.**
Dar. 26/3—6/4/56.**N/C.**
Dar. 5/9—3/10/59.**G.**

BOILERS:
  E4/5.
  HL986 (*new*) 27/3/30.
  2440 (*ex2245*) 22/11/35.
  2984 (*new*) 6/12/38 (50A).
  3017 (*ex2272*) 28/10/41 (50A).
  2850 (*ex2270*) 6/7/45.
  3297 (*ex3400*) 23/10/47 (50A).
  24243 6/12/52 (50A).
  24271 20/3/56 (50A).
  24321 (*new*) 3/10/59 (50A).

SHEDS:
Carlisle.
West Hartlepool 30/3/39.
Springhead 7/5/40.
Neville Hill 28/3/43.
Darlington 14/7/43.
Neville Hill 24/8/44.
West Hartlepool 4/5/47.

RENUMBERED:
  3414 25/8/46.
  63414 3/7/50.

CONDEMNED: 17/5/65.
Sold for scrap to Ellis Metals,
Swalwell, 6/65.

2258

Armstrong Whitworth 6.

To traffic 2/1920.

REPAIRS:
Ghd. 23/8—22/10/23.**G.**
Ghd. 2/12/27—12/3/28.**G.**
Ghd. 3/2—2/4/30.**H.**
Ghd. 27/8—30/9/31.**G.**
Dar. 15/10—15/11/34.**G.**
Dar. 26/8/37—22/1/38.**G.**
Dar. 24/1—7/2/38.**N/C.**
Dar. 8/7—4/8/40.**G.**
Dar. 3—15/7/41.**N/C.**
Dar. 17—31/7/41.**L.**
Dar. 28/10—26/11/42.**G.**
Ghd. 30/6—13/7/44.**L.**
Dar. 27/9—3/11/45.**G.**
Ghd. 8—23/10/46.**L.**
Dar. 13/4—14/5/48.**G.**
Dar. 15/1—8/2/51.**G.**
Dar. 24/4/53.**N/C.**
Ghd. 27/4—29/5/54.**G.**
Ghd. 2—10/6/54.**N/C.**
Ghd. 29/6—31/7/54.**C/L.**
Dar. 6—28/3/57.**G.**
Dar. 31/8—6/10/60.**G.**

BOILERS:
  E4/7.
  AW27 (*ex2279*) 15/11/34.
  2658 (*exB15 779*) 22/1/38.
  HL104 (*ex2263*) 4/8/40.
  D1940 (*ex2251*) 26/11/42.

2258 cont/.
3314 *(ex2251)* 3/11/45 (50A).
3147 *(ex3421)* 14/5/48 (50A).
24173 8/2/51.
24260 29/5/54 (50A).
24293 28/3/57 (50A).
24317 *(new)* 6/10/60 (50A).

SHEDS:
Blaydon.
Darlington 14/5/41.
Northallerton14/9/42.
Newport 28/3/43.
West Hartlepool 27/6/48.

RENUMBERED:
3415 23/10/46.
63415 14/5/48.

CONDEMNED: 15/4/64.
Sold for scrap to Arnott Young, Dinsdale, 6/64.

2259

Armstrong Whitworth 7.

To traffic 2/1920.

REPAIRS:
Ghd. ?/?—12/9/22.**G**.
Ghd. 14/10/24—5/1/25.**G**.
Ghd. 13/7—21/10/26.**H**.
Ghd. 7/12/28—24/1/29.**G**.
Ghd. 3/6—24/7/31.**G**.
Dar. 4/8—5/12/34.**G**.
Dar. 19/8—23/11/38.**G**.
Dar. 25/1—6/2/41.**L**.
Dar. 26/8—30/9/42.**G**.
Dar. 4—26/1/44.**L**.
Dar. 3/1—3/2/45.**G**.
Ghd. 26/3—9/4/46.**L**.
Dar. 30/6—21/8/47.**G**.
Ghd. 15—28/10/48.**L**.
Dar. 24/1—17/3/50.**G**.
Dar. 18/12/50—19/1/51.**C/L**.
Dar. 18/3—8/4/52.**G**.
Dar. 6—24/10/54.**G**.
Dar. 10/10/56.*Weigh*.
Dar. 11/3—5/4/57.**G**.
Dar. 22/1—25/2/60.**G**.
Dar. 2—27/8/62.**C/L**.
After collision.

BOILERS:
E4/6.
D703 *(ex2232)* 24/1/29.
AW19 *(ex2247)* 5/12/34.
2980 *(new)* 23/11/38 (50A).
3305 *(new)* 30/9/42 (50A).
HL112 *(ex3456)* 21/8/47.
2431 *(ex63454)* 17/3/50.
2431 reno.24175 19/1/51.
24216 8/4/52.
24185 24/10/54.

24306 *(new)* 5/4/57 (50A).
24152 25/2/60 (50A).

SHEDS:
Carlisle.
West Hartlepool 23/3/39.
Newport 3/9/42.
Stockton 4/12/43.
Haverton Hill 5/10/47.
Thornaby 14/6/59.

RENUMBERED:
3416 9/4/46.
63416 28/10/48.

CONDEMNED: 15/7/63.
Into Dar. for cut up 16/8/63.

2260

Armstrong Whitworth 8.

To traffic 2/1920.

REPAIRS:
Ghd. 14/12/22—8/3/23.**G**.
Ghd. 5—10/1/24.**L**.
Ghd. 18/2—10/6/27.**G**.
Ghd. 9—20/6/28.**L**.
Ghd. 4—22/1/29.**L**.
Ghd. 14/11/29—22/1/30.**G**.
Ghd. 29/4—6/5/31.**N/C**.
Dar. 21/9—10/10/32.**H**.
Dar. 8/8—10/10/34.**G**.
Dar. 21/4—7/6/37.**G**.
Dar. 21/5—15/6/40.**G**.
Dar. 5/9—9/10/42.**G**.
Dar. 10/6—1/7/44.**G**.
Ghd. 7—22/11/45.**L**.
Dar. 7/2—19/4/47.**G**.
Dar. 4/2—11/3/49.**G**.
Dar. 5—27/4/51.**H/I**.
Dar. 2—7/5/51.**N/C**.
Ghd. 20/6—30/8/51.**C/L**.
Dar. 20/4—9/5/53.**G**.
Dar. 11—18/1/55.**C/L**.
Dar. 3—30/6/55.**G**.
Ghd. 2/12/57—3/1/58.**G**.
Dar. 9—11/11/59.**C/L**.
Dar. 14—20/1/60.**N/C**.
Dar. 20/5—4/7/60.**C/L**.
Dar. 3/7—18/8/61.**G**.

BOILERS:
E4/8.
E4/46 *(ex2297)* 10/10/32.
E4/46 reno.46 10/10/34.
2386 *(ex2247)* 7/6/37.
3145 *(new)* 15/6/40 (50A).
3023 *(ex2269)* 1/7/44 (50A).
3162 *(ex3368)* 11/3/49 (50A).
3162 reno.24187 27/4/51.
24181 9/5/53 (50A).
24284 30/6/55 (50A).
24169 3/1/58 (50A).

24153 18/8/61 (50A).

SHEDS:
Blaydon.
Gateshead 7/11/31.
Blaydon 26/11/31.
Newport 28/3/43.
Middlesbrough 7/11/48.
Thornaby 1/6/58.
Neville Hill 16/12/62.

RENUMBERED:
3417 15/9/46.
63417 11/3/49.

CONDEMNED: 13/2/66.
Sold for scrap to T W Ward, Beighton, 4/66.

2261

Armstrong Whitworth 9.

To traffic 2/1920.

REPAIRS:
Ghd. 6/10/22—4/1/23.**G**.
Ghd. 6—19/9/23.**L**.
Ghd. 26/5—1/9/25.**G**.
Ghd. 22/5—14/6/27.**L**.
Ghd. 7—23/12/27.**L**.
Ghd. 11/9—5/11/28.**G**.
Ghd. 3/3—7/4/32.**G**.
Dar. 1—28/8/34.**G**.
Dar. 27/8—16/10/37.**G**.
Dar. 16/10—14/11/40.**G**.
Dar. 30/1—24/2/43.**G**.
Ghd. 20—30/6/44.**L**.
Dar. 8/2—9/3/46.**G**.
Ghd. 3—13/6/47.**L**.
Dar. 8/7—20/8/48.**G**.
Dar. 26/6—19/7/51.**G**.
Ghd. 7/7—22/8/53.**C/H**.
Ghd. 7—12/12/53.**N/C**.
Ghd. 9/8—7/10/54.**G**.
Dar. 28/5—2/6/56.**N/C**.
Ghd. 24/5—17/6/57.**G**.
Ghd. 7—8/11/57.**N/C**.
Dar. 30/12/60—11/2/61.**G**.
Dar. 6/2—11/3/63.**N/C**.

BOILERS:
E4/9.
2425 *(new)* 7/4/32.
3152 *(new)* 14/11/40 (50A).
2988 *(ex2216)* 24/2/43 (50A).
2985 *(ex1264)* 9/3/46 (50A).
3017 *(ex3373)* 20/8/48 (50A).
24194 19/7/51.
24155 7/10/54 (50A).
24185 17/5/57.
24328 *(new)* 11/2/61 (50A).

SHEDS:
Blaydon.

Borough Gardens 27/1/27.
Dairycoates 12/4/39.
York 6/1/40.
Neville Hill 28/3/43.
Consett 19/6/43.
Sunderland 6/5/62.

RENUMBERED:
3418 1/9/46.
63418 20/8/48.

CONDEMNED: 15/7/63.
Into Dar. for cut up 6/8/63.

2262

Armstrong Whitworth 10.

To traffic 2/1920.

REPAIRS:
Ghd. ?/?—19/10/22.**G**.
Ghd. 26/5—15/9/25.**G**.
Ghd. 20/3—15/5/29.**G**.
Dar. 16/6—2/8/33.**G**.
Dar. 12—26/10/34.**L**.
Dar. 13/5—17/6/35.**L**.
Dar. 19/1—26/2/37.**G**.
Dar. 20/9—27/11/39.**L**.
After collision.
Dar. 7/1—14/2/41.**G**
Dar. 14/10—11/11/43.**G**.
Dar. 3/1—22/3/47.**G**.
Dar. 15—24/6/48.**L**.
Dar. 13/7—31/8/49.**G**.
Dar. 10/6—5/7/52.**G**.
Dar. 12/3—2/4/55.**H/I**.
Dar. 4—5/4/55.**N/C**.
Ghd. 31/3—2/5/58.**G**.
Dar. 6/11—9/12/61.**H/I**.
Dar. 18—20/12/61.**N/C**.
Dar. 30/10—21/11/62.**C/H**.

BOILERS:
E4/10.
D957 *(ex2252)* 15/5/29.
E4/49 *(ex2245)* 2/8/33.
2157 *(ex2221)* 26/2/37.
2643 *(ex1251)* 14/2/41.
2563 *(ex2299)* 11/11/43.
3148 *(ex3422)* 31/8/49 (50A).
24282 *(new)* 5/7/52 (50A).
24267 2/5/58 (50A).
24273 21/11/62 (50A).

SHEDS:
Blaydon.
Dairycoates ?/2/37.
East Hartlepool 27/2/38.
West Hartlepool 17/4/39.
Newport 3/9/42.
West Hartlepool 12/5/48.

RENUMBERED:
3419 12/10/46.

(left) From September 1923 to February 1924 area suffix D was added to the number.

(below) From early February 1924 the suffix was discarded and from the June 1928 painting economies, so was the red lining. This July 1926 photograph shows the photographic difficulty then at being able to reproduce red.

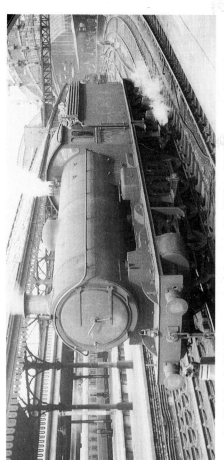

Although lining was dropped from June 1928, the number was still put on the tender to mid-March 1929, as shown by No.2255 ex-Darlington 22nd December 1928.

Ex-works 9th March 1946 from a general repair, No.2261 had LNER restored and it was not re-numbered until 1st September 1946.

No.2224 ex-Darlington on 13th March 1929 was the first to have its number moved to the cab and 12in. LNER on the tender. All acquired this style which was then standard until July 1942.

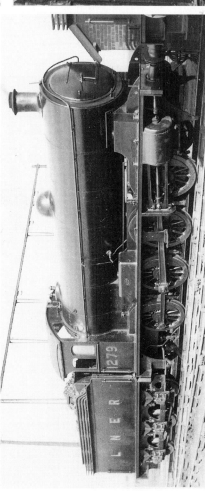

When stocks of the shaded transfers were exhausted, change to yellow painted and unshaded letters and figures was made. No.3394 was so painted ex-works 23rd November 1946. The style was Gill sans but with modified 9.

From July 1942 to January 1946 only NE was applied to the tender due to wartime shortage of manpower. From January 1946 the class became Nos.3340 to 3459 in order of building. No.2286 was changed to 3443 on Sunday 1st December 1946 at Newport shed.

At the end of the LNER, Q6 light repairs were usually done at Gateshead works. These engines did not get a repaint, but No.3384 done at Darlington and ex-works 23rd January 1948 did have regional prefix E added to its number although keeping LNER on its tender.

2262 cont/.
63419 24/6/48.

CONDEMNED: 7/6/65.
Sold for scrap to Ellis Metals,
Swalwell, 7/65.

2263

Armstrong Whitworth 11.

To traffic 3/1920.

REPAIRS:
Ghd. ?/?—8/11/22.**G.**
Ghd. 27/3—30/7/25.**G.**
Ghd. 21/6—10/11/27.**G.**
Ghd. 19/12/29—10/2/30.**G.**
Ghd. 8—26/4/30.**L.**
Ghd. 10/11—2/12/30.**L.**
Dar. 25/10—1/12/33.**G.**
Dar. 25/5—29/6/37.**G.**
Dar. 13/6—6/7/40.**G.**
Dar. 3/2—14/3/42.**G.**
Dar. 13/3—6/4/44.**G.**
Ghd. 8/7—2/8/45.**L.**
Dar. 12/9—19/10/46.**G.**
Dar. 15/11—3/12/48.**G.**
Dar. 13/2—10/3/51.**G.**
Dar. 12—14/3/51.**N/C.**
Dar. 9/2—7/3/53.**G.**
Dar. 9—11/3/53.**N/C.**
Dar. 19/4—14/5/55.**H/I.**
Dar. 21—26/5/55.**N/C.**
Dar. 28/9—14/11/56.**C/L.**
Dar. 20—28/11/56.**N/C.**
Dar. 15—21/8/57.**C/L.**
Dar. 6/5—20/6/58.**G.**
Dar. 16—23/12/59.**N/C.**
Dar. 24/2—4/4/62.**G.**
Dar. 7/5—3/6/65.**C/H.**

BOILERS:
E4/11.
HL983 *(new)* 10/2/30.
   E4/2 *(ex2302)* 1/12/33.
HL104 *(ex2239)* 29/6/37.
   2423 *(ex1285)* 6/7/40.
D1965 *(ex2285)* 14/3/42.
   2567 *(ex2266)* 6/4/44.
   2384 *(ex3341)* 19/10/46.
   2565 *(ex3398)* 3/12/48.
   24178 10/3/51.
   24248 7/3/53.
   24288 20/6/58 (50A).
   24217 4/4/62 (50A).
   24240 3/6/65 (50A).

SHEDS:
Tyne Dock.
Thornton Jct. 14/3/23.
Tyne Dock 3/5/23.
Newport 28/3/43.
Middlesbrough 7/11/48.
Thornaby 1/6/58.

Neville Hill 2/12/62.
Normanton 12/6/66.
Tyne Dock 2/10/66.

RENUMBERED:
   3420 19/10/46.
63420 3/12/48.

CONDEMNED: 5/2/67.
Sold for scrap to, Clayton &
Davie, Dunston, 4/67.

2264

Armstrong Whitworth 12.

To traffic 3/1920.

REPAIRS:
Ghd. 8/12/22—20/2/23.**G.**
Dar. 21/8—13/11/25.**G.**
Dar. 6/2—17/4/28.**G.**
Dar. 25/2—1/4/31.**G.**
Dar. 30/4—30/5/34.**G.**
Dar. 4/5—18/6/37.**G.**
Dar. 6/1—18/2/39.**L.**
Dar. 5/6—3/7/40.**G.**
Dar. 23/12/42—23/1/43.**G.**
Dar. 27/12/44—27/1/45.**G.**
Ghd. 14—30/5/46.**L.**
Dar. 30/12/47—6/2/48.**G.**
Dar. 1/2—3/3/50.**C/L.**
Dar. 2/10—4/11/50.**G.**
Dar. 9—11/11/50.**N/C.**
Ghd. 4—26/10/51.**C/L.**
After collision.
Dar. 16/12/53—9/1/54.**G.**
Ghd. 21/12/56—25/1/57.**G.**
Dar. 23—29/11/60.**N/C.**
Dar. 28/4—20/5/61.**G.**

BOILERS:
   E4/12.
D1568 *(exB15 782)* 1/4/31.
   D558 *(ex2213)* 30/5/34.
AW46 *(ex2260)* 18/6/37.
D1942 *(ex1283)* 3/7/40.
   3147 *(ex2227)* 23/1/43 (50A).
   3153 *(ex3452)* 6/2/48 (50A).
   24156 *(ex63390)* 4/11/50.
   24293 *(new)* 9/1/54 (50A).
   24153 25/1/57 (50A).
   24309 20/5/61 (50A).

SHEDS:
Tyne Dock.
Springhead 17/11/24.
Dairycoates 1/27.
Springhead 20/1/40.
Neville Hill 28/3/43.
Darlington 8/7/43.
West Hartlepool 5/3/45.

RENUMBERED:
   3421 30/5/46.

ᴇ**3421** 6/2/48.
63421 3/3/50.

CONDEMNED: 5/6/66.
Sold for scrap to Hughes,
Bolckow, Blyth, 7/66.

2265

Armstrong Whitworth 13.

To traffic 3/1920.

REPAIRS:
Ghd. 15/3—22/5/23.**G.**
Dar. 25/2—9/7/26.**G.**
Ghd. 25/5—26/7/28.**G.**
Dar. 10/9—23/9/29.**N/C.**
Dar. 28/2—7/4/30.**L.**
Dar. 5/8—29/9/30.**G.**
Dar. 8/8—13/9/33.**G.**
Dar. 22/8—3/10/35.**G.**
Dar. 20/10—22/12/38.**G.**
Dar. 21/3—5/4/40.**N/C.**
Dar. 25/8—24/9/40.**N/C.**
Dar. 8/4—9/5/41.**G.**
Dar. 7/5—19/6/43.**G.**
Ghd. 27/3—12/4/45.**L.**
Dar. 31/10—30/11/46.**G.**
Ghd. 10—26/3/48.**L.**
Dar. 23/6—2/8/49.**G.**
Dar. 10/7—16/8/52.**G.**
Dar. 18—20/8/52.**N/C.**
Dar. 22/11—16/12/55.**G.**
Dar. 22—29/3/56.**C/L.**
Dar. 1—22/4/59.**N/C.**

BOILERS:
   E4/13.
D855 *(ex2238)* 26/7/28.
E4/20 29/9/30.
E4/20 reno.20 3/10/35.
   2989 *(new)* 22/12/38 (50A).
   3004 *(ex2274)* 9/5/41 (50A).
   3148 *(ex3349)* 30/11/46 (50A).
   2567 *(ex63355)* 2/8/49.
   24226 16/8/52 (50A).
   24238 16/12/55 (50A).
   24184 26/3/59 (50A).

SHEDS:
Tyne Dock.
Borough Gardens 8/3/24.
Stockton 19/9/24.
Newport 9/6/30.
Neville Hill 11/9/44.
Newport 4/5/47.
West Hartlepool 7/9/47.

RENUMBERED:
   3422 8/9/46.
63422 2/8/49.

CONDEMNED: 18/5/64.
Into Dar. for cut up 29/7/64.

2266

Armstrong Whitworth 14.

To traffic 3/1920.

REPAIRS:
Ghd. 9/2—18/4/23.**G.**
Ghd. 8/10—30/12/25.**G.**
Ghd. 14/12/27—1/3/28.**G.**
Ghd. 31/7—20/8/29.**L.**
Ghd. 26/2—30/3/32.**G.**
Dar. 16/10—17/12/35.**G.**
Dar. 9/8—30/9/38.**G.**
Dar. 30/9—7/10/38.**N/C.**
Dar. 18/3—26/4/41.**G.**
Dar. 17/2—11/3/44.**G.**
Ghd. 3—30/8/45.**L.**
Dar. 22/8—14/9/46.**G.**
Ghd. 2—17/11/47.**L.**
Dar. 9—30/12/48.**G.**
Dar. 6—15/1/49.**N/C.**
Dar. 12/7—18/8/51.**G.**
Ghd. 29/2—24/3/52.**C/L.**
Dar. 3—31/12/53.**H/I.**
Dar. 13—22/1/54.**N/C.**
Ghd. 24/6—21/9/55.**N/C.**
Dar. 16/8—18/9/56.**G.**
Dar. 24/9—9/10/56.**N/C.**
Dar. 30/10—28/11/58.**G.**
Dar. 12—21/9/60.**N/C.**
Dar. 9/11/61.*Weigh.*
Dar. 6/7—29/8/62.**G.**
Dar. 10/11/64. *Not repaired.*

BOILERS:
   E4/14.
   D234 *(ex1293)* 1/3/28.
   2423 *(new)* 30/3/32.
   2259 *(ex2254)* 17/12/35.
   2440 *(ex2257)* 30/9/38.
   2567 *(ex2291)* 26/4/41.
   2383 *(ex2285)* 11/3/44.
   2569 *(ex2273)* 14/9/46.
   3851 *(new)* 30/12/48 (50A).
   24190 18/8/51 (50A).
   24273 18/9/56 (50A).
   24284 28/11/58 (50A).
   24300 29/8/62 (50A).

SHEDS:
Blaydon.
Newport 28/3/43.
Haverton Hill 13/2/49.
Selby 24/9/50.
Darlington 14/6/59.
Sunderland 18/8/63.

RENUMBERED:
   3423 14/9/46.
63423 30/12/48.

CONDEMNED: 16/11/64.
Cut up at Darlington.

2267

Armstrong Whitworth 15.

To traffic 3/1920.

REPAIRS:
Ghd. 9/2—20/4/23.**G.**
Ghd. 24/3—17/6/27.**G.**
Ghd. 16/5—4/7/30.**G.**
Dar. 19/4—15/5/34.**G.**
Dar. 17/12/36—28/1/37.**G.**
Dar. 5/9—11/10/39.**G.**
Dar. 1—29/4/42.**G.**
Dar. 11—22/2/43.**N/C.**
Dar. 11/1—22/2/45.**G.**
Dar. 6/8—12/9/47.**G.**
Dar. 3/5—15/6/50.**G.**
Dar. 23—26/6/50.**N/C.**
Dar. 27/11—19/12/53.**G.**
Dar. 21—24/12/53.**N/C.**
Ghd. 12/11—7/12/56.**G.**
Dar. 14—30/1/57.**N/C.**
Dar. 9/5—16/6/58.**C/L.**
Dar. 3—23/2/60.**N/C.**
Dar. 31/3—11/5/60.**G.**

BOILERS:
E4/15.
  E4/5 *(ex2257)* 4/7/30.
HL982 *(ex2230)* 15/5/34.
  2388 *(ex2251)* 28/1/37.
  2434 *(ex2224)* 29/4/42.
HL105 *(ex2288)* 22/2/45.
  3009 *(ex3429)* 12/9/47 (50A).
  3311 *(ex3408)* 15/6/50 (50A).
  24205 19/12/53 (50A).
  24190 7/12/56 (50A).
  24285 11/5/60 (50A).

SHEDS:
Blaydon.
Borough Gardens 2/3/27.
Darlington 18/4/35.
Neville Hill 14/12/37.
Darlington 26/6/43.
West Hartlepool 5/3/45.
Middlesbrough 14/8/55.
Thornaby 1/6/58.
Neville Hill 11/11/62.

RENUMBERED:
3424 15/9/46.
63424 15/6/50.

CONDEMNED: 13/1/64.
Into Dar. for cut up 6/2/64.

2268

Armstrong Whitworth 16.

To traffic 3/1920.

REPAIRS:
Ghd. ?/?—13/12/22.**G.**
Ghd. 25/5—25/8/25.**G.**
Ghd. 2/7—24/8/28.**G.**
Ghd. 31/12/30—3/2/31.**L.**
Ghd. 6/7—4/8/32.**G.**
Dar. 1/6—29/7/37.**G.**
Dar. 23/7—21/8/40.**G.**
Dar. 16/4—29/5/43.**G.**
Ghd. 10/8—17/9/45.**L.**
Dar. 5—27/4/46.**L.**
Dar. 27/12/46—22/2/47.**G.**
Dar. 12—15/3/47.**N/C.**
Dar. 10/11—6/12/49.**G.**
Dar. 15/4—3/5/52.**G.**
Dar. 9—13/5/52.**N/C.**
Dar. 8—23/9/53.**C/L.**
Dar. 3—30/9/54.**G.**
Dar. 8/1—1/2/57.**G.**
Dar. 19—22/2/57.**N/C.**
Dar. 19/10—18/11/59.**G.**

BOILERS:
E4/16.
  E4/13 *(ex2265)* 24/8/28.
  D930 *(ex1335)* 4/8/32.
HL106 *(ex1362)* 29/7/37.
  2874 *(ex2239)* 29/5/43.
  2826 *(ex3411)* 22/2/47.
  2992 *(ex63451)* 6/12/49 (50A).
  24220 3/5/52 (50A).
  24217 30/9/54 (50A).
  24168 1/2/57 (50A).
  24271 18/11/59 (50A).

SHEDS:
Carlisle.
Borough Gardens 12/24.
Tyne Dock 10/4/40.
Newport 28/3/43.
Haverton Hill 12/5/48.
Selby 24/9/50.
Tyne Dock 16/6/57.

RENUMBERED:
3425 27/4/46.
63425 6/12/49.

CONDEMNED: 15/4/63.
Into Dar. for cut up 30/4/63.

2269

Armstrong Whitworth 17.

To traffic 4/1920.

REPAIRS:
Ghd. 18/8—9/10/23.**G.**
Ghd. 16/2—13/5/27.**G.**
Ghd. 4/10—12/12/29.**G.**
Dar. 7/6—14/7/34.**G.**
Dar. 2/11—23/12/36.**G.**
Dar. 19—28/10/36.**N/C.**
Dar. 9/4—10/5/40.**G.**
Dar. 13—18/5/40.**N/C.**
Dar. 23/10—2/11/40.**L.**
Dar. 13—28/10/41.**N/C.**
Dar. 29/4—29/5/42.**G.**
Dar. 2—26/5/44.**G.**
Dar. 11/7—24/8/46.**G.**
Dar. 16/8—3/9/48.**G.**
Dar. 29/5—22/6/51.**G.**
Dar. 12/11—5/12/53.**G.**
Dar. 26/3—30/4/56.**G.**
Dar. 3—10/5/56.**N/C.**
Dar. 31/1—18/3/59.**G.**
Dar. 26—31/10/59.**N/C.**
Dar. 19/6—9/8/62.**G.**
Dar. 13—20/8/62.**N/C.**

BOILERS:
E4/17.
AW15 *(ex2300)* 14/7/34.
  2850 *(new)* 23/12/36.
  3138 *(new)* 10/5/40 (50A).
  3023 *(ex1247)* 29/5/42 (50A).
  3015 *(ex2225)* 26/5/44 (50A).
  2429 *(ex2291)* 24/8/46.
  2426 *(ex3389)* 3/9/48.
  24177 22/6/51 (50A).
  24182 5/12/53 (50A).
  24191 30/4/56 (50A).
  24257 18/3/59 (50A).
  24288 9/8/62 (50A).

SHEDS:
Blaydon.
Borough Gardens 7/11/31.
Blaydon 26/11/31.
Darlington 14/6/41.
Stockton 28/3/43.
Newport 13/4/47.
Thornaby 1/6/58.
Neville Hill 2/12/62.
Normanton 12/6/66.
Tyne Dock 2/10/66.

RENUMBERED:
3426 23/6/46.
63426 3/9/48.

CONDEMNED: 22/6/67.
Sold for scrap to Garnham,
Harris & Elton,Chesterfield, 8/67.

2270

Armstrong Whitworth 18.

To traffic 4/1920.

REPAIRS:
Dar. 26/10/22—29/1/23.**G.**
Dar. 28/7—30/10/24.**G.**
Dar. 24/5—9/9/27.**G.**
Dar. 15/7—21/8/29.**N/C.**
Dar. 15/3—7/5/30.**G.**
Dar. 13/4—12/5/34.**G.**
Dar. 28/4—14/9/36.**G.**
Dar. 6—19/1/39.**N/C.**
Dar. 8/11—14/12/39.**G.**
Dar. 7/5—2/6/42.**G.**
Dar. 9/2—8/3/45.**G.**
Ghd. 30/6—18/7/46.**L.**
Dar. 23/10—21/11/47.**G.**
Dar. 15/10—1/11/49.**C/L.**
Dar. 1/11—2/12/50.**G.**
Dar. 4—6/12/50.**N/C.**
Dar. 9—22/3/51.**N/C.**
Dar. 3/12/51—3/1/52.**C/H.**
Dar. 30/6—8/8/53.**G.**
Dar. 10—13/8/53.**N/C.**
Dar. 31/12/54—7/1/55.**N/C.**
Ghd. 20/7—12/8/55.**C/L.**
After collision.
Ghd. 7/11—8/12/55.**C/L.**
Dar. 10/10—6/11/56.**G.**
Dar. 11—17/9/59.**C/L.**
Dar. 6/11—16/12/59.**C/L.**
Dar. 29/12/60—4/2/61.**G.**
Dar. 12/8—13/9/63.**C/L.**

BOILERS:
E4/18.
  D658 *(ex2246)* 7/5/30.
  E4/12 *(ex2251)* 12/5/34.
  2816 *(new)* 14/9/36.
  2850 *(ex2229)* 2/6/42.
  3317 *(ex2295)* 8/3/45 (50A).
  3008 *(ex3382)* 21/11/47 (50A).
  24162 *(ex3452)* 2/12/50.
  24153 8/8/53 (50A).
  24179 6/11/56 (50A).
  24296 4/2/61 (50A).

SHEDS:
Dairycoates.
West Hartlepool 5/3/45.
Consett 1/1/51.
North Blyth 23/5/65.

RENUMBERED:
3427 18/7/46.
63427 1/11/49.

CONDEMNED: 14/6/65.
Sold for scrap to Ellis Metals,
Swalwell, 7/65.

2271

Armstrong Whitworth 19.

To traffic 4/1920.

REPAIRS:
Ghd. 6/12/22—26/2/23.**G.**
Ghd. 31/3—13/8/26.**G.**
Ghd. 23/5—1/8/29.**G.**
Ghd. 21/5—17/6/31.**N/C.**
Ghd. 29/12/31—15/2/32.**L.**
Ghd. 8—26/9/32.**H.**
Dar. 6/6—12/7/34.**G.**
Dar. 15/12/37—11/2/38.**G.**
Dar. 23/7—28/8/40.**G.**
Dar. 8/8—9/9/42.**G.**
Dar. 30/10—25/11/44.**G.**
Dar. 10/1—7/2/46.**L.**
Ghd. 4—19/3/46.**L.**
Dar. 17/4—24/5/47.**G.**
Dar. 14/9—14/10/50.**G.**
Dar. 16—18/10/50.**N/C.**
Dar. 24/6—17/7/54.**G.**
Dar. 19—22/7/54.**N/C.**
Dar. 27/1—28/2/58.**G.**
Dar. 14—22/1/60.**N/C.**
Dar. 24/7—4/10/61.**C/H.**

BOILERS:
E4/19.
2258 *(new)* 1/8/29.
2437 *(ex2245)* 11/2/38.
2638 *(ex2273)* 25/11/44.
2818 *(ex3447)* 24/5/47.
24155 *(ex3446)* 14/10/50 (50A).
24170 17/7/54.
24249 28/2/58 (50A).

SHEDS:
Carlisle.
Blaydon 1/7/24.
Borough Gardens 7/11/31.
Blaydon 26/11/31.
Stockton 14/6/41.
Blaydon 5/10/47.
North Blyth 1/7/56.
Newport 29/9/57.
Thornaby 1/6/58.

RENUMBERED:
3428 19/3/46.
63428 14/10/50.

CONDEMNED: 29/4/63.
Into Dar. for cut up 15/5/63.

2272

Armstrong Whitworth 20.

To traffic 5/1920.

REPAIRS:
Dar. 6/11/22—30/1/23.**G.**

Dar. 18/6—25/9/25.**G.**
Dar. 23/5—18/7/28.**G.**
Dar. 18/2—31/3/30.**G.**
Dar. 21/5—21/6/30.**L.**
Dar. 9/1—8/2/33.**G.**
Dar. 22/1—7/4/36.**G.**
Dar. 26/7—6/9/39.**G.**
Dar. 6—13/9/39.**N/C.**
Dar. 25/8—23/9/41.**G.**
Dar. 2/9—14/10/43.**G.**
Ghd. 31/1—19/2/46.**L.**
Dar. 2/7—30/8/47.**G.**
Ghd. 13—29/12/48.**L.**
Dar. 19/5—13/7/49.**G.**
Ghd. 18/2—3/3/50.**C/L.**
Dar. 7—31/8/51.**G.**
Dar. 2—13/9/52.**C/L.**
Dar. 28/11—31/12/53.**G.**
Ghd. 23/4—25/5/56.**G.**
Dar. 22/6—7/8/59.**G.**
Dar. 17—27/8/59.**N/C.**
Dar. 1—10/9/59.**N/C.**
Dar. 1/2—9/3/61.**C/L.**
Dar. 28/8—4/10/63.**G.**
Dar. 11—25/10/63.**N/C.**

BOILERS:
E4/20.
D239 *(exB15 824)* 25/9/25.
HL987 *(new)* 31/3/30.
D670 *(ex2241)* 8/2/33.
2565 *(ex2274)* 7/4/36.
3017 *(new)* 6/9/39 (50A).
3009 *(ex2302)* 23/9/41 (50A).
2394 *(ex3371)* 30/8/47.
3161 *(ex63459)* 13/7/49 (50A).
24189 31/8/51 (50A).
24166 31/12/53.
24253 25/5/56.
24213 7/8/59 (50A).
24236 4/10/63 (50A).

SHEDS:
Dairycoates.
Tyne Dock 29/7/39.
Blaydon 15/2/41.
Newport 28/3/43.
Neville Hill 12/9/44.
Selby 5/10/47.
Tyne Dock 13/9/59.
Blaydon 19/3/61.
North Blyth 24/2/63.
Tyne Dock 9/1/66.

RENUMBERED:
3429 25/8/46.
63429 29/12/48.

CONDEMNED: 1/7/67.
Sold for scrap to Clayton &
Davie, Dunston, 9/67.

2273

Armstrong Whitworth 21.

To traffic 5/1920.

REPAIRS:
Dar. 4/11/24—27/1/25.**G.**
Dar. 21/12/26—16/3/27.**G.**
Dar. 10/6—13/8/29.**G.**
Dar. 23/6—4/8/32.**G.**
Rail washing gear fitted.
Dar. 8/8—10/9/35.**G.**
Dar. 9/8—30/9/38.**G.**
Dar. 24/6—1/8/40.**G.**
Dar. 16/9—13/10/42.**G.**
Dar. 16/10—2/12/44.**G.**
Dar. 26/6—9/8/46.**G.**
Ghd. 20/11—16/12/47.**L.**
Dar. 11/3—2/4/49.**G.**
Dar. 7—28/9/51.**G.**
Dar. 18/3—13/4/54.**G.**
Dar. 16/2—9/4/56.**G.**
Dar. 6/1/58.*Weigh.*
Ghd. 4/11—19/12/58.**G.**
Dar. 25/11—3/12/59.**N/C.**

BOILERS:
E4/21.
E4/45 *(ex2297)* 16/3/27.
E4/28 *(ex2280)* 13/8/29.
D1942 *(exB15 820)* 4/8/32.
2149 *(ex2288)* 10/9/35.
AW19 *(ex2259)* 30/9/38.
AW46 *(ex2264)* 1/8/40.
2638 *(ex2242)* 13/10/42.
2569 *(ex1285)* 2/12/44.
2817 *(ex2252)* 9/8/46.
2815 *(ex3401)* 2/4/49.
24200 28/9/51.
24259 13/4/54.
24302 *(new)* 9/4/56 (50A).
24292 19/12/58 (50A).

SHEDS:
Selby.
Dairycoates 18/11/29.
Newport 21/5/36.
West Hartlepool 5/12/48.
Newport 13/11/49.
Thornaby 1/6/58.

RENUMBERED:
3430 9/8/46.
63430 2/4/49.

CONDEMNED: 29/4/63.
Into Dar. for cut up 29/4/63.

2274

Armstrong Whitworth 22.

To traffic 5/1920.

REPAIRS:
Dar. 25/1—16/4/23.**G.**
Dar. 27/7—16/10/25.**G.**
Dar. 24/5—13/7/28.**G.**
Dar. 18/2—26/3/31.**G.**
Dar. 13/3—11/4/34.**G.**
Dar. 10/3—27/6/36.**G.**
Dar. 21/1—24/2/39.**G.**
Dar. 4/3—3/4/41.**G.**
Dar. 20/4—22/5/42.**L.**
Dar. 1/9—1/10/43.**G.**
Dar. 25/10—30/11/46.**G.**
Dar. 13—20/2/48.**N/C.**
Dar. 30/10—19/11/48.**G.**
Dar. 24/4—19/5/51.**G.**
Dar. 18/12/51—14/1/52.**C/L.**
Ghd. 23/1—14/2/53.**C/L.**
Dar. 24/6—18/7/53.**H/I.**
Dar. 4—12/8/53.**N/C.**
Dar. 17—24/8/53.**N/C.**
Ghd. 12/12/55—13/1/56.**G.**
Dar. 3/9—2/10/59.**G.**
Dar. 18/3—16/4/63.**G.**
Dar. 2—10/5/63.**N/C.**
Dar. 15—21/5/63.**N/C.**

BOILERS:
E4/22.
D699 *(exB15 813)* 13/7/28.
2565 *(new)* 11/4/34.
D806 *(ex2278)* 27/6/36.
3004 *(new)* 24/2/39 (50A).
3161 *(new)* 3/4/41 (50A).
3143 *(ex3438)* 30/11/46 (50A).
2985 *(ex3418)* 19/11/48 (50A).
24271 *(new)* 19/5/51 (50A).
24277 13/1/56 (50A).
24150 2/10/59 (50A).
24201 16/4/63 (50A).

SHEDS:
Stockton.
Newport 9/6/30.
Borough Gardens 9/5/41.
Neville Hill 28/3/43.
Stockton 19/6/43.
Newport 20/9/44.
West Hartlepool 5/12/48.
Newport 12/12/48.
Dairycoates 4/9/49.
Selby 20/11/49.
Borough Gardens 27/1/52.
Blaydon 14/6/59.
Tyne Dock 24/2/63.
West Hartlepool 2/7/67.

RENUMBERED:
3431 8/9/46.
63431 19/11/48.

CONDEMNED: 7/8/67.
Sold for scrap to Hughes,
Bolckow, Blyth, 9/67.

Whilst the prefix was in use, Darlington repaired and repainted ten Q6. Although they got 12in. number, only 6in. letters were used for **BRITISH RAILWAYS** on the tender, these ten, all in 1948 were: February - E3373 (6th), E3421(6th), E3353 (13th), E3370 (20th), E3396 (27th), E3404 (27th); March - E3342 (5th), E3375 (5th), E3443 (19th), E3405 (31st).

From March 1948 full BR number was used, and from light repairs it was usual to apply it but leave LNER on the tender. No.63449 was ex-Gateshead on 23rd August 1948, figures have now become 10in. but still include modified 6 and 9.

By August 1948 Darlington had settled into the standard style of matching 10in. figures and letters, with 6 and 9 in correct Gill sans. 63418 was ex-works 20th August. This style was then used for another year. Some Q6's e.g. 63385 (*see* page 50) never had this style, going straight from LNER to emblem (2nd December 1950).

2275

Armstrong Whitworth 23.

To traffic 5/1920.

REPAIRS:
Ghd. 30/5—10/8/23.**G.**
Ghd. 14/7—15/10/25.**G.**
Ghd. 10/1—21/3/29.**G.**
Ghd. 28/4—3/6/32.**G.**
Dar. 23/9—16/12/36.**G.**
Dar. 7—13/10/38.**N/C.**
Dar. 21/2—20/3/40.**G.**
Dar. 1/7—21/8/42.**G.**
Dar. 8/10—6/11/43.**L.**
Dar. 8/7—17/8/44.**G.**
Dar. 7/12/46—8/2/47.**G.**
Ghd. 13—30/1/50.**C/L.**
Dar. 8/6—4/8/50.**G.**
Dar. 5—22/11/52.**H/I.**
Dar. 24/11—1/12/52.**N/C.**
Ghd. 22/2—25/3/55.**C/H.**
After collision.
Dar. 28/5—13/8/56.**G.**
Dar. 26/8—19/10/60.**G.**

BOILERS:
E4/23.
    E4/6 *(ex2259)* 21/3/29.
    E4/9 3/6/32.
    2826 *(new)* 16/12/36.
    2819 *(ex2236)* 17/8/44.
    2582 *(exB15 787)* 8/2/47.
    2890 *(ex3371)* 4/8/50.
    2890 *reno.24247* 22/11/52.
    24256 13/8/56 (50A).
    24313 19/10/60 (50A).

SHEDS:
Tyne Dock.
West Hartlepool 5/1/40.
Springhead 10/5/41.
Dairycoates 28/3/43.
Blaydon 27/7/47.
Newport 15/9/57.
Selby 27/10/57.
Stockton 8/6/58.
Haverton Hill 12/10/58.
Thornaby 14/6/59.
West Hartlepool 8/4/62.

RENUMBERED:
    3432 27/10/46.
63432 4/8/50.

CONDEMNED: 17/5/65.
Sold for scrap to M.Baum,
Middlesbrough, 6/65.

2276

Armstrong Whitworth 24.

To traffic 5/1920.

REPAIRS:
Ghd. 9/1—13/3/23.**G.**
Ghd. 12/11/25—17/2/26.**G.**
Ghd. 21/2—6/5/29.**G.**
Ghd. 22/6—5/7/29.**N/C.**
Ghd. 4/8—8/10/31.**H.**
Dar. 10/5—13/6/34.**G.**
Dar. 22/3—5/5/38.**G.**
Dar. 12/11—5/12/40.**G.**
Dar. 12/12/42—11/1/43.**G.**
Dar. 23/6—6/7/43.**L.**
Ghd. 13/7—10/8/44.**L.**
Dar. 25/2—6/4/46.**G.**
Dar. 16—26/4/47.**L.**
Ghd. 19/9—2/10/47.**L.**
Dar. 12/3—2/4/49.**G.**
Dar. 5—14/4/49.**N/C.**
Dar. 10/5—9/6/51.**G.**
Dar. 11—12/6/51.**N/C.**
Dar. 9—13/7/51.**C/L.**
Ghd. 3/3—1/4/53.**C/L.**
Dar. 21/9—18/10/54.**G.**
Dar. 16/12/57—17/1/58.**G.**
Dar. 31/1—6/2/58.**N/C.**
Dar. 7/6—8/7/60.**G.**
Dar. 22/7—20/9/60.**N/C.**

BOILERS:
E4/24.
    E4/23 *(ex2275)* 6/5/29.
    D845 *(ex2289)* 13/6/34.
    2425 *(ex2261)* 5/12/40.
    D1939 *(exB15 820)* 11/1/43.
    2435 *(ex1252)* 6/4/46.
    2653 *(ex3352)* 2/4/49.
    24185 9/6/51.
    24295 *(new)* 18/10/54 (50A).
    24313 *(new)* 17/1/58 (50A).
    24190 8/7/60 (50A).

SHEDS:
Tyne Dock.
Consett 5/5/41.
Sunderland 8/9/63.

RENUMBERED:
    3433 6/4/46.
63433 2/4/49.

CONDEMNED: 30/9/63.
Into Dar. for cut up 7/10/63.

2277

Armstrong Whitworth 25.

To traffic 5/1920.

REPAIRS:
Dar. 15/12/22—28/3/23.**G.**
Dar. 11/9—27/11/25.**G.**
Ghd. 16/3—14/7/27.**G.**
Ghd. 16/5—3/7/30.**G.**
Dar. 1/5—11/6/35.**G.**
Dar. 27/1—29/6/36.**H.**
Dar. 30/8—15/9/38.**N/C.**
Dar. 28/6—4/12/39.**H.**
Dar. 2/9—5/10/40.**G.**
Dar. 2—22/4/42.**L.**
Dar. 7/7—20/8/43.**G.**
Dar. 18/1—15/3/47.**G.**
Dar. 27/3—3/4/47.**N/C.**
Dar. 15—19/4/47.**N/C.**
Ghd. 10—19/8/48.**L.**
Dar. 21/12/49—20/1/50.**G.**
Dar. 8/7—9/8/52.**G.**
Dar. 11—14/8/52.**N/C.**
Ghd. 15/6—6/7/53.**C/L.**
Ghd. 14/9—10/10/53.**C/L.**
Dar. 5/11—3/12/55.**H/I.**
Dar. 12/8—11/9/59.**G.**
Dar. 6/7—30/8/60.**C/L.**
Dar. 8/9—8/11/60.**C/L.**

BOILERS:
E4/25.
    E4/20 *(ex2272)* 27/11/25.
    E4/2 *(ex2254)* 14/7/27.
    D906 *(ex2243)* 3/7/30.
    D504 *(ex2253)* 11/6/35.
    AW12 *(ex2270)* 29/6/36.
    HL112 *(ex2256)* 4/12/39.
    2387 *(ex1288)* 20/8/43.
    2812 *(ex2287)* 15/3/47.
    2826 *(ex3425)* 20/1/50.
    24228 9/8/52.
    24314 11/9/59 (50A).

SHEDS:
Springhead.
Tyne Dock 1/2/27.
Borough Gardens 28/3/43.
Blaydon 14/6/59.
North Blyth 24/2/63.

RENUMBERED:
    3434 13/5/46.
63434 19/8/48.

CONDEMNED: 25/9/63.
Into Dar. for cut up 10/10/63.

2278

Armstrong Whitworth 26.

To traffic 5/1920.

REPAIRS:
Dar. 1/7—3/10/24.**G.**
Dar. 14/9—14/12/27.**G.**
Dar. 14/10—21/11/30.**G.**
Dar. 18/8—18/9/33.**G.**
Dar. 22/4—25/9/36.**G.**
Dar. 4—19/1/39.**N/C.**
Dar. 3/2—4/3/40.**G.**
Dar. 18/3—18/4/42.**G.**
Dar. 25/6—13/7/43.**L.**
Dar. 22/2—17/3/45.**G.**
Ghd. 31/5—18/6/46.**L.**
Dar. 26/11—10/12/46.**L.**
Dar. 30/9—23/10/47.**G.**
Dar. 4/7—26/8/50.**G.**
Dar. 14—18/9/50.**N/C.**
Dar. 24—26/5/52.**N/C.**
Dar. 26/3—25/4/53.**G.**
Dar. 28—29/4/53.**N/C.**
Dar. 28/7—9/9/55.**G.**
Dar. 2/5—10/6/58.**G.**
Dar. 15—21/12/59.**N/C.**
Dar. 2—15/9/60.**N/C.**
Dar. 2/11—2/12/61.**G.**
Dar. 29/4/65.Weigh.

BOILERS:
E4/26.
    E4/33 *(ex2284)* 21/11/30.
    D806 *(exB15 788)* 18/9/33.
    2818 *(new)* 25/9/36.
    2813 *(ex2249)* 4/3/40.
    2876 *(ex2226)* 18/4/42.
    HL107 *(ex2247)* 17/3/45.
    2875 *(exB15 1693)* 23/10/47.
    24150 26/8/50 (50A).
    24254 25/4/53 (50A).
    24299 *(new)* 9/9/55 (50A).
    24220 10/6/58 (50A).
    24312 2/12/61 (50A).

SHEDS:
Dairycoates.
Cudworth 20/3/44.
Dairycoates 13/5/44.
West Hartlepool 5/3/45.
Middlesbrough 14/9/52.
Thornaby 1/6/58.
West Hartlepool 23/6/63.

RENUMBERED:
    3435 18/6/46.
63435 26/8/50.

CONDEMNED: 5/6/66.
Sold for scrap to Hughes
Bolckow, Blyth, 7/66.

WORKS CODES:- Cw - Cowlairs. Dar- Darlington. Don - Doncaster. Ghd - Gateshead. Gor - Gorton. Hsi - Hull Springhead. Inv - Inverurie. Str - Stratford.
REPAIR CODES:- **C/H** - Casual Heavy. **C/L** - Casual Light. **G** - General. **H** - Heavy. **H/I** - Heavy Intermediate. **L** - Light. **L/I** - Light Intermediate. **N/C** - Non-Classified.

2279

Armstrong Whitworth 27.

To traffic 6/1920.

REPAIRS:
Ghd. 25/5—1/8/23.**G.**
Ghd. 3/8—15/10/25.**G.**
Ghd. 3/7—31/8/28.**G.**
Ghd. 1/10—5/11/31.**G.**
Dar. 2/11—19/12/32.**H.**
Dar. 28/8—25/9/34.**G.**
Dar. 7/9—17/12/38.**G.**
Dar. 30/4—7/6/41.**G.**
Dar. 9—16/6/41.**N/C.**
Dar. 30/11—31/12/43.**G.**
Ghd. 3—18/1/46.**L.**
Dar. 28/3—17/5/47.**G.**
Ghd. 9—26/1/49.**L.**
Dar. 6/12/49—6/1/50.**G.**
Dar. 3—20/7/51.**C/L.**
Dar. 15/10—10/11/51.**C/L.**
Dar. 11—27/3/52.**G.**
Dar. 10/9—2/10/54.**H/I.**
Dar. 15/11—22/12/55.**C/L.**
Dar. 12—26/9/57.**N/C.**
Dar. 19/12/57—16/1/58.**G.**
Dar. 21/9—20/10/61.**G.**

BOILERS:
E4/27.
 AW3 *(ex2255)* 25/9/34.
 2985 *(new)* 17/12/38 (50A).
 2989 *(ex2265)* 7/6/41 (50A).
 2999 *(ex1250)* 31/12/43 (50A).
 2656 *(ex63387)* 6/1/50.
 2656 reno.24198 20/7/51.
 24224 27/3/52 (50A).
 24219 16/1/58 (50A).
 24260 20/10/61 (50A).

SHEDS:
Borough Gardens.
Blaydon 29/3/41.
Newport 28/3/43.
Neville Hill 12/9/44.
Selby 5/10/47.
Neville Hill 25/1/53.
Selby 16/6/57.
York 13/9/59.
Neville Hill 6/12/59.
Sunderland 13/10/63.

RENUMBERED:
 3436 25/8/46.
 63436 21/1/49.

CONDEMNED: 24/4/67.
*Sold for scrap to Hughes
Bolckow, Blyth, 7/67.*

2280

Armstrong Whitworth 28.

To traffic 6/1920.

REPAIRS:
Dar. 18/5—25/7/23.**G.**
Dar. 28/12/25—16/4/26.**G.**
Dar. 26/3—16/5/29.**G.**
Dar. 12/9—19/10/32.**G.**
Dar. 29/3—12/7/34.**H.**
Dar. 12/3—9/4/35.**G.**
Dar. 21/5—19/8/37.**G.**
Dar. 27/12/39—29/1/40.**G.**
Dar. 22/3—7/5/41.**N/C.**
Dar. 17/9—27/10/42.**G.**
Dar. 16/3—27/4/44.**L.**
Dar. 31/1—3/3/45.**G.**
Dar. 23/8—22/9/45.**L.**
Dar. 24/9—2/10/45.**N/C.**
Ghd. 26/5—7/6/46.**L.**
Dar. 12—21/8/46.**N/C.**
Dar. 20/8—27/9/47.**G.**
Dar. 28/11/50—6/1/51.**G.**
Dar. 16/2—13/3/54.**G.**
Dar. 22—26/3/54.**N/C.**
Dar. 31/7—18/9/57.**C/L.**
Ghd. 8/4—9/5/58.**G.**
Dar. 14/5—14/6/62.**G.**
Dar. 5/3/64.*Weigh.*
Dar. 28—30/4/64.**N/C.**
Dar. 25/6/64.*Weigh.*
Dar. 21—23/10/64.**N/C.**

BOILERS:
E4/28.
 E4/47 *(ex2299)* 16/5/29.
 E4/37 *(ex2229)* 19/10/32.
 E4/37 reno.37 19/8/37.
 3310 *(new)* 27/10/42 (50A).
 3298 *(ex2243)* 3/3/45 (50A).
 2576 *(ex3363)* 27/9/47.
 2576 reno.24171 6/1/51.
 24160 13/3/54 (50A).
 24283 9/5/58 (50A).
 24299 14/6/62 (50A).

SHEDS:
Neville Hill.
Starbeck 6/5/31.
Neville Hill 28/3/43.
Stockton 23/6/43.
Blaydon 5/10/47.
Dairycoates 4/9/49.
Tyne Dock 1/12/49.
Consett 13/12/59.
Blaydon 11/9/60.
Sunderland 16/6/63.

RENUMBERED:
 3437 7/6/46.
 63437 6/1/51.

CONDEMNED: 5/6/67.
*Sold for scrap to Hughes
Bolckow, Blyth, 8/67.*

2281

Armstrong Whitworth 29.

To traffic 6/1920.

REPAIRS:
Ghd. ?/?—14/12/22.**?.**
Ghd. 13—31/3/25.**L.**
Ghd. 4/11/25—14/1/26.**G.**
Ghd. 15/10—23/11/28.**G.**
Ghd. 7—20/5/31.**N/C.**
Ghd. 18/6—28/8/31.**H.**
Dar. 3/8—6/9/33.**G.**
Dar. 23/9—10/11/37.**G.**
Dar. 6/5—8/6/40.**G.**
Dar. 8/7—16/8/40.**N/C.**
Dar. 23/1—1/3/43.**G.**
Dar. 4—21/8/43.**L.**
Ghd. 9—24/4/45.**L.**
Dar. 8/10—2/11/46.**G.**
Dar. 3—26/11/48.**G.**
Dar. 30/11—8/12/48.**N/C.**
Dar. 12/12/51—10/1/52.**G.**
Dar. 18/12/54—15/1/55.**H/I.**
Dar. 8—31/8/57.**G.**
Dar. 2—3/9/57.**N/C.**
Dar. 10—19/9/57.**N/C.**
Dar. 6/12/60—26/1/61.**C/H.**
Dar. 27/1—26/2/62.**G.**

BOILERS:
E4/29.
 E4/36 *(ex2288)* 23/11/28.
 D957 *(ex2262)* 6/9/33.
 3143 *(new)* 8/6/40 (50A).
 3157 *(ex3344)* 2/11/46 (50A).
 3321 *(ex3361)* 26/11/48 (50A).
 24212 10/1/52 (50A).
 24281 31/8/57 (50A).
 24187 26/2/62 (50A).

SHEDS:
Carlisle.
Blaydon 1/7/24.
Stockton 14/6/41.
Newport 23/9/44.
West Hartlepool 12/12/48.

RENUMBERED:
 3438 8/9/46.
 63438 26/11/48.

CONDEMNED: 12/11/64.
Into Dar. for cut up 23/11/64.

2282

Armstrong Whitworth 30.

To traffic 6/1920.

REPAIRS:
Dar. 15/5—12/8/24.**G.**
Dar. 3/12/27—17/2/28.**G.**
Dar. 3/2—8/3/32.**G.**
Dar. 23/5—16/6/34.**G.**
Dar. 29/7—10/9/37.**G.**
Dar. 12/3—11/4/40.**G.**
Dar. 20—22/5/40.**N/C.**
Dar. 4—17/7/40.**N/C.**
Dar. 27/6—13/8/42.**G.**
Dar. 12/7—18/8/44.**G.**
Dar. 23/8—6/9/44.**N/C.**
Ghd. 18/3—4/4/46.**L.**
Dar. 17/12/47—16/1/48.**G.**
Dar. 11/8—16/9/50.**G.**
Dar. 18—20/9/50.**N/C.**
Dar. 7—30/5/53.**G.**
Dar. 3—5/6/53.**N/C.**
Dar. 15—20/6/53.**N/C.**
Dar. 21/1—16/3/55.**C/L.**
Dar. 23/3—7/4/55.**N/C.**
Dar. 15—28/4/55.**N/C.**
Dar. 6/5—3/6/55.**C/H.**
Dar. 24/12/56—18/1/57.**G.**
Dar. 3/6—8/7/59.**C/H.**
Dar. 9/8—6/9/61.**G.**
Dar. 9—24/5/63.**N/C.**

BOILERS:
E4/30.
 2426 *(new)* 8/3/32.
 2816 *(ex2270)* 13/8/42.
 3141 *(ex2290)* 18/8/44 (50A).
 3843 *(new)* 16/1/48 (50A).
 3843 reno.24153 16/9/50.
 24176 30/5/53.
 24198 3/6/55.
 24304 *(new)* 18/1/57 (50A).
 24278 6/9/61 (50A).

SHEDS:
Neville Hill.
Darlington 14/7/43.
Consett 18/10/43.

RENUMBERED:
 3439 4/4/46.
 63439 16/9/50.

CONDEMNED: 7/4/64.
*Sold for scrap to Arnott Young,
Dinsdale, 6/64.*

2283

Armstrong Whitworth 31.

To Traffic 6/1920.

REPAIRS:
Dar. 11/4—30/6/23.**G.**
Dar. 30/7—28/10/25.**G.**
Dar. 17/3—15/5/28.**G.**
Dar. 28/7—24/9/30.**G.**

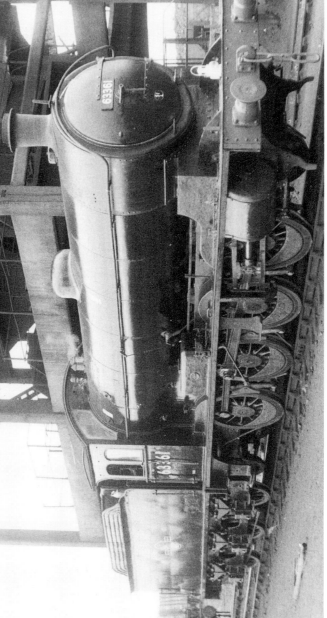

(above) From late September 1949, tender lettering ceased and the BR emblem was put on, all Q6 getting the larger (28in.) size. Note handing to face forward.

(left) From 11th June 1948 engines from Darlington works had cast iron smokebox number plates put on, Nos.63345 and 63389 being the first Q6 to get them. Until at least the end of August plates were cast with modified 6 and 9 on them. 63361 so fitted was out 26th August but from 3rd September 1948, on 63426 the correct Gill sans 6 and 9 were used.

2283 cont/.
Dar. 4/4—15/5/33.**G.**
Dar. 24/7—11/9/36.**G.**
Dar. 29/11/38—11/1/39.**G.**
Dar. 2/6—10/7/41.**G.**
Dar. 13/4—22/5/43.**G.**
Ghd. 8—27/3/45.**L.**
Dar. 31/8—28/9/46.**G.**
Ghd. 23/2—11/3/48.**L.**
Dar. 19/4—12/5/49.**G.**
Dar. 23/5—7/6/49.**N/C.**
Dar 28/11—22/12/51.**G.**
Ghd. 21/12/53—16/1/54.**C/L.**
Dar. 18/11—18/12/54.**G.**
Dar. 7—25/1/55.**N/C.**
Ghd. 21/5—21/6/57.**G.**
Dar. 4—7/8/59.**C/L.**
Dar. 10/2—11/3/61.**C/L.**
Dar. 17/8/61.*Weigh.*
Dar. 18/9—23/10/62.**G.**
Dar. 9—20/11/62.**N/C.**
Dar. 26/3/64.*Weigh.*

BOILERS:
E4/31.
D598 *(ex2216)* 15/5/28.
E4/41 *(ex1284)* 15/5/33.
2815 *(new)* 11/9/36.
2817 *(ex1361)* 10/7/41.
2993 *(ex2250)* 22/5/43 (50A).
2888 *(ex2253)* 28/9/46.
2816 *(ex3411)* 12/5/49.
24276 *(new)* 22/12/51 (50A).
24221 18/12/54 (50A).
24189 21/6/57 (50A).
24284 23/10/62 (50A).

SHEDS:
Selby.
Dairycoates 18/11/29.
Springhead 20/1/40.
Neville Hill 28/3/43.
Darlington 23/6/43.
Neville Hill 24/8/44.
Selby 5/10/47.
Whitby 12/10/52.
Selby 21/12/52.
Stockton 8/6/58.
West Hartlepool 14/9/58.

RENUMBERED:
3440 28/9/46.
63440 12/5/49.

CONDEMNED: 31/12/66.
Sold for scrap to Clayton & Davie, Dunston, 9/2/67.

2284

Armstrong Whitworth 32.

To traffic 7/1920.

REPAIRS:
Dar. 26/2—12/5/23.**G.**
Dar. 9/4—25/8/25.**G.**
Dar. 12—16/10/25.**L.**
Dar. 7/3—10/5/28.**G.**
Dar. 16/9—24/10/30.**G.**
Dar. 1/7—7/8/31.**L.**
Dar. 6/7—31/8/33.**G.**
Dar. 30/4—17/8/36.**G.**
Dar. 28/8—13/10/39.**G.**
Dar. 2—19/8/40.**N/C.**
Dar. 22/9—21/10/41.**G.**
Dar. 5/5—3/6/44.**G.**
Ghd. 12—29/11/45.**L.**
Dar. 7/1—22/2/47.**G.**
Ghd. 19/12/48—4/1/49.**L.**
Dar. 18/10—24/11/50.**G.**
Ghd. 19/3—17/4/53.**C/H.**
Ghd. 5/4—14/5/54.**G.**
Ghd. 28/7—5/9/58.**G.**
Dar. 23/6—5/8/61.**C/L.**
After collision.

BOILERS:
E4/32.
E4/33 *(ex2285)* 10/5/28.
D946 *(exB15 788)* 24/10/30.
2152 *(exB15 786)* 31/8/33.
1967 *(ex2300)* 21/10/41.
2390 *(ex2297)* 3/6/44.
24161 24/11/50.
24251 14/5/54 (50A).
24298 5/9/58 (50A).

SHEDS:
Stockton.
Selby 3/7/30.
Newport 19/6/39.
Stockton 1/2/43.
Blaydon 5/10/47.
Sunderland 24/2/63.

RENUMBERED:
3441 24/11/46.
63441 4/1/49.

CONDEMNED: 23/12/63.
Into Dar. for cut up 6/2/64.

2285

Armstrong Whitworth 33.

To traffic 7/1920.

REPAIRS:
Dar. 31/10/22—18/1/23.**G.**
Dar. 10—22/3/23.**L.**
Dar. 10/12/24—30/3/25.**G.**
Dar. 19/12/27—24/2/28.**G.**
Dar. 5—18/10/28.**N/C.**
Dar. 24/3—15/5/30.**G.**
Dar. 11/5—16/6/33.**G.**
Dar. 25/4—31/5/35.**G.**
Dar. 13/9—15/11/37.**G.**

Dar. 4/4—1/5/40.**G.**
Dar. 27/1—4/3/42.**G.**
Dar. 18/1—10/2/44.**G.**
Dar. 13/11—10/12/45.**L.**
Dar. 18/1—29/3/47.**G.**
Dar. 8/7—17/8/49.**G.**
Dar. 20/8—8/9/51.**H/I.**
Dar. 10—11/9/51.**N/C.**
Dar. 15/12/53—6/1/54.**G.**
Dar. 11—12/1/54.**N/C.**
Dar. 18/6—31/7/56.**G.**
Dar. 11—16/8/56.**N/C.**
Dar. 4—7/2/57.**C/L.**
Dar. 5—12/6/57.**C/L.**
Dar. 6/8—4/9/59.**G.**

BOILERS:
E4/33.
D504 *(exB15 822)* 24/2/28.
D598 *(ex2283)* 16/6/33.
D1965 *(exB15 787)* 31/5/35.
2383 *(ex2213)* 4/3/42.
2149 *(ex2222)* 10/2/44.
2570 *(ex3413)* 29/3/47.
2988 *(ex63448)* 17/8/49 (50A).
2988 reno.24204 8/9/51.
24177 6/1/54 (50A).
24203 31/7/56.
24319 *(new)* 4/9/59 (50A).

SHEDS:
Stockton.
Newport 5/5/31.
Middlesbrough 15/5/48.
Thornaby 1/6/58.

RENUMBERED:
3442 8/12/46.
63442 17/8/49.

CONDEMNED: 15/7/63.
Into Dar. for cut up 21/8/63.

2286

Armstrong Whitworth 34.

To traffic 7/1920.

REPAIRS:
Dar. 9/1—28/3/23.**G.**
Dar. 17/8—26/10/25.**G.**
Dar. 8/3—9/5/28.**G.**
Dar. 15/7—16/8/29.**N/C.**
Dar. 3/11—10/12/31.**G.**
Dar. 10/7—24/8/34.**G.**
Dar. 11/12/36—20/1/37.**G.**
Dar. 25/9—3/11/39.**G.**
Dar. 14/5—2/7/42.**G.**
Dar. 2—30/8/44.**G.**
Dar. 31/10—1/12/45.**G.**
Ghd. 27/2—8/3/47.**L.**
Dar. 17/2—19/3/48.**G.**
Dar. 4—15/3/49.**C/L.**
Dar. 27/9—28/10/50.**G.**

Dar. 9/6/53.*Weigh.*
Dar. 8/12/53—8/1/54.**G.**
Dar. 15—19/1/54.**N/C.**
Ghd. 20/8—21/9/56.**G.**
Dar. 1—11/3/57.**C/L.**
Dar. 18/3—22/4/59.**G.**
Dar. 5—25/5/59.**N/C.**
Dar. 12/3—13/4/62.**G.**
Dar. 10—13/4/64.**N/C.**

BOILERS:
E4/34.
2261 *(ex1249)* 24/8/34.
D1569 *(ex1264)* 20/1/37.
D1956 *(ex2234)* 2/7/42.
2653 *(ex2233)* 30/8/44.
2637 *(ex1291)* 1/12/45.
3856 *(new)* 19/3/48 (50A).
3856 reno.24160 28/10/50.
24195 8/1/54.
24177 21/9/56 (50A).
24291 22/4/59 (50A).
24212 13/4/62 (50A).

SHEDS:
Stockton.
Selby 3/7/30.
Newport 17/8/39.
Neville Hill 30/5/48.
Newport 6/2/49.
Haverton Hill 13/2/49.
West Auckland 14/6/59.
Thornaby 2/2/64.
West Hartlepool 15/11/64.

RENUMBERED:
3443 1/12/46.
E3443 19/3/48.
63443 15/3/49.

CONDEMNED: 18/10/65.
Sold for scrap to W. Willoughby, Choppington, 11/65.

2287

Armstrong Whitworth 35.

To traffic 8/1920.

REPAIRS:
Ghd. 11/10—13/12/23.**G.**
Ghd. 1/6—14/9/26.**G.**
Ghd. 10/12/28—7/2/29.**G.**
Ghd. 15/12/30—28/1/31.**L.**
Ghd. 29/6—29/7/32.**G.**
Dar. 24/1—18/3/38.**G.**
Dar. 28—30/3/38.**N/C.**
Dar. 28/5—1/7/41.**G.**
Dar. 16/11—16/12/42.**H/I.**
Dar. 27/1—21/2/44.**G.**
Dar. 4—6/3/44.**N/C.**
Dar. 28/12/46—15/2/47.**G.**
Dar. 26/2—3/3/47.**N/C.**
Dar. 9/9—11/10/49.**G.**

2287 cont/.
Ghd. 22/11/49—9/1/50.**C/L.**
After collision.
Dar. 23/1—22/2/52.**C/L.**
Dar. 8/7—15/8/53.**G.**
Dar. 17—18/8/53.**N/C.**
Dar. 9/7—23/8/56.**H/I.**
Dar. 4—8/2/57.**N/C.**
Dar. 14/9—21/10/59.**G.**
Dar. 7/1/65.*Weigh.*

BOILERS:
E4/35.
E4/6 *(ex2275)* 29/7/32.
2258 *(ex2271)* 18/3/38.
2441 *(ex2220)* 1/7/41.
HL104 *(ex2258)* 16/12/42.
2812 *(ex2240)* 21/2/44.
2393 *(ex3354)* 15/2/47.
2640 *(ex3403)* 11/10/49.
2640 *reno.24223* 22/2/52.
24187 15/8/53 (50A).
24209 21/10/59 (50A).

SHEDS:
Borough Gardens.
Dairycoates 12/4/39.
Cudworth 20/3/44.
Dairycoates 29/9/46.
Blaydon 20/7/47.
Borough Gardens 17/12/50.
Blaydon 14/6/59.
Sunderland 24/2/63.

RENUMBERED:
3444 7/1/47.
63444 11/10/49.

CONDEMNED: 17/5/65.
Sold for scrap to M.Baum,
Middlesbrough, 6/65.

2288

Armstrong Whitworth 36.

To traffic 9/1920.

REPAIRS:
Ghd. 20/7—11/9/23.**G.**
Ghd. 21/12/25—8/3/26.**G.**
Ghd. 15/4—9/6/26.**L.**
Ghd. 20/9—5/11/28.**G.**
Ghd. 16—23/8/29.**N/C.**
Ghd. 10/9—14/10/31.**G.**
Dar. 30/7—24/8/35.**G.**
Dar. 23/9—22/10/35.**L.**
Dar. 27/4—3/8/37.**G.**
Dar. 24/8—27/9/39.**G.**
Dar. 11—30/3/40.**N/C.**
Dar. 6—17/6/41.**N/C.**
Dar. 11—12/11/41.**N/C.**
Dar. 1/9—2/10/42.**G.**
Dar. 14/12/44—13/1/45.**G.**
Dar. 5—13/4/46.**L.**

Dar. 16/1—29/3/47.**G.**
Dar. 17/5—23/6/50.**G.**
Dar. 26/6—12/7/50.**N/C.**
Dar. 30/1—28/2/53.**G.**
Dar. 2—3/3/53.**N/C.**
Dar. 31/8—24/9/55.**G.**
Dar. 19—20/6/57.**N/C.**
Ghd. 25/2—3/4/58.**G.**
Dar. 6—8/1/60.**N/C.**
Dar. 2—27/10/61.**G.**
Dar. 28/1/65.*Weigh.*

BOILERS:
E4/36.
2149 *(new)* 5/11/28.
AW28 *(ex1362)* 24/8/35.
D930 *(ex2268)* 3/8/37.
AW13 *(ex1262)* 27/9/39.
HL105 *(ex2235)* 2/10/42.
2437 *(ex2271)* 13/1/45.
2566 *(ex3457)* 29/3/47.
3847 *(ex3375)* 23/6/50 (50A).
24186 28/2/53 (50A).
24300 *(new)* 24/9/55 (50A).
24290 3/4/58 (50A).
24169 27/10/61 (50A).

SHEDS:
Borough Gardens.
Newport 9/10/34.
Neville Hill 30/5/48.
Newport 6/2/49.
Thornaby 1/6/58.
Neville Hill 16/12/62.
Sunderland 13/10/63.
Tyne Dock 19/6/66.

RENUMBERED:
3445 8/12/46.
63445 23/6/50.

CONDEMNED: 26/6/66.
Sold for scrap to Hughes
Bolckow, Blyth, 8/66.

2289

Armstrong Whitworth 37.

To traffic 9/1920.

REPAIRS:
Dar. 23/10—22/12/23.**G.**
Dar. 10/8—23/12/26.**G.**
Dar. 17/4—11/6/29.**G.**
Dar. 20/10—25/11/31.**G.**
Dar. 26/4—18/5/34.**G.**
Dar. 24/7—9/9/36.**G.**
Dar. 2/12/38—20/1/39.**G.**
Dar. 15/10—13/11/40.**G.**
Dar. 24/12/42—23/1/43.**G.**
Dar. 25/1—23/2/45.**G.**
Ghd. 11—30/4/46.**L.**
Dar. 30/4—31/5/47.**G.**
Dar. 31/8—5/10/50.**G.**

Dar. 19/3—18/4/53.**L/I.**
Dar. 20—22/4/53.**N/C.**
Dar. 14/6—8/7/55.**G.**
Dar. 4—13/12/56.**C/L.**
Dar. 9/1—8/2/58.**G.**
Dar. 10—12/2/58.**N/C.**
Dar. 10/11/60—12/1/61.**C/L.**
Dar. 24/8—16/9/61.**G.**
Dar. 20—28/9/61.**N/C.**

BOILERS:
E4/37.
D845 *(exB15 821)* 11/6/29.
D1945 *(exB15 825)* 18/5/34.
2431 *(ex2250)* 20/1/39.
HL110 *(ex2219)* 13/11/40.
2433 *(ex2232)* 23/1/43.
2423 *(exB15 823)* 23/2/45.
3159 *(ex3450)* 31/5/47 (50A).
24157 *(ex3432)* 5/10/50.
24199 8/7/55 (50A).
24246 8/2/58 (50A).
24311 16/9/61 (50A).

SHEDS:
Newport.
Stockton 7/2/48.
Haverton Hill 6/2/49.
West Auckland 14/6/59.
Thornaby 2/2/64.
West Hartlepool 27/9/64.

RENUMBERED:
3446 8/9/46.
63446 5/10/50.

CONDEMNED: 5/6/66.
Sold for scrap to Hughes
Bolckow, Blyth, 7/66.

2290

Armstrong Whitworth 38.

To traffic 10/1920.

REPAIRS:
Ghd. 15/2—10/4/24.**G.**
Dar. 28/3—4/6/28.**G.**
Ghd. 16/12/30—26/1/31.**G.**
Dar. 26/1—23/2/34.**G.**
Dar. 29/4—8/6/37.**G.**
Dar. 22/4—17/5/40.**G.**
Dar. 23/6—15/7/41.**L.**
Dar. 30/4—3/6/42.**G.**
Dar. 14/6—8/7/44.**G.**
Dar. 21/2—19/4/47.**G.**
Dar. 12/11—9/12/48.**L.**
Dar. 17/11—12/12/49.**G.**
Ghd. 30/1—23/2/51.**L/I.**
After derailment.
Ghd. 14/2—14/3/52.**C/L.**
Dar. 28/4/52.*Weigh.*
Dar. 25/8—16/9/53.**G.**
Ghd. 17/5—26/6/54.**C/H.**

After derailment.
Ghd. 29/6—2/7/54.**N/C.**
Ghd. 6/1—9/2/55.**C/L.**
After collision.
Dar. 6/4—22/5/56.**H/I.**
Dar. 28—31/5/56.**N/C.**
Dar. 14/4—15/5/59.**G.**
Dar. 12—17/10/59.**N/C.**
Dar. 10—31/8/61.**C/L.**

BOILERS:
E4/38.
E4/32 *(ex2284)* 4/6/28.
E4/21 *(ex2301)* 26/1/31.
2570 *(new)* 23/2/34.
3141 *(new)* 17/5/40 (50A).
2818 *(ex2226)* 8/7/44.
2639 *(ex3367)* 19/4/47.
4030 *(new)* 12/12/49 (50A).
4030 *reno.24182* 23/2/51.
24229 16/9/53 (50A).
24280 15/5/59 (50A).

SHEDS:
Borough Gardens.
Doncaster 27/12/25.
Borough Gardens 28/3/28.
Selby 28/3/43.
Newport 6/2/49.
Thornaby 1/6/58.

RENUMBERED:
3447 14/6/46.
63447 9/12/48.

CONDEMNED: 29/4/63.
Into Dar. for cut up 16/5/63.

2291

Armstrong Whitworth 39.

To traffic 10/1920.

REPAIRS:
Ghd. 20/8—11/10/23.**G.**
Ghd. 16—27/11/23.**L.**
Ghd. 28/10/26—10/5/27.**G.**
Ghd. 17/9—13/11/29.**G.**
Ghd. 7/4—10/5/32.**G.**
Dar. 11/3—16/4/35.**G.**
Dar. 13/10—30/11/37.**G.**
Dar. 7/1—11/2/41.**G.**
Dar. 10/5—15/6/43.**G.**
Dar. 26/3—3/5/46.**G.**
Ghd. 4—13/7/48.**L.**
Dar. 8/4—6/5/49.**G.**
Dar. 10—17/5/49.**N/C.**
Dar. 2/2—10/3/50.**C/L.**
After derailment.
Dar. 8/1—1/2/52.**G.**
Dar. 11—24/9/53.**C/L.**
Dar. 28/7—9/9/54.**G.**
Dar.16—27/9/54.**N/C**
Dar. 11/12/56—5/1/57.**G.**

2291 cont/.
Dar. 27/7—28/8/59.**G.**
Dar. 21/7—9/11/61.**C/L.**
Dar. 6/4—17/5/62.**C/L.**

BOILERS:
E4/39.
2429 *(new)* 10/5/32.
2567 *(exB15 791)* 30/11/37.
2652 *(ex2231)* 11/2/41.
2429 *(ex2294)* 15/6/43.
2988 *(ex2261)* 3/5/46 (50A).
3023 *(ex3417)* 6/5/49 (50A).
24211 1/2/52 (50A).
24278 9/9/54 (50A).
24209 5/1/57 (50A).
24322 *(new)* 28/8/59 (50A).

SHEDS:
Borough Gardens.
Dairycoates 24/4/39.
West Hartlepool 2/3/40.
Springhead 25/5/40.
Dairycoates 28/3/43.
Blaydon 20/7/47.
Dairycoates 4/9/49.
Selby 24/11/49.
Tyne Dock 13/9/59.
Consett 13/12/59.

RENUMBERED:
3448 3/5/46.
63448 13/7/48.

CONDEMNED: 8/11/63.
Into Dar. for cut up 25/11/63.

2292

Armstrong Whitworth 40.

To traffic 10/1920.

REPAIRS:
Ghd. 14/11/23—16/1/24.**G.**
Ghd. 26/5—4/6/25.**L.**
Ghd. 13/9—6/12/27.**G.**
Ghd. 2/8—12/9/30.**G.**
Dar. 22/12/32—20/1/33.**G.**
Dar. 18/5—7/7/36.**G.**
Dar. 28/10—30/11/39.**G.**
Dar. 22/4—2/6/43.**G.**
Dar. 25/6—19/7/45.**L.**
Dar. 23/1—8/3/47.**G.**
Dar. 11—24/3/47.**N/C.**
Ghd. 12—23/8/48.**L.**
Dar. 2—26/11/49.**G.**
Dar. 3—22/12/51.**G.**
Dar. 9/6—3/7/54.**G.**
Dar. 5—6/7/54.**N/C.**
Dar. 13—15/7/54.**N/C.**
Dar. 8/10—7/11/56.**G.**
Dar. 20/4—21/5/59.**G.**
Dar. 26/5—17/6/59.**N/C.**

BOILERS:
E4/40.
2161 *(exB15 819)* 20/1/33.
2260 *(ex1262)* 2/6/43.
4022 *(new)* 26/11/49 (50A).
24278 *(new)* 22/12/51 (50A).
24209 3/7/54 (50A).
24303 *(new)* 7/11/56 (50A).
24315 *(new)* 21/5/59 (50A).

SHEDS:
Borough Gardens.
Selby 28/3/43.
Neville Hill 11/9/44.
Selby 5/10/47.
York 13/9/59.
Neville Hill 6/12/59.

RENUMBERED:
3449 20/10/46.
63449 23/8/48.

CONDEMNED: 15/7/63.
Into Dar. for cut up 7/8/63.

2293

Armstrong Whitworth 41.

To traffic 11/1920.

REPAIRS:
Ghd. 21/8—15/10/23.**G.**
Ghd. 18/3—20/7/26.**G.**
Ghd. 3/2—11/4/27.**G.**
Ghd. 2/7—17/10/29.**G.**
Ghd. 21—26/11/29.**N/C.**
Dar. 1/6—6/7/33.**G.**
Dar. 24/1—24/2/38.**G.**
Dar. 16/12/40—15/1/41.**G.**
Dar. 19/5—29/6/43.**G.**
Ghd. 10/5—5/6/45.**L.**
Dar. 27/3—23/5/47.**G.**
Ghd. 30/9—13/10/48.**L.**
Dar. 25/4—19/5/50.**G.**
Ghd. 25/11—20/12/52.**C/L.**
Dar. 22/9—24/10/53.**C/L.**
Dar. 23/2—20/3/54.**G.**
Dar. 22—25/3/54.**N/C.**
Dar. 18/4—14/5/56.**H/I.**
Dar. 25/11—22/12/58.**G.**
Dar. 3—12/1/59.**N/C.**
Dar. 14/1—13/2/63.**G.**

BOILERS:
E4/41.
E4/10 *(ex2262)* 17/10/29.
D940 *(ex2216)* 6/7/33.
3159 *(new)* 15/1/41 (50A).
2259 *(ex3362)* 23/5/47.
4061 *(new)* 19/5/50 (50A).
4061 reno.24251 20/12/52.
24184 20/3/54 (50A).
24164 22/12/58 (50A).
24154 13/2/63 (50A).

SHEDS:
Tyne Dock.
Newport 28/3/43.
Neville Hill 12/9/44.
Selby 5/10/47.
Neville Hill 6/2/49.
Selby 27/1/52.
Thornaby 14/6/59.
West Hartlepool 8/4/62.

RENUMBERED:
3450 8/9/46.
63450 13/10/48.

CONDEMNED: 31/12/66.
*Sold for scrap to W.Willoughby,
Choppington, 9/2/67.*

2294

Armstrong Whitworth 42.

To traffic 11/1920.

REPAIRS:
Ghd. 6/6—30/8/24.**G.**
Dar. 30/3—24/8/26.**G.**
Ghd. 4/9—19/11/29.**G.**
Ghd. 30/7—15/9/32.**G.**
Dar. 20/1—29/2/36.**G.**
Dar. 24/6—16/9/38.**G.**
Dar. 25/1—26/2/41.**G.**
Dar. 6/4—5/5/43.**G.**
Dar. 29/5—4/6/43.**N/C.**
Ghd. 17—27/4/45.**L.**
Dar. 12/12/46—25/1/47.**G.**
Ghd. 13/7—9/8/48.**L.**
Dar. 5—29/10/49.**G.**
Dar. 31/10—4/11/49.**N/C.**
Dar. 9—31/5/52.**G.**
Ghd. 21/1—20/2/54.**C/L.**
Dar. 4—12/8/54.**C/L.**
Dar. 7/2—5/3/55.**N/C.**
Dar. 31/3—15/4/55.**N/C.**
Dar. 24/6—21/7/55.**G.**
Dar. 2—8/8/55.**N/C.**
Dar. 3—21/12/57.**G.**
Dar. 23—27/12/57.**N/C.**
Dar. 16/6—5/8/60.**G.**
Dar. 19/8—15/9/60.**N/C.**

BOILERS:
E4/42.
E4/13 *(ex2268)* 15/9/32.
AW24 *(exB15 788)* 29/2/36.
2149 *(ex2273)* 16/9/38.
2429 *(ex1254)* 26/2/41.
2820 *(exB15 796)* 5/5/43.
2992 *(ex2302)* 25/1/47 (50A).
2857 *(ex63377)* 29/10/49.
24227 31/5/52 (50A).
24157 21/7/55.
24159 21/12/57.
24327 *(new)* 5/8/60 (50A).

SHEDS:
Borough Gardens.
Springhead 16/2/25.
Borough Gardens 1/2/27.
Newport 9/5/41.
Neville Hill 12/9/44.
Selby 5/10/47.
Thornaby 14/6/59.
West Hartlepool 8/4/62.

RENUMBERED:
3451 8/9/46.
63451 9/8/48.

CONDEMNED: 1/1/64.
Into Dar. for cut up 15/1/64.

2295

Armstrong Whitworth 43.

To traffic 11/1920.

REPAIRS:
Ghd. ?/?—4/5/22.**G.**
Ghd. 25/7—23/10/25.**G.**
Ghd. 4/4—7/6/28.**G.**
Ghd. 28/10—4/12/30.**G.**
Dar. 19/1—19/2/34.**G.**
Dar. 27/8—13/10/36.**G.**
Dar. 15—21/10/36.**N/C.**
Dar. 15/8—15/9/39.**G.**
Dar. 9/11—8/12/42.**G.**
Dar. 12/4—8/5/43.**L.**
After collision.
Dar. 22/1—23/2/45.**G.**
Ghd. 19/6—9/7/46.**L.**
Ghd. 10—16/7/46.**N/C.**
Dar. 14/4—3/5/47.**L.**
Dar. 27/11—24/12/47.**G.**
Dar. 21/9—21/10/50.**G.**
Ghd. 26/6—18/7/52.**C/L.**
Dar. 19/6—11/7/53.**G.**
Dar. 6—30/7/55.**H/I.**
Dar. 2—5/8/55.**N/C.**
Dar. 25/10—11/12/57.**C/L.**
Dar. 30/1—20/2/58.**N/C.**
Dar. 26/11—22/12/58.**G.**
Dar. 20—21/8/59.**N/C.**
Dar. 30/11—4/12/59.**N/C.**
Dar. 26/5—15/6/61.**C/L.**
After collision.
Dar. 3—6/4/62.**N/C.**

BOILERS:
E4/43.
D238 *(ex1361)* 7/6/28.
2569 *(new)* 19/2/34.
2561 *(ex1249)* 15/9/39.
3317 *(new)* 8/12/42 (50A).
3153 *(ex2250)* 23/2/45 (50A).
2813 *(ex3359)* 24/12/47.
24159 *(ex3435)* 21/10/50.
24257 11/7/53 (50A).
24301 22/12/58 (50A).

When No.63407 was ex-works 2nd August 1957 it was the first Q6 to have BR crest in place of the emblem, and the whole class duly acquired the crest. None however were fitted with BR's Automatic Warning System.

Like the emblem, the crest was handed for the lion to face forward, but under the rules of heraldry (which now applied to the grant of arms) it was a serious gaffe to have the lion facing to the right. After about a year, correct crests were used. The rebuilt tender, ex-works 18th October 1957 was not corrected at the 3rd October 1958 general repair, and with its subsequent moves to 63384, 63389 and 63445, seems to have missed out on repainting.

CLASS Q 6

2295 cont/.
SHEDS:
Borough Gardens.
Neville Hill 28/3/43.
Darlington 26/6/43.
West Hartlepool 5/3/45.
Middlesbrough 14/9/52.
Thornaby 1/6/58.

RENUMBERED:
3452 30/6/46.
63452 21/10/50.

CONDEMNED: 29/4/63.
Into Dar. for cut up 16/5/63.

2296

Armstrong Whitworth 44.

To traffic 12/1920.

REPAIRS:
Dar. 11/6—12/9/24.G.
Dar. 2/4—29/6/27.G.
Dar. 25—29/7/27.L.
Dar. 2/9—23/10/29.G.
Dar. 30/11/31—28/1/32.G.
Dar. 22/5—20/6/34.G.
Dar. 27/8—15/10/36.G.
Dar. 31/10—8/11/38.N/C.
Dar. 12/7—17/8/39.G.
Dar. 24/11—14/12/39.H.
Dar. 15/12/41—13/1/42.G.
Dar. 13/3—6/4/44.G.
Ghd. 2—18/6/45.L.
Dar. 19/2—16/3/46.G.
Dar. 2/3—7/4/48.G.
Dar. 10/1—3/2/51.G.
Dar. 23/1—21/2/53.H/I.
Dar. 31/1—15/3/55.C/L.
Ghd. 13/12/55—12/1/56.C/L.
Ghd. 11/6—13/7/56.G.
Ghd. 26—28/2/57.C/L.
Dar. 6/2—6/3/59.C/L.
Dar. 2/12/59—1/1/60.G.
Dar. 25/3—29/4/63.G.
Dar. 16/12/63—14/1/64.C/L.

BOILERS:
E4/44.
D916 (ex2226) 20/6/34.
2819 (new) 15/10/36.
2976 (ex2218) 13/1/42 (50A).
2815 (ex1362) 6/4/44.
2262 (ex2239) 16/3/46.
HL110 (ex3396) 7/4/48.
24172 (ex3359) 3/2/51.
24275 13/7/56 (50A).
24277 1/1/60 (50A).
24269 29/4/63 (50A).

SHEDS:
Newport.
Blaydon 8/7/39.

Newport 28/3/43.
West Hartlepool 11/7/48.
Haverton Hill 7/11/48.
Selby 24/9/50.
Tyne Dock 17/8/52.
Consett 1/9/57.
Borough Gardens 20/7/58.
Blaydon 25/1/59.
Tyne Dock 24/2/63.

RENUMBERED:
3453 16/3/46.
63453 7/4/48.

CONDEMNED: 2/10/66.
Sold for scrap to A Draper,
Hull, 11/66. Cut up 12/12/66.

2297

Armstrong Whitworth 45.

To traffic 12/1920.

REPAIRS:
Dar. 5/6—16/8/23.G.
Dar. 5/10/26—10/2/27.G.
Dar. 27/8—25/10/29.G.
Dar. 13/7—22/8/32.G.
Dar. 2/4—9/5/35.G.
Dar. 24/2—2/7/38.G.
Dar. 2—18/7/38.N/C.
Dar. 23/4—22/5/41.G.
Dar. 14/2—8/3/44.G.
Dar. 8/8—5/9/45.L.
Ghd. 12—29/12/45.L.
Dar. 30/3—8/5/46.L.
Dar. 17/3—26/4/47.G.
Ghd. 8—20/8/48.L.
Dar. 30/11—29/12/49.G.
Dar. 10/9—4/10/52.G.
Dar. 3/8—17/9/55.G.
Dar. 19—20/9/55.N/C.
Ghd. 20/6—8/8/58.G.
Dar. 30/10—7/11/58.N/C.
Dar. 26/3—19/5/59.C/H.
Dar. 5/11—6/12/62.G.
Dar. 10—13/12/62.N/C.

BOILERS:
E4/45.
D872 (ex2224) 10/2/27.
E4/46 (ex2298) 25/10/29.
D796 (exB15 823) 22/8/32.
AW32 (ex2242) 9/5/35.
2640 (ex2219) 2/7/38.
2390 (ex1292) 22/5/41.
HL104 (ex2287) 8/3/44.
2431 (ex3347) 26/4/47.
4038 (new) 29/12/49 (50A).
24236 4/10/52 (50A).
24201 17/9/55 (50A).
24170 8/8/58.
24302 6/12/62 (50A).

SHEDS:
Dairycoates.
West Hartlepool 5/3/45.

RENUMBERED:
3454 13/4/46.
63454 20/8/48.

CONDEMNED: 5/6/66.
Sold for scrap to Hughes
Bolckow, Blyth, 7/66.

2298

Armstrong Whitworth 46.

To traffic 12/1920.

REPAIRS:
Dar. 14/2—30/4/24.G.
Dar. 26/7—20/10/27.G.
Dar. 2—20/8/29.G.
Dar. 21/5—7/7/31.G.
Dar. 5/5—1/6/34.G.
Dar. 11/10—26/11/38.G.
Dar. 28/11—2/12/38.N/C.
Dar. 2/4—1/5/41.G.
Dar. 28/8—25/9/43.G.
Dar. 17/3—3/5/47.G.
Dar. 11/10—5/12/47.L.
Dar. 26/8—17/9/48.L.
Dar. 18/4—12/5/50.G.
Ghd. 24/3—22/4/52.C/H.
Dar. 27/3—2/5/53.G.
Dar. 4—5/5/53.N/C.
Ghd. 16/11—29/12/55.C/L.
Dar. 10/9—5/10/56.G.
Dar. 12/9—8/10/59.G.
Dar. 15—24/10/59.N/C.
Dar. 3/12/62—4/1/63.G.
Dar. 2/12/65—10/1/66.C/H.

BOILERS:
E4/46.
D690 (ex2229) 20/8/29.
2563 (new) 1/6/34.
2582 (ex2230) 1/5/41.
2261 (exB15 782) 25/9/43.
3002 (ex3372) 12/5/50 (50A).
3002 reno.24229 22/4/52.
24235 2/5/53 (50A).
24152 5/10/56 (50A).
24316 (new) 8/10/59 (50A).
24186 4/1/63 (50A).

SHEDS:
Neville Hill.
Consett 19/6/43.
Tyne Dock 23/5/65.

RENUMBERED:
3455 1/9/46.
63455 17/9/48.

CONDEMNED: 22/6/67.
Sold for scrap to Garnham,
Harris & Elton,Chesterfield, 8/67.

2299

Armstrong Whitworth 47.

To traffic 1/1921.

REPAIRS:
Dar. 3/7—25/9/23.G.
Dar. 8/2—26/9/26.G.
Dar. 28/1—28/2/29.G.
Dar. 21/7—30/8/32.G.
Dar. 17/10—17/11/34.G.
Dar. 19/2—20/3/37.G.
Dar. 12/7—24/8/39.G.
Dar. 21/4—17/5/41.G.
Dar. 27/7—4/9/43.G.
Ghd. 15/11—5/12/45.L.
Dar. 6/5—19/6/47.G.
Ghd. 2—13/1/49.L.
Dar. 11/1—8/2/50.G.
Dar. 15/7—23/8/52.G.
Dar. 19/1—12/2/55.H/I.
Dar. 14—26/2/55.N/C.
Ghd. 29/8—13/9/55.C/L.
Ghd. 20/1—21/2/58.G.
Ghd. 26/6—10/7/58.C/L.
Dar. 12/6—29/7/61.G.
Dar. 9/7—17/8/62.C/L.
Dar. 15/1—4/2/63.N/C.
Dar. 17/1/64.Weigh.

BOILERS:
E4/47.
D182 (exB15 823) 28/2/29.
2441 (new) 30/8/32.
D1568 (ex1276) 20/3/37.
2563 (ex2298) 17/5/41.
HL112 (ex2277) 4/9/43.
2423 (ex3446) 19/6/47.
4050 (new) 8/2/50 (50A).
24283 (new) 23/8/52 (50A).
24224 21/2/58 (50A).
24310 29/7/61 (50A).

SHEDS:
Springhead.
Newport 22/5/24.
Neville Hill 8/9/44.
Selby 5/10/47.
Borough Gardens 27/1/52.
Blaydon 14/6/59.
Consett 27/9/59.
Sunderland 6/5/62.

RENUMBERED:
3456 22/12/46.
63456 13/1/49.

CONDEMNED: 15/12/64.
Sold for scrap 2/65.

95

2300

Armstrong Whiteworth 48.

To traffic 1/1921.

REPAIRS:
Ghd. 28/7—14/8/23.**L.**
Ghd. 28/2—19/5/25.**G.**
Ghd. 16/4—18/6/28.**G.**
Ghd. 3/10—14/11/30.**G.**
Dar. 16/5—16/6/34.**G.**
Dar. 30/3—13/5/38.**G.**
Dar. 14—27/5/38.**N/C.**
Dar. 9/6—19/7/41.**G.**
Dar. 22—26/7/41.**N/C.**
Dar. 27/2—26/3/43.**L.**
Dar. 13/12/43—8/1/44.**G.**
Dar. 9/1—8/3/47.**G.**
Dar. 16/8—10/9/49.**G.**
Dar. 12/9—1/10/49.**N/C.**
Dar. 3—7/10/49.**N/C.**
Dar. 2—24/12/52.**G.**
Dar. 20/5—25/6/55.**G.**
Dar. 28/6—2/7/55.**N/C.**
Ghd. 29/4—6/6/58.**G.**
Dar. 2—23/5/61.**C/L.**
Dar. 30/11/61. *Not repaired.*

BOILERS:
E4/48.
E4/43 *(ex2295)* 18/6/28.
E4/15 *(ex2267)* 14/11/30.
D1967 *(ex1254)* 16/6/34.
  2258 *(ex2287)* 19/7/41.
  2566 *(ex2214)* 8/1/44.
HL111 *(ex3390)* 8/3/47.
  2570 *(ex3442)* 10/9/49.
24245 24/12/52.
24237 25/6/55.
24282 6/6/58 (50A).

SHEDS:
Borough Gardens.
Blaydon 29/3/41.
Newport 28/3/43.

Darlington 29/9/44.
West Hartlepool 5/3/45.

RENUMBERED:
3457 24/11/46.
63457 10/9/49.

CONDEMNED: 18/12/61.
Cut up at Darlington.

2301

Armstrong Whiteworth 49.

To traffic 3/1921.

REPAIRS:
Dar. 28/7—22/10/24.**G.**
Dar. 12/1—29/4/27.**G.**
Ghd. 1/8—12/9/30.**G.**
Dar. 30/5—30/6/34.**G.**
Dar. 1/7—27/8/37.**G.**
Dar. 30/8—6/9/37.**N/C.**
Dar. 19/7—14/8/40.**G.**
Dar. 30/9—24/10/42.**G.**
Dar. 11/9—5/10/44.**G.**
Dar. 3—11/8/45.**L.**
Dar. 3—13/4/46.**N/C.**
Dar. 8/1—1/3/47.**G.**
Dar. 23/3—20/4/50.**G.**
Dar. 24—29/4/50.**N/C.**
Dar. 23/5—9/6/51.**C/L.**
Dar. 16/9—9/10/52.**G.**
Ghd. 15/3—15/4/55.**G.**
Dar. 11/6—30/7/58.**G.**
Dar. 14—18/8/59.**N/C.**
Dar. 27—30/10/59.**C/L.**
Dar. 20/2—30/3/62.**G.**
Dar. 27/1—18/3/64.**C/L.**
Dar. 22/9—11/11/65.**C/H.**

BOILERS:
E4/49.
E4/21 *(ex2273)* 29/4/27.
E4/50 *(ex2300)* 12/9/30.
  2387 *(ex1276)* 30/6/34.

2658 *(ex2258)* 14/8/40.
3311 *(new)* 24/10/42 (50A).
HL103 *(ex2255)* 5/10/44.
2439 *(ex3393)* 1/3/47.
2812 *(ex63434)* 20/4/50.
2812 reno.24193 9/6/51.
24237 9/10/52.
24298 *(new)* 15/4/55 (50A).
24299 30/7/58 (50A).
24282 30/3/62 (50A).
24332 11/11/65 (50A).

SHEDS:
Dairycoates.
Springhead 17/5/23.
Borough Gardens 23/5/27.
Tyne Dock 10/5/40.
Newport 28/3/43.
Borough Gardens 16/3/48.
Blaydon 14/6/59.
Sunderland 17/2/63.
Tyne Dock 19/6/66.

RENUMBERED:
3458 10/11/46.
63458 20/4/50.

CONDEMNED: 1/7/67.
Sold for scrap to Clayton & Davie, Dunston.

2302

Armstrong Whitworth 50.

To traffic 3/1921.

REPAIRS:
Ghd. 24/7—25/9/24.**G.**
Dar. 18/8—22/12/26.**G.**
Ghd. 23/6—11/8/30.**G.**
Dar. 2/10—8/11/33.**G.**
Dar. 8/5—6/7/36.**G.**
Dar. 1/2—15/3/39.**G.**
Dar. 13/8—11/9/41.**G.**
Dar. 2/10—4/11/43.**G.**

Dar. 9/11—14/12/46.**G.**
Ghd. 16/3—9/4/48.**L.**
Dar. 4—26/5/49.**G.**
Dar. 2—20/7/51.**G.**
Dar. 14/9—7/10/53.**G.**
Dar. 20—27/10/53.**N/C.**
Dar. 9/12/55—6/1/56.**H/I.**
Dar. 11/7—4/9/56.**C/L.**
Dar. 15/12/58—21/1/59.**G.**
Dar. 9/3—14/4/61.**C/L.**
Dar. 27/8—5/10/62.**G.**

BOILERS:
E4/50.
E4/2 *(ex2277)* 11/8/30.
2392 *(ex1280)* 8/11/33.
3009 *(new)* 15/3/39 (50A).
2992 *(ex1311)* 11/9/41 (50A).
3161 *(ex3431)* 14/12/46 (50A).
2435 *(ex3433)* 26/5/49.
24195 20/7/51.
24163 7/10/53 (50A).
24302 21/1/59 (50A).
24283 5/10/62 (50A).

SHEDS:
Borough Gardens.
Doncaster 24/12/25.
Borough Gardens 11/8/26.
Tyne Dock 1/3/40.
Newport 28/3/43.
Stockton 1/3/48.
Middlesbrough 25/6/50.
West Auckland 29/8/54.
North Blyth 6/10/63.
Tyne Dock 19/12/65.

RENUMBERED:
3459 16/11/46.
63459 9/4/48.

CONDEMNED: 30/10/66.
Sold for scrap to A.Draper, Hull, 12/66. Cut up 15/5/67.

Most duly had the right hand crest corrected for the lion to face the left. 63372 and 63457 were the only exceptions as they were the first withdrawals, 16th May 1960 (accident damage) and 18th December 1961 respectively. No more went until April 1963 when steady withdrawal began and the last three Nos.63344, 63387 and 63395 were taken out of stock 9th September 1967. 63395 was sold 29th October 1967 for private preservation.

63373 (on its side) and 63355 suffered this mishap on 20th May 1955 on the Tebay line with the result that such heavy engines were quickly transferred from Kirkby Stephen shed. After recovery and whilst both were being repaired in Darlington works, on 26th June 1955 they were re-allocated to Middlesbrough.

(opposite) This class of 120 engines was built by the NER (70) and Armstrong Whitworth (50) from February 1913 to March 1921. Here one of them, number unknown, is delivering three more Stanier Class 5 locomotives, built by Armstrong Whitworth, to the LMS in August 1935 and almost certainly using the Newcastle to Carlisle line.

The LNER built ten similar engines, Nos.624, 625, 626, 628, 629, 630, 631, 632, 633 and 634 at Darlington from 18th March to 3rd May 1924. The differences between the two batches was only in detail. The 1924 engines started off with a chimney lacking a windjabber and set further forward, but they all had Gresley anti-vacuum valves from new. The two batches also differed throughout in type of lubrication for their cylinders.

Nos.901, 902, 904 and 905 continued to have steam circulating for superheater element protection until 1927/28. When new they had pyrometer to indicate steam temperature but by Grouping, this was no longer required and had been removed leaving only the stub on the smokebox. No.903 kept its first boiler until October 1935 but it is not known if it actually got the Gresley anti-vacuum valve at that shopping or at an earlier works visit.

CLASS Q 7

901

Darlington

To traffic 10/1919.

REPAIRS:
Dar. 30/11/23—28/2/24.**G**.
Dar. 23/3/27—18/1/28.**G**.
Wheels to Doncaster for dynamic balance.
Dar. 31/7—14/8/28.**L**.
Dar. 10/2—27/3/31.**G**.
Dar. 8/7—20/8/36.**G**.
Dar. 16/1—22/2/39.**G**.
Dar. 8/4—8/6/40.**N/C**.
Dar. 5—16/6/41.**N/C**.
Dar. 6/3—9/4/42.**G**.
Dar. 27/1—24/3/45.**G**.
Dar. 4—5/4/45.**L**.
Ghd. 5—26/6/46.**L**.
Dar. 25/11—19/12/47.**G**.
Dar. 29/12/47—6/1/48.**N/C**.
Ghd. 17/12/48—14/1/49.**L**.
Ghd. 27/1—2/2/49.**C/L**.
Ghd. 17/2—7/4/49.**C/L**.
Dar. 24/5—29/6/51.**G**.
Vac. ejector fitted. Modification for iron ore train working
Dar. 13—25/10/51.**N/C**.
.Air reservoir added.
Dar. 14/4—15/5/54.**G**.
Dar. 22/9—30/10/54.**C/L**.
New cylinders.
Dar. 29/3—16/4/57.**C/L**.
Dar. 14/10—9/11/57.**G**.
Westinghouse equip. removed.
Dar. 11—15/11/57.**N/C**.
Dar. 8—18/8/58.**C/L**.
Dar. 13/12/60—28/1/61.**G**.
New fire box tube plate & full set (150/24) of new tubes.
Dar. 4—15/6/62.**N/C**.
Complete AWS fitted.
Dar. 2—12/10/62.**C/L**.
Dar. 10/4/63. *In for storage.*

BOILERS:
D962.
D1616 *(ex626)* 18/1/28.
  2556 *(exB16 914)* 20/8/36.
D1492 *(ex631)* 22/2/39.
  3246 *(new)* 9/4/42 (49A).
  2692 *(ex3467)* 19/12/47.
  24023 29/6/51 (49A).
  24027 15/5/54 (49A).
  24020 9/11/57 (49A).
  24022 28/1/61 (49A).

SHEDS:
Dairycoates.
Haverton Hill 19/7/28.
Stockton 5/5/31.
West Hartlepool 19/3/37.
Darlington 25/11/38.
Tyne Dock 28/3/43.

RENUMBERED:
  3460 27/10/46.
  63460 29/6/51.

WITHDRAWN: 3/12/62.
For preservation. Sent to Str. for storing 12/8/64.
First steaming after restoration 8/8/90.

902

Darlington

To traffic 10/1919.

REPAIRS:
Dar. 21/2—30/4/24.**G**.
Dar. 25—30/6/25.**N/C**.
'Touching up' for Centenary exhibition.
Ghd. 11/7/27—2/2/28.**G**.
Ghd. 2—20/8/28.**L**.
Ghd. 2—16/12/30.**N/C**.
Ghd. 7—20/7/31.**L**.
Ghd. 8/9—10/10/31.**L**.
Ghd. 17/5—30/6/32.**G**.
Dar. 4/11/35—28/1/36.**H**.
Dar. 19/7—31/8/37.**G**.
Dar. 3/11/37—5/1/38.**L**.
After collision.
Dar. 20/2—1/3/40.**N/C**.
Dar. 6—15/3/40.**N/C**.
Dar. 29/1—10/3/41.**G**.
Dar. 24/4—16/5/44.**G**.
Ghd. 26/3—13/4/46.**L**.
Dar. 4/3—26/4/47.**G**.
Dar. 10—17/5/47.**N/C**.
Dar. 12/6—8/7/50.**G**.
Dar. 2—27/2/54.**G**.
Ghd. 31/12/54—4/2/55.**C/L**.
After derailment.
Dar. 19—28/4/55.**C/L**.
Dar. 12/1—8/2/56.**N/C**.
Dar. 8/2—1/3/57.**C/L**.
Dar. 6/8—4/9/57.**G**.
Dar. 16—23/8/60.**N/C**.
Dar. 10/11/60—15/3/61.**G**.
Dar. 4—22/12/61.**C/L**.
Collision damage repaired.

Complete AWS fitted.
Dar. 30/3—11/4/62.**C/L**.

BOILERS:
D976.
D1034 *(exB16 846)* 2/2/28.
D1622 *(ex629)* 30/6/32.
D1619 *(ex633)* 31/8/37.
  3166 *(new)* 10/3/41 (49A).
  3440 *(new)* 16/5/44 (49A).
  3269 *(exB16 1457)* 26/4/47 (49A).
  3167 *(exB16 61442)* 8/7/50 (49A).
  24019 27/2/54 (49A).
  24000 4/9/57 (49A).

SHEDS:
Dairycoates.
Tyne Dock 24/4/26 (T).
Tyne Dock 2/3/27 (P).
Blaydon 17/6/56.
Tyne Dock 16/6/57.

RENUMBERED
  3461 27/10/46.
  63461 8/7/50.

CONDEMNED: 10/12/62.
Into Dar. for cut up 1/3/63.

903

Darlington

To traffic 10/1919.

REPAIRS:
Ghd. 16—21/6/23.**L**.
Dar. 18/10—20/11/23.**L**.
Ghd. 27/4—7/8/25.**G**.
Ghd. 2/8—4/10/29.**G**.
Dar. 11/11/32—16/1/33.**H**.
Dar. 8/10—27/11/35.**G**.
Dar.18/4—21/6/39.**L**.
Dar. 8/7—4/8/40.**G**.
Dar. 5—13/8/40.**N/C**.
Dar. 22/3—27/4/43.**G**.
Ghd. 2—25/5/45.**L**.
Dar. 22/6—30/11/46.**G**.
Ghd. 12/4—21/5/48.**L**.
Dar. 15/11—16/12/49.**G**.
Dar. 19/1—14/2/53.**G**.
Dar. 23/2—5/3/53.**N/C**.
Dar. 4—11/8/54.**N/C**.
Dar. 19/3—25/4/56.**G**.
Dar. 24/10—2/12/60.**G**.
Dar. 26/10—8/11/62.**N/C**.
Complete AWS fitted.

BOILERS:
D977.
D1111 *(exB16 2376)* 27/11/35.
D1610 *(ex624)* 4/8/40.
D1616 *(ex629)* 27/4/43.
  3424 *(ex632)* 30/11/46 (49A).
  3483 *(exB16 61457)* 16/12/49 (49A).
  24001 14/2/53 (49A).
  24052 25/4/56 (49A).
  24100 2/12/60 (49A).

SHEDS:
Tyne Dock.
Blaydon 17/6/56.
Tyne Dock 8/3/59.

RENUMBERED:
  3462 2/11/46.
  63462 21/5/48.

CONDEMNED: 2/12/62.
Into Dar. for cut up 25/2/63.

904

Darlington

To traffic 11/1919.

REPAIRS:
Dar. 20/11/24—26/2/25.**G**.
Dar. 27/11/25—13/4/26.**L**.
Wheels to Doncaster for dynamic balancing.
Dar. 10/8—29/11/27.**G**.
Dar. 29/10—8/12/31.**G**.
Dar. 5/11—20/12/35.**G**.
Dar. 24/3/37.*Weigh*.
Dar. 26/4—28/5/37.**L**.
Dar. 8/5—27/6/39.**G**.
Dar. 11—15/9/39.**N/C**.
Dar. 30/10/39.**N/C**.
Dar. 14/11/39.**N/C**.
Dar. 24/10—4/11/40.**N/C**.
Dar. 20—27/6/41.**N/C**.
Dar. 20/3—22/4/42.**G**.
Dar. 11/5—1/7/42.**H**.
Dar. 27/6—2/8/44.**G**.
Dar. 2/12/46—11/1/47.**G**.
Ghd. 28/1—16/2/49.**L**.
Dar. 1/6—1/7/50.**G**.
Ghd. 14/1—1/3/52.**C/H**.
Modification for iron ore train working. Vac. ejector fitted.
Ghd. 8/4—13/5/53.**C/H**.
Dar. 26/7—4/9/54.**G**.
Dar. 6—8/9/54.**N/C**.
Dar. 14—24/9/56.**C/L**.

WORKS CODES:- Cw - Cowlairs. Dar- Darlington. Don - Doncaster. Ghd - Gateshead. Gor - Gorton. Hsi - Hull Springhead. Inv - Inverurie. Str - Stratford.
REPAIR CODES:- **C/H** - Casual Heavy. **C/L** - Casual Light. **G** - General. **H** - Heavy. **H/I** - Heavy Intermediate. **L** - Light. **L/I** - Light Intermediate. **N/C** - Non-Classified.

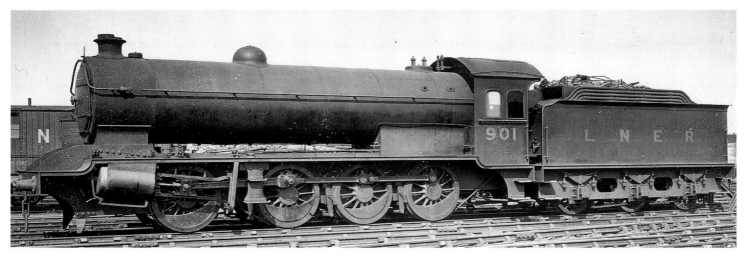

Nos.901 to 905 duly changed to Gresley anti-vacuum valve. The boiler on this class was to Diagram 49 and the same as used by Class B16 so there was much interchanging. Diagram 49 boiler barrels had three plates.

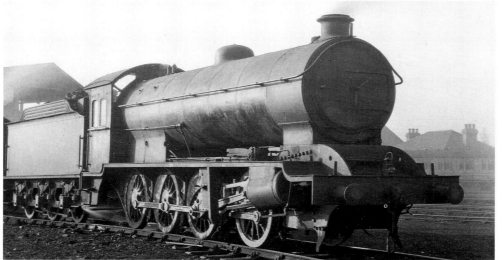

In 1939 the boiler was re-designed with two plates to Diagram 49A, on which the dome was placed 2ft 8in. further back and had a flatter top to its cover. No.902 ex-works 10th March 1941 was the first Q7 with a 49A boiler and No.625 had one from 10th November 1945. All fifteen duly carried Diagram 49A boiler and had the type at withdrawal.

After having a Diagram 49A boiler from January 1949 to April 1952, No.63474 then reverted to a Diagram 49 boiler until 14th February 1957 as seen here. Seven others also reverted to Diagram 49 for a period after having carried a 49A. After having a 49A from November 1955 to January 1959, No.63470 then had a Diagram 49 from ex-works 13th February 1959 to as late as 22nd January 1962 and was the last Q7 with that type.

As customary on their heavy mineral engines, the North Eastern fitted Nos.901 to 905 with steam reversing gear.

The LNER-built batch also had reversing gear of the same type with two-handle control. The boiler handrail housed one operating rod, with lever and linkage down to the steam valve being in view.

Unlike Q6 Class, which all retained the original arrangement of control for the steam reversing gear, the fifteen Q7's changed to a lower position for the control rod. At first this alteration coincided with Diagram 49A boiler being fitted; No.901 was done ex-works 9th April 1942, but delay in fitting the Diagram 49A's broke this combination on other engines.

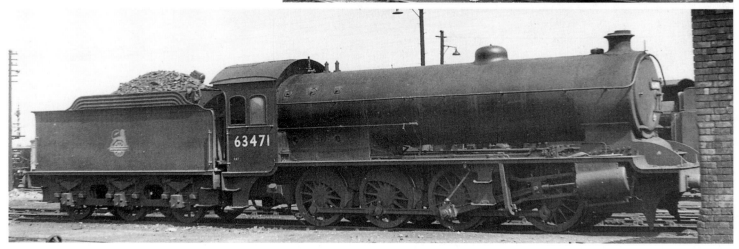

No.63471 did not get its first 49A boiler until it was ex-works 21st November 1958, but this 25th June 1950 photograph shows it had already been changed to the lower control position probably when out 24th December 1949. Note that the change enabled the handrail to be made continuous.

904 cont/.
Dar. 13—22/12/56.**C/L.**
Dar. 26/4—28/5/58.**G.**
Westinghouse equipment
removed.
Dar. 29/9—27/10/60.**C/L.**
Dar. 28/2—7/4/62.**G.**
Complete AWS fitted.

BOILERS:
 D980.
D1221 *(exB16 937)* 29/11/27.
D1665 *(ex626)* 20/12/35.
D1513 *(ex630)* 27/6/39.
 3269 *(new)* 22/4/42 (49A).
 3486 *(new)* 2/8/44 (49A).
 3052 *(exB16 1380)* 11/1/47 (49A).
 2885 *(ex3472)* 1/7/50.
 2885 reno.24079 1/3/52.
 24072 4/9/54 (49A).
 24019 28/5/58 (49A).
 24104 7/4/62 (49A).

SHEDS:
Dairycoates.
Haverton Hill 19/7/28.
Stockton 5/5/31.
Darlington 18/1/36.
Tyne Dock 28/3/43.
Sunderland 14/6/59.
Tyne Dock 13/12/59.

RENUMBERED:
 3463 24/11/46.
63463 16/2/49.

CONDEMNED: 3/12/62.
Into Dar. for cut up 5/3/63.

905

Darlington

To traffic 11/1919.

REPAIRS:
Dar. 15/3—19/6/23.**G.**
Dar. 4/9—18/12/25.**G.**
Ghd. 26/9—12/11/28.**G.**
Dar. 29/10—15/11/29.**L.**
Dar. 17/6—20/8/31.**G.**
Dar. 2/12/35—18/1/36.**G.**
Dar. 19—29/1/36.**N/C.**
Dar. 18/8—27/9/38.**H.**
Dar. 8/11—14/12/39.**G.**
Dar. 24/1—24/2/41.**N/C.**
Dar. 24/11—11/12/41.**L.**
Dar. 1/9—1/10/42.**G.**
Dar. 3/1—2/2/45.**L.**
Ghd. 17/5—2/6/45.**L.**
Dar. 18/7—31/8/46.**G.**
Dar. 24/3—5/7/47.**L.**
Dar. 28/4—27/5/50.**G.**
Dar. 8—14/6/50.**N/C.**
Dar. 6—31/10/53.**G.**

Dar. 5—14/8/54.**N/C.**
Dar. 16/9—7/10/54.**N/C.**
Dar. 9—16/8/56.**C/L.**
Dar. 24/4—18/5/57.**G.**
Dar. 20—21/5/57.**N/C.**
Dar. 20/10—24/11/60.**G.**
Dar. 17/1—14/2/62.**C/H.**
Complete AWS fitted.

BOILERS:
 D983.
D1577 *(exB16 1378)* 12/11/28.
D1204 *(exB16 1373)* 20/8/31.
 2783 *(new)* 18/1/36.
D1588 *(ex628)* 14/12/39.
 2558 *(exB16 936)* 1/10/42.
 2265 *(exB16 2363)* 31/8/46.
 3424 *(ex63462)* 27/5/50 (49A).
 24000 31/10/53 (49A).
 24051 18/5/57 (49A).
 24042 24/11/60 (49A).

SHEDS:
Dairycoates.
Haverton Hill 19/7/28.
Stockton 5/5/31.
Selby 13/8/34.
Tyne Dock 28/3/43.
Blaydon 17/6/56.
Sunderland 25/1/59.
Tyne Dock 13/12/59.

RENUMBERED:
 3464 7/7/46.
63464 27/5/50.

CONDEMNED: 3/12/62.
Into Dar. for cut up 25/2/63.

624

Darlington

To traffic 19/3/24.

REPAIRS:
Dar. 27/1—13/5/27.**G.**
Dar. 20/12/28—8/1/29.**N/C.**
Dar. 7/10—19/11/29.**G.**
Dar. 23/3—4/5/33.**G.**
Dar. 4/8—3/9/36.**G.**
Dar. 7/2—22/3/39.**G.**
Dar. 7/5—12/6/40.**H.**
Dar. 4/6—19/7/41.**G.**
Dar. 27/3—25/6/45.**G.**
Ghd. 20/8—9/9/46.**L.**
Dar. 13/5—18/6/48.**G.**
Dar. 23/3—2/4/49.**C/L.**
Dar. 20/1—24/2/51.**G.**
Modified for iron ore train
working. Vac. ejector fitted.
Dar. 26/2—7/3/51.**N/C.**
Ghd. 4/6—12/7/52.**N/C.**
Air reservoir added. Position of
air pumps changed.

Ghd. 5—8/9/52.**N/C.**
Dar. 28/10—13/12/52.**H/I.**
Dar. 15—16/12/52.**N/C.**
Ghd. 20/6—22/7/55.**G.**
Ghd. 5—11/8/55.**N/C.**
Dar. 12—30/8/57.**C/L.**
Dar. 28/1—22/2/58.**G.**
Westinghouse equipment
removed.
Dar. 24—26/2/58.**N/C.**
Dar. 13/5—10/6/60.**C/L.**
After collision. Vac. ejector
removed.
Dar. 28/10—30/11/60.**C/L.**
Dar. 19/6—5/8/61.**G.**
Dar. 9—15/8/61.**N/C.**
Dar. 13—28/9/62.**N/C.**
Complete AWS fitted.

BOILERS:
 D1610.
D1623 *(ex630)* 19/11/29.
D1667 *(exB16 849)* 4/5/33.
D1610 *(exB16 930)* 3/9/36
D1442 *(exB16 911)* 12/6/40.
 2775 *(ex630)* 25/6/45.
 2267 *(exB16 1458)* 18/6/48.
 24013 *(ex63463)* 24/2/51 (49A).
 24046 22/7/55 (49A).
 24027 22/2/58 (49A).
 24050 5/8/61 (49A).

SHEDS:
Dairycoates.
Doncaster 22/9/24
For coal trials.
Dairycoates 27/2/25.
Stockton 19/7/28.
Selby 27/11/30.
Tyne Dock 28/3/43.

RENUMBERED:
 3465 10/11/46.
63465 18/6/48.

CONDEMNED: 3/12/62.
Into Dar. for cut up 24/4/63.
Final Mileage 699,693

625

Darlington

To traffic 18/3/24.

REPAIRS:
Dar. 29/9/26—26/1/27.**G.**
Dar. 25/9/29—20/1/30.**G.**
Dar. 11/5—26/6/33.**G.**
Dar. 7/5—9/7/35.**L.**
Dar. 17/10/35.*Weigh.*
Dar. 25/2—2/4/36.**G.**
Dar. 16/1—23/2/39.**G.**
Dar. 22/10—8/12/42.**G.**
Dar. 9/10—10/11/45.**G.**

Ghd. 14—26/4/47.**L.**
Dar. 23/3—30/4/48.**L.**
Dar. 12/11—17/12/48.**G.**
Dar. 27/2—25/4/50.**C/H.**
After collision.
Dar. 14—20/12/50.**C/L.**
Dar. 24—27/10/51.**C/L.**
Dar. 21/3—17/4/52.**G.**
Dar. 11—21/11/53.**C/L.**
Dar. 5—30/7/55.**G.**
Ghd. 16/5—22/6/56.**C/L.**
After derailment.
Dar. 31/10—29/11/57.**G.**
Dar. 3—11/11/59.**N/C.**
Dar. 24/5—9/9/61.**G.**
Dar. 24/9—9/10/62.**N/C.**
Complete AWS fitted.

BOILERS:
D1614.
D1610 *(ex624)* 20/1/30.
D1595 *(exB16 1385)* 26/6/33.
 2556 *(ex901)* 23/2/39.
 3248 *(ex628)* 10/11/45 (49A).
 3243 *(exB16 1414)* 17/12/48 (49A).
 3243 reno. 24039 27/10/51.
 24052 17/4/52 (49A).
 24069 30/7/55 (49A).
 24108 *(new)* 29/11/57 (49A).
 24077 9/9/61 (49A).

SHEDS:
Dairycoates.
Stockton 19/7/28.
Haverton Hill 3/4/30.
West Hartlepool 6/12/37.
Darlington 4/11/38.
Tyne Dock 28/3/43.
Sunderland 23/9/56.
Tyne Dock 13/12/59.

RENUMBERED:
 3466 10/11/46.
63466 30/4/48

CONDEMNED: 3/12/62.
Into Dar. for cut up 24/4/63.
Final mileage 879,342.

626

Darlington

To traffic 1/4/24.

REPAIRS:
Dar. 7/2—25/5/27.**G.**
Ghd. 18/7—29/8/30.**G.**
Dar. 16/10—29/11/35.**G.**
Dar. 9/12/37—10/2/38.**H.**
Dar. 21/2—4/4/39.**G.**
Dar. 26/3—30/4/41.**G.**
Dar. 15/6—8/7/44.**G.**
Dar. 5/7—18/8/45.**L.**
Ghd. 30/4—18/5/46.**L.**

(right) **On that same date, 25th June 1950, No.3467 still had the original control arrangement for its steam reversing gear, although this would probably be changed when in for a general repair from 4th to 28th October 1950. This one did not get its first Diagram 49A boiler until July 1953.**

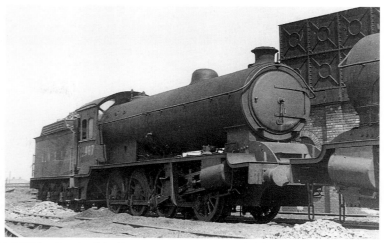

(below) **Compared with Q6, the Q7 boiler and firebox was 12in. longer and to avoid increasing rear overhang, the working space in the cab was reduced accordingly. Normal length side sheets were used and so the spectacle plate was inset 9in. from cab sides and roof. This allowed a box to be made on the left hand running plate which housed a spare gauge lamp and two headlamps. The cab side windows had to be narrower and put off-centre.**

Both batches began by having a wheel and handle for fastening the smokebox door.

Curiously, the change from wheel to a second handle was an early occurrence on this class, No.901 being altered in June 1920 and No.902 in April 1924. No.905 (*see page 114, second top*) was also changed by June 1923. As shown by the illustration on the previous page, centre, the wheel could still be seen into the 1930's but by 1937 all had two handles, No.633 to June 1937 being the last with a wheel.

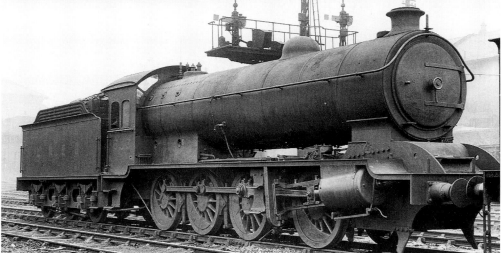

Until after the 1939-45 war, all had smokebox door with a wide flat flange fitting flush with the front plate.

Beginning with No.634 ex-works 13th April 1946, a smokebox door with pressed joint ring was fitted, and all duly changed to that type.

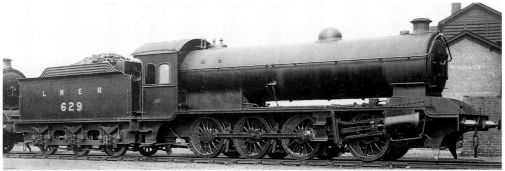

Until after October 1933, when the system was discarded all were fitted with Raven fog signalling apparatus. The toggled striker to make contact with the track ramps can be seen below the cab.

626 cont/.
Dar. 29/10—28/11/47.**G**.
Dar. 4—28/10/50.**G**.
Dar. 30/10—3/11/50.**N/C**.
Dar. 12/6—10/7/53.**G**.
Ghd. 4—31/3/55.**C/L**.
Dar. 23/1—20/2/56.**G**.
Dar. 4/5—2/6/59.**G**.
Dar. 11—26/6/59.**N/C**.
Dar. 2—9/7/59.**N/C**.
Dar. 27/7—18/8/59.**N/C**.
Dar. 18/12/61—17/1/62.**C/L**.
Complete AWS fitted.

BOILERS:
D1616.
D1665 *(new)* 25/5/27.
  2267 *(exB16 942)* 29/11/35.
D1595 *(ex625)* 4/4/39.
D1619 *(ex902)* 30/4/41.
  2692 *(exB16 2379)* 8/7/44.
  2557 *(exB16 1453)* 28/11/47.
  24004 *(ex3464)* 28/10/50.
  24011 10/7/53 (49A).
  24076 20/2/56 (49A).
  24103 2/6/59 (49A).

SHEDS:
Dairycoates.
Stockton 19/7/28.
Selby 27/11/30.
West Hartlepool 6/9/41.
Newport 3/9/42.
Darlington 14/9/42.
Tyne Dock 28/3/43.
Sunderland 23/9/56.
Tyne Dock 20/8/61.

RENUMBERED:
  3467 17/11/46.
  63467 28/10/50.

CONDEMNED: 25/11/62.
Into Dar. for cut up 5/4/63.
Final mileage 683,154.

628

Darlington

To traffic 3/4/24.

REPAIRS:
Dar. 15/6—19/10/26.**G**.
Dar. 29/1—4/4/29.**G**.
Dar. 26/3—26/4/34.**G**.
Dar. 29/9—2/12/36.**G**.
Dar. 21/6—1/8/39.**G**.
Dar. 18/4/41.*Weigh.*
Dar. 17/2—27/3/42.**G**.
Dar. 7/6—7/7/45.**G**.
Ghd. 16/8—2/9/46.**L**.
Dar. 15/5—2/7/48.**G**.
Dar. 12/3—19/4/51.**G**.

Ghd. 16/5—13/6/52.**C/L**.
Dar. 6/1—13/2/54.**G**.
Dar. 15—17/2/54.**N/C**.
Dar. 19—24/2/54.**N/C**.
Dar. 2/8—3/9/56.**G**.
Dar. 2/3—2/4/60.**G**.
Dar. 4/5—13/6/61.**C/L**.
Dar. 21/5—10/7/62.**C/L**.
Complete AWS fitted.

BOILERS:
D1619.
D1450 *(exB16 2367)* 26/4/34.
D1588 *(exB16 936)* 2/12/36.
D1665 *(ex904)* 1/8/39.
  3248 *(new)* 27/3/42 (49A).
  3245 *(exB16 848)* 7/7/45 (49A).
24015 *(exB16 1426)* 19/4/51 (49A).
  24025 13/2/54.
  24011 3/9/56 (49A).
  24013 2/4/60 (49A).

SHEDS:
Dairycoates.
Stockton 19/7/28.
Selby 27/11/30.
York 3/9/32.
Tyne Dock 28/3/43.
Blaydon 17/6/56.
Tyne Dock 16/6/57.

RENUMBERED:
  3468 24/11/46.
  63468 2/7/48.

CONDEMNED: 25/11/62.
Into Dar. for cut up 2/4/63.
Final mileage 702,000.

629

Darlington

To traffic 8/4/24.

REPAIRS:
Ghd. 2/7—6/8/26.**L**.
Ghd. 9—23/3/27.**L**.
Ghd. 19/10/27—15/2/28.**G**.
Ghd. 27/12/29—16/1/30.**L**.
Ghd. 3/2—8/3/32.**G**.
Dar. 30/12/32—6/2/33.**L**.
Dar. 9/6—3/8/37.**G**.
Dar. 23/10—21/11/40.**G**.
Dar. 2/2—1/3/43.**G**.
Ghd. 2—23/2/45.**L**.
Dar. 13/3—18/4/46.**G**.
Ghd. 23/8—17/9/47.**L**.
Dar. 28/7—3/9/48.**G**.
Dar. 1/5—9/6/51.**G**.
Modified for iron ore train
working. Vac. ejector fitted.
Dar. 27/9—10/10/51.**N/C**.
Air resevoir added.

Ghd. 26/3—25/4/53.**C/L**.
Dar. 9/3—3/4/54.**G**.
Dar. 5—8/4/54.**N/C**.
Dar. 24/8—25/9/56.**G**.
Ghd. 27/8—10/10/58.**C/L**.
Dar. 11/8/59.**N/C**.
Dar. 24/9—4/12/59.**G**.
Westinghouse equipment
removed.
Dar. 13/6—17/8/60.**C/H**.
Dar. 31/1—23/2/61.**C/L**.
Dar. 3/11—6/12/61.**C/L**.
Complete AWS fitted.

BOILERS:
D1622.
D1633 *(ex633)* 8/3/32.
D1551 *(exB16 843)* 3/8/37.
D1616 *(ex634)* 21/11/40.
  3035 *(exB16 2381)* 1/3/43 (49A).
  3271 *(exB16 1383)* 18/4/46 (49A).
  2775 *(ex3465)* 3/9/48.
  24021 9/6/51 (49A).
  24090 3/4/54 (49A).
  24042 25/9/56 (49A).
  24076 4/12/59 (49A).

SHEDS:
Dairycoates.
Tyne Dock 24/4/26 (T).
Tyne Dock 2/3/27 (P).
Annfield Plain 14/10/29.
Tyne Dock 1/3/40.
Sunderland 25/1/59.
Tyne Dock 20/8/61.

RENUMBERED:
  3469 10/11/46.
  63469 3/9/48.

CONDEMNED: 2/12/62.
Into Dar. for cut up 5/4/63.
Final mileage 641,280.

630

Darlington

To traffic 16/4/24.

REPAIRS:
Dar. 2/7—26/10/26.**G**.
Dar. 17/6—20/8/29.**G**.
Dar. 1/9—10/10/33.**G**.
Dar. 3/1—7/2/36.**L**.
Dar. 15/9—28/10/36.**G**.
Dar. 4/5—30/6/39.**G**.
Dar. 5/8—6/9/41.**G**.
Dar. 2—30/8/44.**G**.
Ghd. 13—28/2/46.**L**.
Dar. 27/6—16/8/47.**G**.
Dar. 5/1—5/4/50.**G**.
Ghd. 29/4—22/5/52.**C/L**.
Dar. 23/12/52—23/1/53.**G**.

Ghd. 7—8/10/54.**C/L**.
Dar. 18/10—12/11/55.**G**.
Dar. 14—15/11/55.**N/C**.
Ghd. 10—17/1/58.**C/L**.
Dar. 12/1—13/2/59.**G**.
Dar. 10/2—7/3/61.**C/L**.
Dar. 22/1—23/2/62.**G**.
Complete AWS fitted.

BOILERS:
D1623.
  2263 *(new)* 20/8/29.
D1243 *(exB16 930)* 10/10/33.
D1513 *(ex631)* 28/10/36.
D1573 *(exB16 1384)* 30/6/39.
  2775 *(exB16 2382)* 6/9/41.
  2778 *(ex631)* 30/8/44.
  2718 *(exB16 845)* 16/8/47.
  2891 *(ex3471)* 5/4/50.
  2891 *reno.24060* 22/5/52.
  24062 23/1/53.
  24103 *(new)* 12/11/55 (49A).
  24035 13/2/59.
  24059 23/2/62 (49A).

SHEDS:
Dairycoates.
Stockton 24/5/28.
Selby 27/11/30.
Tyne Dock 28/3/43.
Blaydon 17/6/56.
Tyne Dock 8/6/58.

RENUMBERED:
  3470 17/11/46.
  63470 5/4/50.

CONDEMNED: 3/12/62.
Into Dar. for cut up 15/3/63.
Final mileage 938,671.

631

Darlington

To traffic 3/5/24.

REPAIRS:
Ghd. 11/7—9/9/27.**G**.
Ghd. 7/1—12/2/31.**G**.
Dar. 5/7—14/8/33.**G**.
Dar. 30/7—1/9/36.**G**.
Dar. 3—6/5/37.**N/C**.
Dar. 8/12/38—25/1/39.**G**.
Dar. 15/9—22/10/41.**G**.
Dar. 13/11—22/12/42.**G**.
Dar. 8/6—1/7/44.**G**.
Dar. 5—14/12/45.**L**.
Dar. 23/5—28/6/47.**G**.
Dar. 1—14/7/47.**N/C**.
Dar. 3/11—24/12/49.**G**.
Dar. 28/12/49—4/1/50.**N/C**.
Dar. 6—24/5/52.**G**.
Dar. 26—27/5/52.**N/C**.

631 cont/.
Dar. 3—9/6/52.**N/C**.
Ghd. 3/2—21/3/53.**C/L**.
Dar. 10/2—10/3/55.**G**.
Ghd. 13/11—14/12/56.**C/H**.
Dar. 8/10—21/11/58.**G**.
Dar. 27/11—8/12/58.**N/C**.
Dar. 15/3—14/4/62.**G**.
Complete AWS fitted.
Dar. 3—15/5/62.**N/C**.

BOILERS:
D1628.
D1218 *(exB16 937)* 12/2/31.
D1513 *(exB16 2379)* 14/8/33.
D1492 *(exB16 1371)* 1/9/36.
D1577 *(exB16 841)* 25/1/39.
  2778 *(exB16 930)* 22/10/41.
D1667 *(exB16 2378)* 1/7/44.
  2891 *(exB16 1406)* 28/6/47.
  2556 *(ex3473)* 24/12/49.
  24057 24/5/52.
  24035 10/3/55.
  24101 21/11/58 (49A).
  24064 14/4/62 (49A).

SHEDS:
Tyne Dock.
Borough Gardens ?/?
Gateshead 29/5/33.
Selby 10/2/38.
Tyne Dock 28/3/43.
Blaydon 17/6/56.
Tyne Dock 8/3/59.

RENUMBERED:
  3471 17/11/46.
  63471 24/12/49.

CONDEMNED: 17/12/62.
Into Dar. for cut up 19/4/63.
Final mileage 755,322.

632

Darlington

To traffic 30/4/24.

REPAIRS:
Ghd. 24/12/25—5/2/26.**L**.
Ghd. 24/9—8/11/28.**G**.
Dar. 5/4—5/5/34.**G**.
Dar. 1/11—15/12/37.**G**.
Dar. 6—13/6/40.**N/C**.
Dar. 24/12/40—19/2/41.**G**.
Dar. 26/8—9/12/43.**G**.
Dar. 10/8—7/9/46.**G**.
Ghd. 15/11—5/12/47.**L**.
Dar. 8/3—20/4/50.**G**.
Ghd. 14/2—5/4/51.**C/L**.
Dar. 2—28/2/53.**G**.
Dar. 2—3/3/53.**N/C**.
Dar. 5/12/55—4/1/56.**G**.

Dar. 11—25/9/56.**C/L**.
Dar. 30/5—6/6/57.**C/L**.
Dar. 27/10—15/12/59.**G**.
Dar. 9/2—17/3/61.**C/L**.
Dar. 23/1—28/2/62.**C/L**.
Complete AWS fitted.

BOILERS:
D1631.
D1133 *(exB16 2364)* 5/5/34.
D1633 *(ex629)* 15/12/37.
D1551 *(ex629)* 19/2/41.
  3424 *(new)* 9/12/43 (49A).
  2885 *(ex633)* 7/9/46.
  2718 *(ex3470)* 20/4/50.
  24076 28/2/53 (49A).
  24013 4/1/56 (49A).
  24085 15/12/59 (49A).

SHEDS:
Tyne Dock.
Annfield Plain 1/27.
Tyne Dock 14/10/29.
Blaydon 17/6/56.
Tyne Dock 8/3/59.

RENUMBERED:
  3472 24/11/46.
  63472 20/4/50.

CONDEMNED: 2/12/62.
Into Dar. for cut up 18/4/63.
Final mileage 600,905.

633

Darlington

To traffic 3/5/24.

REPAIRS:
Ghd. 12/5—4/8/27.**G**.
Ghd. 13/3—22/4/31.**G**.
Dar. 18/6—18/7/34.**G**.
Dar. 25/6—12/8/37.**G**.
Dar. 13/8/37.**N/C**.
Dar. 28/12/39—30/1/40.**G**.
Dar. 2/2—6/3/43.**G**.
Dar. 16/11—30/12/44.**L**.
Dar. 23/2—22/3/46.**G**.
Ghd. 31/8—24/9/47.**L**.
Dar. 10/8—10/9/49.**G**.
Dar. 28/9—12/10/49.**N/C**.
Ghd. 12—20/10/49.**N/C**.
Dar. 7/3—5/4/52.**G**.
Modified for iron ore train
working. Vac. ejector fitted.
Dar. 26/10—27/11/54.**G**.
Dar. 29/11—2/12/54.**N/C**.
Ghd. 20/2—5/4/56.**C/L**.
Ghd. 7—26/9/56.**C/L**.
Dar. 12/11—7/12/57.**N/C**.
Westinghouse equipment
removed.

Dar. 9—11/12/57.**N/C**.
Dar. 7/6—30/8/60.**C/L**.
Dar. 25/4—1/6/62.**G**.
Complete AWS fitted.
Dar. 14—21/6/62.**N/C**.

BOILERS:
D1633.
D1628 *(ex631)* 22/4/31.
D1619 *(ex628)* 18/7/34.
D1201 *(exB16 932)* 12/8/37.
D1465 *(exB16 914)* 30/1/40.
  2885 *(exB16 846)* 6/3/43.
  2556 *(ex625)* 22/3/46.
  2879 *(ex3474)* 10/9/49.
  24046 5/4/52 (49A).
  24101 *(new)* 27/11/54 (49A).
  24107 *(new)* 7/12/57 (49A).
  24034 1/6/62 (49A).

SHEDS:
Tyne Dock.
Borough Gardens ?/?
Gateshead 29/5/33.
York 3/4/35 (T).
York 19/3/37 (P).
Tyne Dock 28/3/43.
Sunderland 21/6/59.
Tyne Dock 13/12/59.

RENUMBERED:
  3473 24/11/46.
  63473 10/9/49.

CONDEMNED: 17/12/62.
Into Dar. for cut up 10/4/63.
Final mileage 701,441.

634

Darlington

To traffic 8/5/24.

REPAIRS:
Ghd. 2/6—16/8/28.**G**.
Ghd. 3/9—12/10/32.**G**.
Dar. 23/9—22/10/36.**N/C**.
Dar. 7/4—3/6/37.**G**.
Dar. 9/8—18/9/40.**G**.
Dar. 13/4—23/6/43.**G**.
Dar. 13/3—13/4/46.**G**.
Dar. 21/12/48—22/1/49.**G**.
Dar. 3—18/2/49.**N/C**.
Dar. 1—26/4/52.**G**.
Dar. 28/4—9/5/52.**N/C**.
Dar. 2/12/54—5/1/55.**H/I**.
Dar. 19—25/1/55.**N/C**.
Ghd. 12/1—24/2/56.**C/L**.
After derailment.
Dar. 14/2—6/4/57.**G**.
Dar. 8—9/4/57.**N/C**.
Dar. 23/4—7/5/57.**N/C**.
Dar. 7—14/2/58.**C/L**.

Dar. 19/12/60—4/2/61.**G**.
Dar. 12—24/10/62.**N/C**.
Complete AWS fitted.

BOILERS:
D1634.
D1034 *(ex902)* 12/10/32.
D1616 *(ex901)* 3/6/37.
D1111 *(ex903)* 18/9/40.
D1525 *(exB16 922)* 23/6/43.
  2879 *(exB16 1378)* 13/4/46.
  3248 *(ex63466)* 22/1/49 (49A).
  24051 26/4/52.
  24090 6/4/57 (49A).
  24052 4/2/61 (49A).

SHEDS:
Tyne Dock.
Sunderland 23/9/56.
Tyne Dock 15/1/61.

RENUMBERED:
  3474 24/11/46.
  63474 22/1/49.

CONDEMNED: 17/12/62.
Into Dar. for cut up 18/4/63.
Final mileage 610,558.

Only the first five had windjabber when they were new, the 1924 built engines having chimney with a plain rim.

There was clearly some flexibility as to the type of chimney because ex-works 10th October 1933 No.630 had changed to one with a windjabber. Note standard whistle gear was a twin mounting with organ pipe on the right hand side and small bell shape on the fireman's side.

No.901 became No.3460 from 27th October 1946, and by 1945 had been changed to a chimney without windjabber but with straighter sides than those first fitted on the 1924 batch. Although the twin whistle mounting is still there, the bell shape on the left hand side has been removed and its pipe blanked off.

No.63468 (ex-628) changed to a chimney with a windjabber. Diagram 49A boilers had only a single whistle, mounted above an isolating valve and directly on to the firebox.

Corrosion affected both types of chimney and in the 1956-59 period No.63472 had to have its chimney top trimmed down.

As the Q7 chimney and that of the B16 were interchangeable, use was made of the spares kept for the latter class, chimney with windjabber could thus be seen through to withdrawal. This 4th August 1962 photograph of No.63472 shows it less than four months before its withdrawal on 2nd December.

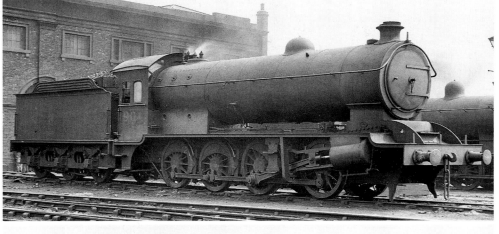

Until October 1933, NER design buffers with taper shank and circular flange, also NER drawhook, were fitted. From 1932, lifting holes were drilled in the front end of the frames. A single steel plate buffer beam was used throughout.

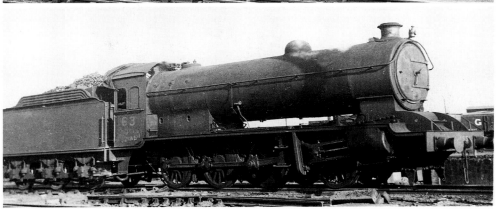

Starting with No.630, ex-works 10th October 1933, Group Standard buffers and drawhook were fitted and these added 5in. to the overall length of the engine and tender combined. By the end of the LNER most had been changed, but No.63466 still had the NER design at least to the end of 1950, (see page 115, middle right and bottom).

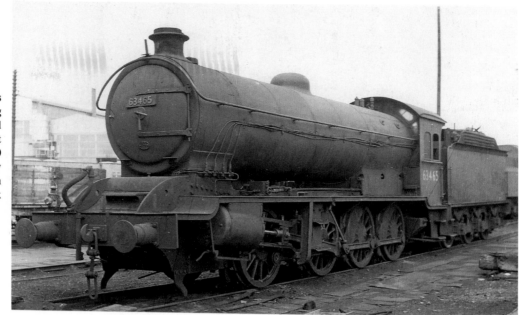

With the GS drawhook it was usual to have loose 3-link coupling but in July 1952 No.63465 gained screw adjustable type which it still had in this 14th May 1960 photograph. This change was only made on the five modified for iron ore train working from Tyne Dock to Consett.

The first five had, and kept, NER type mechanical lubricator for cylinders and valves. There was one on each side mounted on the running plate (*see* illustrations page 101, second from bottom, *and* page 107, second from bottom). Axles were fed from oil boxes. The 1924 engines had a quite different lubrication arrangement. The two NER mechanical lubricators, in the same positions, now fed the axles. Cylinder and valves were fed by a 4-feed sight feed Detroit lubricator in the cab, on the fireman's side, with the pipes along the side of the boiler (*see* this page, top)

Beginning with No.63474, ex-works 22nd January 1949, all were fitted with positive drive to mechanical lubricators but the boxes were never moved nearer to the drive as they were on Class Q6.

This photograph needs explanation. No.632 was maintained by Gateshead until that works closed at the end of January 1933 and it is last recorded out from repair there on 8th November 1928. This is too early for the number to have been moved to cab, which would be done during its first Darlington repair 5th April to 5th May 1934, yet the frames do not have the lifting holes which Darlington had been cutting from 1932.

Until December 1949 sandboxes for running in reverse were in the cab and needed long pipes to the point of application.

(above) Starting with No.63462, ex-works 16th December 1949, rear sandboxes were fixed on the frames below the cab which reduced the pipe length and made it easy to fill the boxes from ground level.

This change of sandbox position was made on both sides, and to all the class. This shows the much more accessible filling position.

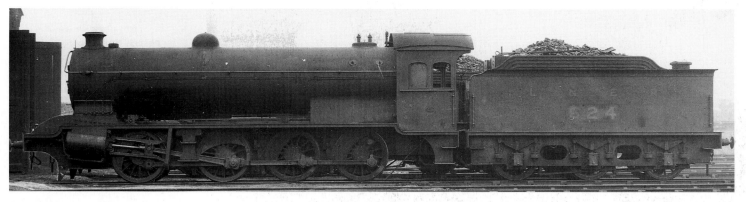

Both batches had the latest design of 4125 gallons self-trimming tender but no water pick-up apparatus. The only changes were with others in the class.

Until after the end of the LNER, all had only steam brake on the engine with linkage to tender brake blocks. Not until September 1948 (on No.63469) was a separate cylinder provided for tender brake but all were so fitted by June 1951.

These engines had long worked iron ore trains up to Consett, but in 1951, large hopper bogie wagons were introduced which had air-operated bottom-opening doors. Separate air supplies were needed, one for holding the doors closed and the other for opening them. Five Q7 were fitted with the equipment for working these trains, three in 1951 followed by two more in 1952. The first, No.63465 out 24th February 1951 had one air pump on each side of the smokebox. A vacuum ejector for the train brakes was also added.

The other four fitted for ore train working were 63460 (29th June 1951), 63463 (1st March 1952), 63469 (9th June 1951), and 63473 (5th April 1952) their pumps sited by the firebox on both sides.

(below) It was found that an air reservoir was needed and this was added to the first three on the left hand running plate, between pump and cab, fitting dates were as follows: 63460 (25th October 1951), 63465 (12th July 1952) and 63469 (10th October 1951). The other two had it included when they were modified. No.63465 had its pumps moved to the firebox position from 12th July 1952.

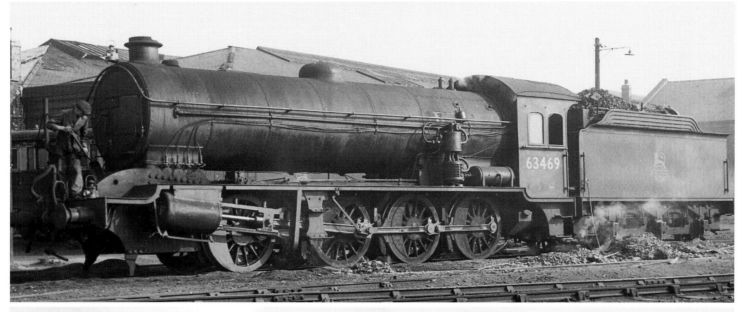

Included in the modifications was a change of couplings from loose 3-link type to screw adjustable for better control of the very heavy trains.

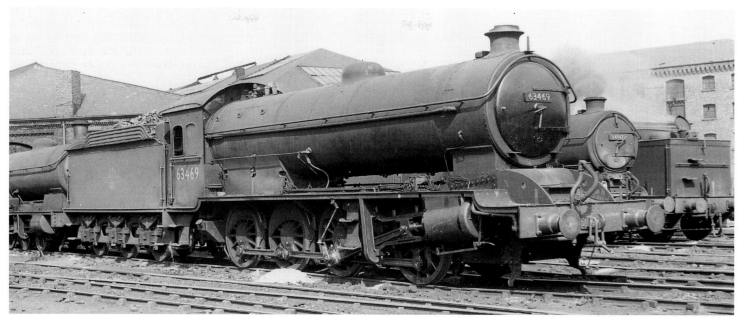

(above) **During 1957-59 the Q7's were superseded on the ore trains by the BR 9F 2-10-0 engines and the air equipment was transferred to them. Dates into works for removal of pumps and piping were: 63460 (14th October 1957), 63463 (26th April 1958), 63465 (28th January 1958), 63469 (24th September 1959), 63473 (12th November 1957). These five however retained their vacuum equipment for train braking, although No.63465 was out 10th June 1960 without it following a front-end collision.**

(right) **Starting with 63469, ex-works 6th December 1961, all were fitted with BR Automatic Warning System. This needed vacuum brake and the eleven (including 63465) without it had it fitted. This is No.63461 fitted with AWS and vacuum brake 22nd December 1961. Note these were able to have a straight standpipe.**

The AWS included battery boxes for the electrical part and these were placed on the right hand running plate in front of the cab. No.63462 was the last to get AWS, ex-works 8th November 1962. Then from 25th November to 17th December 1962 the whole class was inexplicably taken out of stock. No.63460 was reserved for preservation in the National Collection, but by the end of April 1963 the other fourteen had been cut up at Darlington.

Nos.901 to 905 had this NER goods livery from new until their first LNER repair.

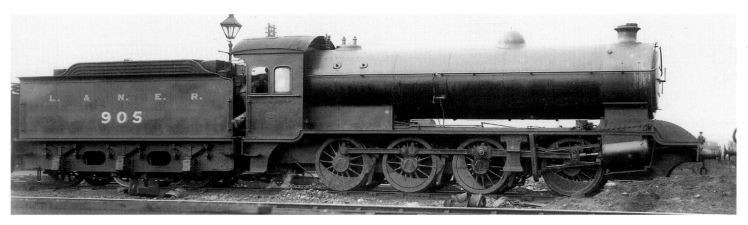

No.905, ex-Darlington on 19th June 1923 was the only one to get any of the 1923 styles of lettering. The other four went straight to LNER (*see* page 101, top) at these dates: 901 (28th February 1924), 902 (30th April 1924), 903 (7th August 1925), and 904 (26th February 1925).

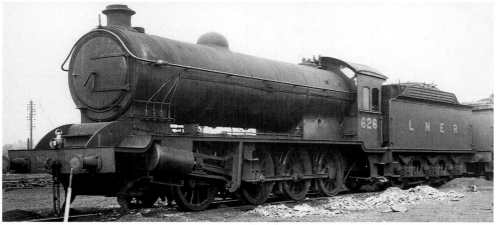

(*above*) By the time the 1924 engines were built Group painting and lettering had been standardised as this and until after June 1928 they had single red lining.

Starting with No.628, ex-works 4th April 1929, the number was moved from the tender to cab side and 12in. LNER was then used. This style continued until July 1942.

Wartime exigencies caused tender lettering to be cut to only NE from July 1942 to January 1946.

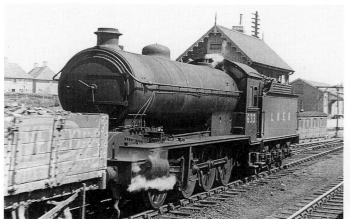

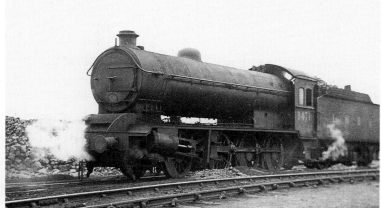

(above) **1946 also saw the class re-numbered from 3460 to 3474, but LNER was restored to No.629, 632, 633 and 634 before they got new numbers.**

(above, right) **The new numbers for 3462 and 3464 were put on in transfers, but painted and unshaded Gill sans was used for Nos.3460, 3461, 3463, 3467, 3470 and 3471. Nos.3465, 3466 and 3468 did not have LNER restored.**

(right) **Still with NE on tender, from a light repair 30th April 1948, No.63466 had its BR number in 12in. figures on the cab and usual 4 ½in. on the front buffer beam in Gill sans but with modified 6. This was carried until it went in for repair 12th November 1948.**

The first to have BRITISH RAILWAYS lettering were 63465 (18th June 1948) and 63468 (2nd July 1948) still with 12in. figures but 10in. letters. Both had smokebox number plate; this, and the cab figures included modified 6.

The next change was to 10in. cab figures to match the tender lettering and to true Gill sans 6. This had been made when 63466 was ex-works 17th December 1948 and it had the true 6 on the smokebox plate. Only Nos.63469 (3rd September 1948) and 63474 (22nd January 1949) got this style.

The smokebox numberplate was normally fitted below the top hinge strap, but at first No.63474 had its plate above the strap. The illustration on page 100 shows it was duly brought into line with the others.

Beginning with No.63473, out 10th September 1949, tender lettering had been discarded, and until 1957 all got the 28in. size emblems, handed to face forward on both sides.

63463 was one of the five fitted with vacuum brake and two air compressors to work iron ore trains from Tyne Dock up to Consett and here in July 1953, at Annfield Plain, is on one of them, banked by another Q7 on the section at 1 in 35 and 1 in 42, with the special 56 ton bogie hopper wagons. The air equipment was taken off in May 1958 and 63463 moved to Sunderland 14th June 1959 but on 13th December went back to Tyne Dock from where it was withdrawn on 3rd December 1962.

63465 had started at Hull Dairycoates but from 22nd September 1924 to 27th February 1925 worked coal trials from Doncaster shed. It left Hull 19th July 1928 for Stockton, then went to Selby 27th November 1930. Its final transfer was 28th March 1943 to Tyne Dock. Ex-works 24th February 1951, No.63465 was the first to be fitted for working these newly introduced 56-ton hopper wagons. Here, on the section to South Pelaw Junction, a Q7 could work unaided. 63465 had the air equipment taken off in February 1958 but still worked from Tyne Dock until it was withdrawn from there 3rd December 1962.

Five more similar engines, Nos.127 to 131, were built between September and November of the same year, also by Yorkshire Engine Co. These five had cab roof ventilators and, at the front end only, the sandbox fillers were now through the running plate.

After the H&B was merged into the North Eastern from 1st April 1922 the running numbers had 3000 added but to the LNER this conflicted with ex-Great Northern engines having the same numbers. So, from 29th February (No.2512) to 24th October 1924 (No.2507), Q10 class became Nos.2498 to 2512. No.3128 changed to 2509 at Hull Springhead on Friday 23rd May.

Until 1924, all still had their 1907-built domeless boiler with Belpaire firebox and these were beginning to need replacing. After discarding the idea to fit Class Q6 boilers (which would have needed frame alterations), Darlington designed a domed boiler with round-top firebox and re-boilering began with No.2505 ex-works 27th October 1924. Neither the original nor the replacement pattern of boiler carried a superheater. The process was completed when No.2512 was ex-works on 31st March 1928. This boiler was given LNER Diagram No.51.

CLASS Q 10

3117/2498

Yorks. Eng. Co. 899.

To traffic 2/1907.

REPAIRS
Hsi. 1/21.**G**.
Dar. 23/2—28/5/24.**G**.
Dar. 27/5—28/9/26.**G**.
Rebuilt to Part 2.
Dar. 12/11/30—9/1/31.**G**.

BOILER:
D1809 *(new)* 28/9/26.

SHED:
Springhead.

RENUMBERED:
2498 28/5/24.

CONDEMNED: 1/10/31.
Cut up at Darlington.

3118/2499

Yorks. Eng. Co. 900.

To traffic 3/1907.

REPAIRS:
Hsi. 3/22.**G**.
Hsi. 24/8/23.**G**.
Dar. 18/9/25—19/2/26.**G**.
Dar. 17/12/27—13/3/28.**G**.
Rebuilt to Part 2.

BOILER:
D1994 *(new)* 13/3/28.

SHEDS:
Springhead.
Selby 18/11/29.
Mexborough 2/1/31.
Selby 31/7/31.

RENUMBERED:
2499 7/4/24.

CONDEMNED: 6/8/31.

3119/2500

Yorks. Eng. Co. 901.

To traffic 3/1907.

REPAIRS:
Hsi. 1/19.**G**.
Dar. 23/3—23/6/23.**G**.
Dar. 31/3—20/6/27.**G**.
Rebuilt to Part 2.

BOILER:
D1817 *(new)* 20/6/27.

SHEDS:
Springhead.
Cudworth 1/7/24.
Dairycoates 23/10/29.
Mexborough 1/1/31.
Dairycoates 27/4/31.

RENUMBERED:
2500 7/7/24.

CONDEMNED: 2/5/31.
Cut up at Darlington.

3120/2501

Yorks. Eng. Co. 902.

To traffic 3/1907.

REPAIRS:
Hsi. 11/21.**G**.
Dar. 23/3—23/6/23.**G**.
Dar. 27/10/25—19/2/26.**G**.
Dar. 10/12/27—21/3/28.**G**.
Rebuilt to Part 2.

BOILER:
D1997 *(new)* 21/3/28.

SHEDS:
Springhead..
Dairycoates 27/5/27.
Springhead. 22/10/28.
Dairycoates 6/7/29.
Mexborough 1/1/31.
Dairycoates 6/8/31.

RENUMBERED:
2501 16/6/24.

CONDEMNED: 13/8/31.
Cut up at Darlington.

3121/2502

Yorks. Eng. Co. 903.

To traffic 8/1907.

REPAIRS:
Hsi. 1/22.**H**.
Dar. 7/6—3/11/22.**G**.
Dar. 21/4—26/4/26.**G**.
Rebuilt to Part 2.
Dar. 18/3—28/5/30.**G**.

BOILER:
D1805 *(new)* 26/4/26

SHEDS:
Springhead..
Dairycoates 27/5/27.
Springhead. 22/10/28.
Mexborough 2/1/31.
March 15/7/31.
Dairycoates 24/10/31.

RENUMBERED:
2502 4/6/24.

CONDEMNED: 4/11/31.
Cut up at Darlington.

3122/2503

Yorks. Eng. Co. 904.

To traffic 4/1907.

REPAIRS:
Hsi. 12/21.**G**.
Dar. 24/11/22—10/9/23.**G**.
Dar. 7/11/24—23/3/25.**G**.
Dar. 11/8—28/9/25.**L**.
Dar. 2/7—26/11/26.**G**.
Rebuilt to Part 2.
Dar. 22/4—16/7/30.**G**.

BOILER:
D1808 *(new)* 26/11/26

SHEDS:
Springhead..
Dairycoates 7/4/30.
Selby 29/12/30.
March 8/8/31.
Selby 22/10/31.

RENUMBERED:
2503 30/5/24.

CONDEMNED: 30/10/31.
Cut up at Darlington.

3123/2504

Yorks. Eng. Co. 905.

To traffic 5/1907.

REPAIRS:
Hsi. 7/21.**G**.
Hsi. 4/7/23.**G**.
Dar. 4/6—5/11/24.**G**.
Rebuilt to Part 2.
Dar. 16/2—30/3/26.**G**.
Dar. 5/11/29—30/1/30.**G**.

BOILER:
D1674 *(new)* 5/11/24.

SHEDS:
Springhead..
Selby 18/11/29.
Doncaster 1/1/31.
Mexborough 6/1/31.
March 15/7/31.
Selby 22/10/31.

RENUMBERED:
2504 15/3/24.

CONDEMNED: 30/10/31.
Cut up at Darlington.

3124/2505

Yorks. Eng. Co. 906.

To traffic 5/1907.

REPAIRS:
Hsi. 11/21.**G**.
Dar. 11/5/23—27/10/24.**G**.
Rebuilt to Part 2.
Dar. 18/9—13/11/28.**G**.

BOILER:
D1661 *(new)* 27/10/24.

SHEDS:
Springhead..
Selby 18/11/29.
Mexborough 1/1/31.
Selby 30/7/31.

RENUMBERED:
2505 15/10/24.

WORKS CODES:- Cw - Cowlairs. Dar- Darlington. Don - Doncaster. Ghd - Gateshead. Gor - Gorton. Hsi - Hull Springhead. Inv - Inverurie. Str - Stratford.
REPAIR CODES:- **C/H** - Casual Heavy. **C/L** - Casual Light. **G** - General. **H** - Heavy. **H/I** - Heavy Intermediate. **L** - Light. **L/I** - Light Intermediate. **N/C** - Non-Classified.

(above) **Curiously, the only chimneys with capuchon were pure H&B type on which the original deep all-around rim had been modified. No.131, with one of these chimneys, was the first of the H&B 0-8-0's to arrive at Darlington for repair, seen here in the shed sidings where it arrived on 2nd June 1922.**

(left) **Until they were re-boilered they kept the H&B smokebox which was flush fitting with twin handles for fastening, aided by three dog clips on the lower part. The upper lamp iron was on the door so steps to reach it were not needed. The door did not have a knob on it.**

With the domed boiler, Darlington put on the NER design of smokebox which had flat flange and straps spaced further apart. The lamp iron was moved to the front plate above the door and to help reach it, steps were added below the door. All except Nos.3126 and 2504 kept the twin handles for fastening the door. A knob was also now provided.

The Belpaire firebox boilers had Ramsbottom safety valves without an enclosure, and a single bell-shape whistle was mounted on the firebox, between the safety valves and cab front.

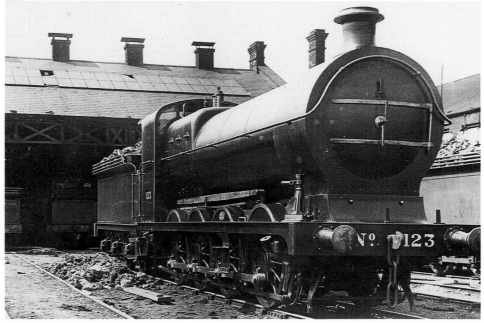

The domed boilers had Ross 'pop' safety valves with circular casing at their base, and the whistle had one organ pipe and one bell-shape on a twin mounting.

(below) When No.2504 was re-boilered it was fitted with an exhaust steam injector on the left hand side. The supply pipe left the smokebox low down and there was a grease separator below the running plate between third and fourth axles. Only 2504 was so fitted and it is not known if this item was kept to its 30th October 1931 withdrawal.

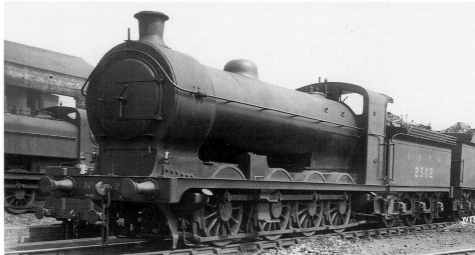

2505 cont/.
CONDEMNED: 6/8/31.
Cut up at Darlington.

3125/2506

Yorks. Eng. Co. 907.

To traffic 6/1907.

REPAIRS:
Hsi. 7/18.**G.**
Dar. 23/3—30/5/23.**G.**
Dar. 8/4—6/10/25.**G.**
Dar. 29/7—20/10/27.**G.**
Rebuilt to Part 2.

BOILER:
D1988 *(new)* 20/10/27.

SHEDS:
Springhead..
Selby 18/11/29.
Mexborough 1/1/31.
Selby 6/8/31.

RENUMBERED:
2506 26/6/24.

CONDEMNED: 13/8/31.
Cut up at Darlington.

3126/2507

Yorks. Eng. Co. 908.

To traffic 6/1907.

REPAIRS:
Hsi. 10/21.**G.**
Dar. 13/11/22—30/4/23.**G.**
Dar. 5/5—29/10/24.**G.**
Rebuilt to Part 2.
Dar. 23/6—27/8/28.**G.**

BOILER:
D1670 *(new)* 29/10/24.

SHEDS:
Springhead..
Selby 18/11/29.
Doncaster 1/1/31.
Mexborough 6/1/31.
Selby 10/8/31.

RENUMBERED:
2507 24/10/24.

CONDEMNED: 13/8/31.
Cut up at Darlington.

3127/2508

Yorks. Eng. Co. 942.

To traffic 9/1907.

REPAIRS:
Hsi. 4/22.**G.**
Dar. 28/8—21/12/23.**G.**
Dar. 8/12/26—30/3/27.**G.**
Rebuilt to Part 2.
Dar. 16/6—17/9/30.**G.**

BOILER:
D1815 *(new)* 30/3/27.

SHEDS:
Springhead..
Cudworth 31/1/25.
Selby 18/11/29.
Mexborough 2/1/31.
March 14/9/31.
Selby 23/10/31.

RENUMBERED:
2508 18/3/24.

CONDEMNED: 30/10/31.
Cut up at Darlington.

3128/2509

Yorks. Eng. Co. 943.

To traffic 10/1907.

REPAIRS:
Hsi. 12/20.**G.**
Dar. 19/6—4/12/22.**G.**
Dar. 15/12/24—23/2/25.**G.**
Rebuilt to Part 2.
Dar. 16/11/27—20/2/28.**G.**
Dar. 27/6—22/9/30.**G.**

BOILER:
D1704 *(new)* 23/2/25.

SHEDS:
Springhead..
Selby 18/11/29.
March 10/8/31.
Selby 21/9/31.

RENUMBERED:
2509 23/5/24.

CONDEMNED: 1/10/31.
Cut up at Darlington.

3129/2510

Yorks. Eng. Co. 944.

To traffic 10/1907.

REPAIRS
Hsi. ?/?—?/2/22.**G.**
Dar. 10/12/24—29/4/25.**G.**
Dar. 4/8—29/10/27.**G.**
Rebuilt to Part 2.

BOILER:
D1991 *(new)* 29/10/27.

SHEDS:
Springhead.
Dairycoates 23/10/29.
Mexborough 2/1/31.
Dairycoates 30/7/31.

RENUMBERED:
2510 4/6/24.

CONDEMNED: 6/8/31.
Cut up at Darlington.

3130/2511

Yorks. Eng. Co. 945.

To traffic 10/1907.

REPAIRS:
Hsi. ?/?—20/12/22.**G.**
Dar. 1/7/24—19/1/25.**G.**
Rebuilt to Part 2.
Dar. 21/3—8/6/27.**G.**
Dar. 4/6—15/8/29.**G.**

BOILER:
D1685 *(new)* 19/1/25.

SHEDS:
Springhead.
Selby 18/11/29.
Dairycoates 29/12/30.
March 8/8/31.
Dairycoates 18/9/31.

RENUMBERED:
2511 25/7/24.

CONDEMNED: 1/10/31.
Cut up at Darlngton.

3131/2512

Yorks. Eng. Co. 946.

To traffic 11/1907.

REPAIRS:
Hsi. ?/?—?/9/21.**G.**
Dar. 7/6/22—19/4/23.**G.**
Dar. 4/8—27/11/24.**G.**
Dar. 24/12/25—28/4/26.**G.**
Dar. 28/12/27—31/3/28.**G.**
Rebuilt to Part 2.

BOILER:
D2003 *(new)* 31/3/28.

SHEDS:
Springhead.
Dairycoates 12/11/29.

RENUMBERED:
2512 29/2/24.

CONDEMNED: 1/10/31.
Cut up at Darlington.

No.2504 was also odd in having a wheel and handle for smokebox door fastening. Only one other got a wheel, No.3126 ex-Darlington 30th April 1923 and that was on an H&B smokebox door.

None was fitted with Raven fog signalling apparatus although that system outlasted this class. There were no track ramps installed on the H&B line where they worked to late 1929 and the expense of fitting could not be justified.

All were fitted with steam brake only, and no alterations were made. This engine was ex-Darlington 21st December 1923 as No.3127ᴅ which can still be seen faintly after its patching to 2508 on 18th March 1924 at Springhead.

The tender, holding 4 tons of coal and 3300 gallons water was larger than the H&B had used before but then became standard for later purchases of 4-4-0 and 0-6-0 engines. Until the first repair at Darlington, the coal rails were open (*see* page 124, bottom) but were then plated on the inside of the rails.

On at least eight of the fifteen tenders the H&B had changed the axle boxes to Iracier type, which could be identified by their shield shape, instead of square lid. Darlington also exchanged the tenders on the first two it repaired. Into works No.121 took a tender with Iracier boxes (*see* below) whilst No.131 had plain boxes (*see* page 120, top). Ex-works they were the other way round as 2502 and 2512 (*see* page 121, centre and top, opposite).

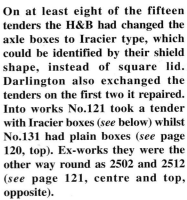

By 1922 the original livery and lining (*see* page 5 and page 118, top) had disappeared, probably being a 1914-18 war casualty and, judging by this (*see* also page 121, top), unlined black had taken its place.

Whilst still North Eastern, Darlington put N.3121E. (3rd November 1922) and N.3128E. (4th December 1922) into their goods livery. See the middle illustration on page 118 for the latter after 23rd May 1924 patching to 2509. The next five out were in this style, and if they had red lining the camera failed to show it. They were Nos.3131 (19th April), 3126 (30th April), 3125 (30th May), 3119 (23rd June) and 3120 (23rd June), all 1923. These were the last to have the 20-ton re-railing jack left on. Two more got the H&B/NE number at Darlington during 1923, Nos.3122 (10th September) and 3127 (21st December). They had just LNER but had suffix D added (*see* page 123, second from bottom).

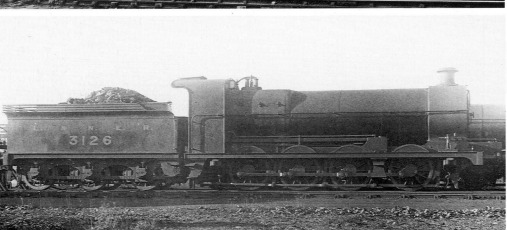

H&B No.129 had a general repair at Springhead in February 1922 and by 19th December 1922 this engine had been altered to 3129. On 4th June 1924 this was then patched to 2510 as shown, using H&B transfers. It went to Darlington 10th December 1924 and was out 29th April 1925 (*see* page 120, middle) without a change of boiler. Meanwhile, Springhead gave general repairs to three others which presumably came out as Nos: N.3130E. (20th December 1922), LNER 3123 (4th July 1923), and LNER 3118 (24th August 1923).

With the 1924 numbering established, this became standard style until the June 1928 painting economies took effect. L&NER 3131 was patched to 2512 on 29th February 1924 and went to Darlington on 4th August 1924. It was ex-works 27th November as shown.

The re-boilering had no effect on the livery and was just completed before red lining was discarded, by Nos.2499, 2501 and 2512 being done in March 1928. Note the deeper windows which the round top firebox allowed. This was the final livery for Nos.2499, 2500, 2501, 2506, 2510 and 2512.

Whilst still with number on the tender, two Q10's went into unlined black. They were 2505 (13th November 1928) and 2507 (27th August 1928), and this was their final guise.

Only seven acquired cab numbering of which only the first one done, No.2511 (15th August 1929), was able to have 12in. figures, with full shading.

Six more got cab figures: 2504 (30th January), 2502 (28th May), 2503 (16th July), 2508 (17th September), 2509 (22nd September), all 1930, and No.2498 (9th January 1931). The narrow cab sides only allowed 12in. figures to be used with their shading removed.

(below) Despite their upgrading, the trade depression and lack of even normal mineral traffic in 1930 and 1931 led to all fifteen being withdrawn from 2nd May 1931, and when No.2502 was withdrawn on 4th November 1931, Class Q10 was extinct. The boilers had only between seven to four years service and so were put to further use on Class Q5 Part 2.